HARDING,

HIS PRESIDENCY AND LOVE LIFE REAPPRAISED

S. Joseph Krause

AuthorHouse™
1663 Liberty Drive
Bloomington, IN 47403
www.authorhouse.com
Phone: 1-800-839-8640

Published by AuthorHouse 11/19/13

ISBN: 978-1-4918-1906-7 (sc)
ISBN: 978-1-4918-1905-0 (e)

Library of Congress Control Number: 2013917280

TABLE OF CONTENTS

PART I:

PART II:

PART III:

PART IV:

PART V:

PART VI:

PART VII:

PART VIII:

PART IX:

PART X:

PART I:

INTRO. FROM BAD TO GOOD

CHAPTER 1

"Harding The Worst?"

Warren G. Harding's aborted term in office (Mar., 1921—Aug., 1923) has the distinction of being assigned the consensus low point in the American Presidency. It has been a given that his administration was "shoddy" and he himself an example of "obvious incompetence."[1] There was a renewed interest in Harding (equally negative) following discovery of his love letters to Carrie Phillips in 1964. As noted by Andrew Sinclair, a British biographer of that era, Harding's name in itself "has become a byword as the worst American President, the prime example of incompetence and sloth and feeble good nature."[2]

Harding's status has been so categorically negative that a question rarely addressed is whether the reputation matches the overall record. For, interestingly, this same biographer, critical as he otherwise was, additionally observed that Harding was actually "a hardworking and shrewd Ohio politician ...always his own master" who had the wisdom to use supposed faults, "compromise and humility, as political tactics." So, in the final analysis, he became a man "of great presence, ambition, and political talent." (Ibid., 297f.).

Francis Russell, a major post-1965 biographer, likewise makes Harding out to be the "worst President," but he similarly hedges his condemnation by saying not that Harding <u>was</u> the worst, but, rather, that it was "by a twist or two of fate" (i.e., not his fault, and not his due) that he "has come" to be so regarded (i.e., not that he should be).[3] In general, however, praise for Harding—usually tempered—has been in short supply. Even in Sinclair's estimation, seeming weakness put to political advantage becomes more like clever machination than outright merit.

The most cynical criticism of Harding has been that by Samuel Hopkins Adams, whose Incredible Era seems much like a belated extension of his satiric novel Revelry (of 1926) in creating a rollicking caricature of Harding. Adams, who had made a reputation for himself as a muckraking journalist, was so sarcastically dismissive of Harding that his glib denunciations become in themselves dismissible. He characterized Harding, Mencken-style, as "an amiable, well-meaning, third-rate Mr. Babbitt, with the equipment of a small-town, semi-educated journalist."

Of course, Harding, early on, had been labeled a "third-rater," and worse, by politicians and the Press alike, though many reporters would reverse themselves once they saw him taking charge of the Presidency. Not so, muckraking Adams, who was unrelenting in discrediting Harding, even when he deserved credit, as was the case with Adams' downplaying Harding's role in the Conference he had called on the Limitation of Armaments (1921).

Viewed by Adams, Harding, for example, "falters when confronted by opposition to the hope of disarmament," and, instead of taking the "opportunity …to forward the cause," he assumedly had it "forced upon him." The Conference actually was an early foreign policy success, and an unexpected one from a President whose origins were located in rural Ohio.

Published in 1939, with the nation still Depression-conscious, Adams' book seems to have been reviving both the stale pre-presidential estimates of Harding and the outdated scandal obsession of the late '20s. Though he did acquaint himself with major facts in the Harding biography, Adams was not loathe to offer opinion as fact, or disparagement by comedic tag-line. ("Harding's conception of public service was to give a friend a job.")

Overall, one comes away with the impression that Adams enjoyed indulging his sense of humor at Harding's expense. In the process, he probably did more than other biographers to propagate the image of

Harding as our worst President. Thus, the reason for giving Adams much attention is that what a lay reader casually interested in Presidents might know about Harding would be a lot like the description Adams had given him.[4]

Harding had indeed become a President easy to discredit, once those post-mortem scandals began to raise their ugly heads. In the same year that Herbert Hoover and Charles Evans Hughes were eulogizing Harding at the belated dedication of his Memorial in Marion, Ohio (16 June, 1931), Frederick Lewis Allen would juxtapose Harding's very presidential appearance (of "Washingtonian nobility and dignity") with William Allen White's calling him "almost unbelievably ill-informed." To this, Allen added that not only was Harding's mind "vague and fuzzy," but he was the epitome of "helplessness when confronted by questions of policy to which mere good nature could not find an answer."[5]

In the latest account of Harding's designation as "worst," Phillip G. Payne embodies it in his title, Dead Last, but it is only by indirection that he deals with how well that evaluates Harding's showing as President. As indicated in his subtitle, Payne, instead, concentrates on "The Pubic Memory of Warren G. Harding's Legacy," which is researched in depth, and well. Payne offers variations on the thesis that Harding's vision of a return to "Normalcy" amounted to the triumph of "Boosterism," a culture, which, springing from small town America, celebrated the virtue of self-promotion.

As Payne puts it, "Harding's reputation was tied not only to national events and conceptions of the log cabin myth, but also to the boosterism still to be found in the Harding Memorial Association." Regarding boosterism per se, Payne sees Harding as "Babbitt before being Babbitt was really all that bad." Since Sinclair Lewis's Babbitt was not published until 1922, Payne would also have Harding being Babbitt before there was a Babbitt he could have been identified with, particularly if tied to the pre-presidential Harding.[6]

What Payne overlooks—not part of his subject—is that Lewis' Babbitt was an exemplar of the widely recognized "Revolt From The Village," a disillusioning motif that became rather prevalent in late 19th

and early 20th Century American Literature. Sherwood Anderson's Winesburg, Ohio (1919) was a major illustration of "Revolt" literature, of which Ohio's Warren Harding would have been a fitting object. It gave him a certain cultural identity.

Although a notable ranking of our Presidents by specialists on the Presidency raised Harding from humble number 42, to number 38, two below George W. Bush, it is not so much that those scholars found Harding to be that much better, as that they found four others they thought were worse. Hence, it is still the case that, to the present day, for another President to be placed in the same class with Harding is the sorriest denigration that could be visited upon him.

So it was when Gerald Ford, ever smarting from his defeat by Jimmy Carter, would place Carter "very close to Warren G. Harding," on the understanding that both shared the rank of worst.[7] In effect, Harding's name, in itself, becomes an icon for failure. As the worst case image is summed up by Phillip Payne, "for the most part Harding [has] remained a historical example of a flawed Babbitt and a self-indulgent philanderer" (Dead Last, 192).

The old adage, nihil nisi bonum, not only didn't apply to Harding, it acquired inverse momentum during the years following his death, as the stain of corruption began to spread. On the other hand, later assessments, given distance, often attempt to balance the bad against the good that can be said of him, though the bad usually predominates.

Robert K. Murray, commenting on Francis Russell's ponderous biography, notes that, while giving Harding credit for being "neither a fool nor a tool," Russell takes the reader through 663 pages that would have us believe "just the opposite." Furthermore, this comes after Russell had made an appeal for rectifying unfair treatment of Harding, as in noting that he was "personally honest" and did not, for example, "use his privileges" to advantage his newspaper.

Murray, it so happens, takes an opposite tack. After more than 500 pages that focus mainly on Harding's flaws, he isolates matters that are worthy of high praise: "In concrete accomplishments, his administration was superior to a sizable portion of those in the nation's history. Indeed, in establishing the political philosophy and program for an entire decade, his 882 days in office were more significant than all but a few similar short periods in the nation's experience."[8] Decrying the emphasis on Harding's negatives, they being the ones most remembered, Murray concludes, "The record notwithstanding, its myths still command more attention than its realities" (Ibid., 537). The situation has not greatly changed for Harding, if at all. Embarrassment from partial disclosure of his love letters to Carrie Phillips doesn't improve his reputation.

This introductory Part One deals with preliminaries providing context for what follows. It includes the review of Harding biography and his status as "worst" President just indicated. From there, I proceed, e.g., to: a summation of commonly accepted information about his political rise (some already documented); a misconception of the reason for his critical break-up with a favored mistress; an inquiry into his relationship with both sustained mistresses; corruption in his Administration, which didn't touch him personally; and his impressive accomplishments as President, mostly overlooked, as has been his triumphant first year in Office when he was regarded as a virtual prodigy. As needed, ad hoc objectives accompany chapter subjects.

I introduce new information about his political life mainly from his private correspondence with his friend Frank Edgar Scobey, and correspondingly new information about his personal life from Nan Britton's account of her time as his mistress. On the other hand, a lot inheres in what one makes of known material, which, taken by itself, may not say much. Hence, my idea is that it is often necessary to provide relevant substance to the factual in order to derive its full meaning. It is often a question of what the facts mean beyond what they flatly state; good in itself, but possibly not quite the whole story.

As my discussion proceeds, some references not specifically tied down to a given source are offered as part of the generally accepted information already out there, derivable from chief biographers—e.g., Francis Russell, Robert Murray, or Carl Anthony, information from whom is cited when called for.

CHAPTER 2

"Need of a Fresh Look"

HISTORIANS LOOKING FOR A VALID appraisal of Harding as President seem to have had difficulty getting it proportionally balanced, which is reason enough for having a fresh look. My objective, though confined in scope, is to elicit a fuller understanding of who Warren G. Harding was, based on data indicating that, "worst" has been a typical oversimplification that has falsely trailed his reputation.

The thesis I come away with is that a key unrecognized irony of his political career, is that contrary to the common appraisal, WGH was an effective President, who made an enviable record of accomplishments. On the other hand, despite his known kindliness, the man, as opposed to the President, didn't lead a completely upstanding life behind that façade. Contrary to the good opinion that the President-worshipping public had of his character, it was in his private life that Harding joins the class of adulterous Presidents who get a low rating for something that doesn't count politically.

Harding's love life was fraught with complications and contradictions, mostly of his own making, which did him no good. Looked at from the point of view of complication, the moral flaws in Harding's private life were understandable, though not necessarily excusable. He was understood to be living in a celibate marriage, and hence found sex elsewhere, in two significant instances based on love. The key, however, is that flagrant as his personal flaws might have been, they had nothing to do with his Presidency, save for the newspaper cartoons he inspired.

In short, quite decent in the one area, he was less than decent in the other, but for reasons. This is the view that emerges as one assembles the facts regarding WGH the man and his separable role as the politician.—Separable with one exception, that being the intrusiveness of a wife who thrived on politics, mostly to her husband's advantage.

My idea is to uncover additions to the Harding profile, yet outstanding, in areas of significant interest. Specifically, this means bringing new data and corresponding insights to bear upon major aspects of his political and personal lives. Simply put, my subject divides into two major segments, with this, the first, having to do with steps in Harding's political life, and the second with comparable steps in his private life, mostly narrowed down to his relationships with the three principal women in his life.

These are matters that need factual explication in greater detail than has hitherto been given them, an endeavor especially relevant in light of the image Harding has unjustly acquired. After all, what is generally thought of Harding hasn't changed much over the years, as indicated by the presidential rankings.

However, taken from candid information Harding divulged in correspondence with his long-time friend, Frank Edgar Scobey, for example, my findings clarify the attributes (good and bad) which this much maligned Twenty-Ninth President brought to the Office. It shows him buckling down to overcome his own sense of inadequacy, and the low opinion of the Press, as well as the influence of the Cabal of Senators who supposedly designed his Nomination.

Given new information, as indicated, there is the matter of how one puts it together. In the case of Harding, one must deal with a large umbrella of collateral data, the use of which depends on how it is construed. For one thing, factual evidence acquires meaning from context; e.g., its connection to events in the subject's life and times. Needless to say, the facts themselves often lie between the lines in unstated inferences, which the following episode illustrates. Hardly subtle, it speaks for itself.

After Warren had spent a few trying years in his marriage to Florence Kling, he was psychologically upset, and having chronic indigestion. He sought help at J. P. Kellogg's famed Sanitarium, but did not return cured. Suggestive as that might be, there was more to the story.

On his return from the 'San,' he had an affair with an unhappily married woman, Susan Hodder, who just happened to have been Florence's next door neighbor and, growing up, her best friend. No connection has been made between these events brought out singularly by Carl Anthony.

But with Warren having had an affair with Susan, of all women, there is a clear inference that he was trying to tell Florence something he couldn't have said any better orally. If so, Florence wasn't taking the bait. Desperation personified, Warren's affair with Susan suggests an effort to compensate for the inertia that kept him married to a woman with an aversion to sex.

Warren had been discovering how difficult a woman Florence was for him to live with in marriage. She was, in fact, literally driving him crazy, exemplified by the bizarre means of insult he undertook to shake her up. Obviously, he was avoiding the painfulness of flatly saying he hoped she would—for goodness sake—agree to a divorce.

The countless adulteries that followed should have compelled any sane woman to have thrown him out. Florence was eminently sane, but she had one insane fixation: hold on to Warren, no matter what. A hard featured lady, she had unexpectedly snagged the handsomest man in town. The irony is that, regarding Susan, he might have known he'd probably fail of his purpose, and went through with it anyway. It was that kind of a relationship.

Carl Anthony's Florence Harding: The First Lady, The Jazz Age, and The Death of America's Most Scandalous President (hereafter Florence) is a valuable source for primary biographic information about Florence and Warren, particularly for details regarding his notorious adulteries. It was Anthony, for example, who brought out Susan Hodder's long-standing friendship with Florence, which gave the critical bite to Warren's relationship with his wife's close friend. He also tied down the fact that the adultery had taken place (Florence, 61).

The facts speak for themselves, but lacking was an effort to clinch the story by bringing out the meaning of what happened, and how it applied to a larger scenario in the lives of this ill-matched couple. They remained married; Warren saw other women; and Florence became his trusted political advisor.

Regarding the political Harding, my idea, simply put, is for clarification: specifically, to identify the bases for where he did well as President, and where he went astray, which in both cases, differ from characteristics usually attributed to him.

Neither a lawyer nor a general, and at times given to inertia, how, then, did Warren G. Harding become an aspirant for the Presidency? The truth is he didn't. At least, he didn't want to be, until the Nomination was handed to him. Better yet, how could he become the good President which nobody believed was possible? On the hidden side, how would adultery translate into a need of love? Questions worth exploring anew.

CHAPTER 3

"Harding's Ascent in Brief"

First, however, as terminus a quo, a summation of the generally known data on Harding's career on the national scene, the documentation for which has already been established.

His national career began as a U.S. Senator, who became unexpectedly vaulted into contention for the Republican Nomination for President. He inauspiciously won it, by default, and, to everyone's surprise, went on to win the Presidency as well, though not really competent for dealing with what awaited him there.

As might well have been predicted, his win did not win him confidence, least of all from his own Party. Rather, as predicted, in his innocence, it placed him at the disposal of ambitious politicians, who on becoming close associates—indeed, friends—were able to both enhance and damage his career.

Chief among those influential friends were the two associates in his Administration who became closest to him; namely, Harry M. Daugherty and Albert B. Fall. Daugherty, originally a small-time Ohio political hack, failed gubernatorial candidate, and savvy lobbyist, engineered Harding's Nomination and Election to the Presidency. He became Harding's strong-armed Attorney General, who, upon being charged with allegations of corruption, would barely escape conviction.

Albert B. Fall had been a fellow Senator much admired by Harding for his expertise in foreign affairs, who, despite an anti-conservationist bias, would be precariously made Interior Secretary. Like Daugherty,

Fall was susceptible to graft, a political perk mostly taken for granted. Though, not quite as skilled at evasion, he would, in time, be unable to elude conviction. There are questions as to how trustful Harding handled these two friends, which, when explored, are revealing. It seemed more like, having sized him up, they saw how easy it was to handle him.

Special attention is required for Fall, whose influence on Harding enabled him to get a free hand for negotiating the oil leases, which became a pernicious political issue that, after Harding's death, surfaced as a hallmark of his ill-fated reputation. That being none other than Teapot Dome.

Overall, the leeway given Daugherty and Fall, among other members of Harding's Administration (e.g., like Jess Smith, Daugherty's unofficial aid and grafter-in-chief) illuminates a core problem that resulted from the decent, trustful side of Harding's nature. His leniency could be taken advantage of, but, it could, by an interesting dichotomy, also work well for him in other respects. For example, the free hand he gave Andrew W. Mellon in Treasury enabled him to bring businessman efficiency to that important post.

In short, when it comes to evaluating Harding the President and Harding the man, one finds there was much good mingled with the bad, much bad mingled with the good. Though there was reason for the latter to prevail, by the time the good could be discerned, it no longer mattered, giving way only to sadness in limited quarters. An essentially simple man turns out to be complicated in his simplicity.

Under scrutiny, the case for a balanced view of Harding encompasses the basic good-bad imbalance that prevailed in his career and private life, the sum total of which lifts the stigma of outright failure signified by "worst"—a designation that, at best, becomes a surface impression, at worst, a non sequitur. Particularly revealing was Harding's manner of coming to terms with the Presidential responsibilities suddenly thrust upon him, which he was woefully unprepared to meet.

This was particularly evident in the matter of patronage, for which he had a wholesome distaste, until he finally applied himself and used his harmonizing talent to master it. Similarly, Harding's realization of how ill-equipped he was for his new role was what goaded him to work hard at it in order to prove himself worthy of it.

If stripped of all other attributes, Harding, after all, remained a politician, and a good one. He knew how little other things would count if he failed to make good at the job, but he also understood that he had to inhabit the role and make it work for him. He looked around and saw that he grew tall because the people had a natural regard for their President, because he was their President. But he had to make the effort to sell himself in that role.

His appearance was helpful. He was tall and had a certain sad look about him that signified seriousness of attitude. It was natural, not put on, and he was able to make the most of that. He likewise capitalized on his ability to make an admirable orator of himself in an age when oratory, ipso facto, gave an impression of importance. He had a voice that resonated. Importantly, as an ex-newspaper man, Harding early on knew how to elicit the approval of the Press.

But probably the most remarkable thing about Harding's ascending to the Presidency was the question of how he ever got there on such meager credentials, none actually for high office. He had started out as the thirty-four year old manager of a newspaper from an obscure small town in rural Ohio where, in a mainly Democratic district, he ran for the State Senate as a Republican in 1899, and won. He ran for a second term in 1901 and won that too.

He made himself popular enough with fellow Republican Senators that they elected him floor leader, a post reserved for those who had distinguished themselves for being Party-dependable. Also helpful was his affability, which was used to cultivate friends among the Senate leadership. Top Republicans in the State became impressed with how good he was at reconciling differences between party factions, which smoothed the way for legislation they favored.

In 1903 that got him nominated to be Lieutenant Governor on the winning ticket headed by Myron T. Herrick. For Harding, this was a big-time connection, as it enabled him to climb the ladder of influence. Herrick, a self-made businessman elected president of the American Bankers Association, had established friendships with distinctive politicians like William McKinley, Mark Hanna, and Joseph Foraker, whom Herrick's ambitious Lieutenant Governor also got to know, and be known by.

In his new post, Harding served as moderator of the Ohio Senate, which gained him additional connections with the Party elite. His voice had platform appeal, and he began to make a name for himself as a popular orator. That positioned him for statewide speaking engagements on the Chautauqua circuit, where he soon found himself in constant demand.

He lost a run for Governor in 1910 because he wasn't a particularly enthusiastic candidate. But, by running, he still got himself known to be an important enough Republican to place William Howard Taft's name in re-nomination for President in 1912. From there, Harding moved up to candidacy for the United States Senate in 1914, and, benefiting from an anti-Catholic bias, defeated his opponent, Timothy Hogan, by an attention-getting majority of 102,000 votes.

But there was nothing in his nondescript career which could augur particularly well for his becoming the Republicans' second-choice Candidate for President. With Harding being not so much as a dark horse, his gaining the Nomination was taken as a jaw-dropping achievement. To seasoned 'pols' the fact that Harding did make it seemed more like a fluke, to be topped by a greater one on his winning the Presidency itself, and doing so by an impressive majority.

So little having been expected of him, his election seemed due more to the mood of the country following Wilson's internationalism, than to any thought of Harding's supposed merits. Beyond his commanding appearance and humble origins, all he had to offer was the background of a clean, mid-American farm boy. Thus, backed by an attractive history and an ability to make himself personally likeable in political circles, he had the ingredients to make himself equally popular with the electorate. He was, in fact, not shy about using those assets as a means of projecting to the people that he was one of them. Oratory came naturally to him, and, shallow though it might have seemed on substance, it was—at the least—a big attention getter.

If the question persisted—as it did with the Press—about how

Harding happened to have gone so far on so little, one would have been hard pressed to find anything in particular to account for it. He had a special likeability and an ability to make a favorable impression on influential politicians, who had mostly preferred other candidates for President.

Harding had a lot to live up to, and there was a lot to be understood about how this small-time politician managed to climb so high. Being so inexperienced, could he be entrusted with the reins of power? The little that was thought of him, the greater his esteem if he exceeded it. Who would have thought that he could turn out to be as much challenging as challenged?

CHAPTER 4

"Ah, The Women: Carrie Then Nan"

QUITE AS IMPORTANT AS CONSIDERATIONS of competence, this contender for the Presidency had baggage. He was insatiably attracted to the Women, a subject of primary interest about which, as with the Presidency, there is a catalogue of generally known information that is covered in the summation that follows.

There is much to be said, above and beyond what has already been written—and avoided—regarding Warren Harding's sexual addiction. But, again, it is best to consider what is generally recognized. To begin with, that a man with his addiction should marry a woman disenchanted with sex made little sense. Less yet was his staying married to her. Aside from his tendency to wander, he did mostly settle down to the two mistresses whom he loved alternatively—as well as concurrently.

Within limits, what unhappiness this President had in the White House and at home was often relieved by these women. They were, respectively, Carrie Phillips, the attractive wife of a Marion, Ohio businessman and friend, and Nan Britton, a home-town idolizing young lady. A reason for the need to expand upon a sensitive area of Harding's personal life is that the tendency among biographers and others has—until quite recently—been to downplay sex as little more than a simple fact of Harding's life, albeit a risky obsession for him as President.

Unlike his wife, his mistresses had nothing to do with his life as President, but they had lots to do with his private life prior to and during his Presidency. Caught in a joyless job, and lacking a sex life at home, Harding looked for compensating extra-mural joy.

Unlike the attention given Carrie Phillips, the case of Nan Britton has mainly been kept in the shadows. Though this was a vital relationship, the tendency among biographers has mostly been to shy away from bringing Nan very much into the picture. For one thing, she was crowded out by Carrie, seen by Harding specialists as the "love of his life," though, as instanced by his affair with Nan, Carrie was one of two. Harding's appetite was big enough; in fact insatiable. The more he got, the more he wanted.

On the other hand, while everyone writing on Harding has been obliged to mention the most controversial subject in his biography—that recorded by Nan in her autobiographical memoir, The President's Daughter—no one has bothered to do much with a work which gives a detailed picture of Harding in love by the lone first-hand observer to tell what it was like. A reason for the avoidance is based on questions regarding the observer's reliability.

On just this point, Phillip Payne has observed that, "Despite the numerous and heavy-handed references to flappers and prudes in the various [early] accounts [of Nan's book] no one took the analysis any further" (Dead Last, 127). Nor has anyone, before or since then, done an analysis of the revelatory details Nan sets forth of her affair with Warren G. Harding. The book has routinely been alluded to, but treated, for the most part casually, and, if explored at all, superficially, and never in-depth. A biographical step-child, it has been kept at arm's length. However, its content is of high value for filling out the picture of what President Harding was doing in his off-time.

Ideally, in order to give expanded treatment to Nan's racy story, one would want her credibility to be sufficiently established by external evidence. Yet, deliberately cloaked in secrecy by the principals (their love letters urgently destroyed) and suppressed by others aware of their affair, much of such evidence is by its very nature impossible to come by. After all, only the two principals could have known what transpired in their intimacy, and only Nan, who kept a record of those events, survived to tell what they were. Nonetheless, for all the questions raised about Nan's book, so far no concrete evidence has emerged to invalidate her credibility.

Since a sticking point has been the lack of substantial evidence for validating her credibility, the implicit reasoning seems to be: why touch it, if there is no confirming allusion to it from the principals apart from Nan's story per se? There is, however, enough external evidence and much internal evidence to support its authenticity, even if Nan was writing this book with a stated point to make, and her narrative is tempered by the mentality of a young woman very much in love.

All else set aside, for those who tend to accept Nan's account, on however limited a basis—as most biographers do—a central basis for conviction is the believability factor. In essence, the situations Nan describes are offered with a kind of detailed certainty that cannot easily be faked. Frederick Lewis Allen was so taken by Nan's book that he asked: how could she possibly have made it up, and, how could a reader not believe the frank details of what she wrote about?

As one reads the "confessions of [Harding's] mistress," Allen observed, "one is struck by the shabbiness of the whole affair." But, infamous as her account might be, that in itself does not cast doubt upon the truth of Nan's story. Allen asks a critical question: "is it easy to imagine any one making up out of whole cloth a supposedly autobiographical story compounded of such ignoble adventures?" (Only Yesterday, 128f.).

The same point has been advanced by others who have found that Nan's account simply compels belief, as with Francis Russell's asserting, "Although [Harding's] affair with Nan Britton could not be documented to the satisfaction of Dr. George Harding [Warren's brother] nevertheless the gushing, redundant pages of her book ring true. Such enthusiastic artlessness could hardly be counterfeited."

Russell found Nan's book to be very "convincing not only through its elaboration of details but by its very naiveté."[9]

As will be seen, a hard bitten journalist like H.L. Mencken, assuredly nobody's fool, was emphatically of the same opinion. For him, Nan's account was "so palpably true that it convinces instantly" ("Saurnalia," Baltimore Sun, 18 July, 1927, p.15.)

Not that intuitive conviction constitutes proof. But, if one wants to pursue the authenticity of Nan's account, what cannot be overlooked is the most controversial part of her story: namely, her claim that Warren fathered her daughter. The girl did exist, and she was informed of her parentage. Nan provided photographs of her, and no man other than Warren Harding was known to have had a physical relationship with Nan at the time she was seeing Harding, and became pregnant. Any concession on this point from the Harding family or the Harding Memorial Association would have been strongly resisted; and it was. There was big money involved, very big for that time—and Warren Harding's name.

Nan's chronology, however, especially regarding her tense last visit with Harding in January, 1923, comports with that provided from other sources—e.g., William Allen White, to be cited later. As for Nan's daughter, Elizabeth Ann, accompanying one of the photographs Nan published of the girl, is the quote she gives from a letter by Harding's sister Abigail (aka Daisy) who, on seeing the photograph wrote, "The cheek and eye are similar to those of yours truly…"[10]

Daisy fully acknowledged the truth of Nan's relationship with her brother, as did her sister Carolyn (aka Carrie). Their acknowledgements, which Nan published while the sisters were still alive, went out uncontradicted by them.

Nan's offer to verify her hotel trysts with Warren would not be taken up by their brother, Dr. George Tryon Harding III, Nan's chief antagonist, himself a pre-marital virgin. His quarrel with Nan was most acute over the $50,000 (assumed, unreliably, to have been one-tenth of Harding's estate) that she wanted for the cost of raising the child she'd had with Warren—plus an additional $2,500 to cover debts.

One result of her grueling four hour interview with brother

George was that Nan would be dismissed as a crass "gold-digger." But there were no charges of slander or libel from the Harding family over Nan's allegation that Warren was the father of her child. Nor, overall, has any evidence been adduced that undercuts the truth of a number of the incidents Nan describes.

Though those disclosures were difficult to ignore, they have remained, till recently, unchallenged, over such basic matters, for example, as date and place—just what brother George had been pressing Nan for. The result is that biographical evasion becomes an extension of the Harding family's effort to shield Warren's reputation from being further scandalized.

In fact, the family's rejection of Nan's appeal for the financial assistance needed to raise Warren's child would become an essential reason for her public confessional, beyond the reason she avows on behalf of children born out of wedlock. Had it not been for that icy dismissal by Warren's prudish brother George (familiarly known as "Deac," short for church Deacon) Nan would likely not have had to come forth on her own to seek income from a risky book no publisher would take.

While there is no way to verify an account of the private intimacy of a pair of lovers, beyond what one of them is willing to tell, Nan did put it out there for all to read, and anyone to refute, which, however, very few readers came forth to do, none effectively. There has been a recent attempt at rebuttal, to be shortly examined in context. Meanwhile, there remains a large uncovered story to be located in Nan Britton's Memoir of her affair with Warren Harding. I shall draw upon it, as needed to fill out the picture of his life, seen up close.

And speaking of sources, in Parts IV, V, and VII, in which I deal respectively with the three principle women in Harding's life, I make use of a good deal of the data reliably established by Francis Russell and Carl Anthony, which doesn't have to be re-established, but becomes a platform for developing the line of thought I have in mind. Supporting information, particularly relevant for Florence, is provided from the Scobey correspondence. My aim is to apply what can be learned from this data to how these women affected the private life of Warren Harding.

CHAPTER 5

"The Memoir's Validity"

THE ONLY PERSONS TO SERIOUSLY go after Nan in her time were: a) Joseph DeBarthe, whose slanderous The Answer to 'The President's Daughter, (1928) failed to prove his point of Harding's sterility, and b) John D. Sumner, on behalf of the Society for the Suppression of Vice. Sumner's case to prohibit publication of Nan's book was dismissed in court, with Nan being awarded $2,500 in damages. Robert Ferrell, another nay-sayer, speculatively contends that Nan did not write her book. But he strangely contradicts himself by first asserting, "Much of what Ms. Britton wrote was believable," only to propose that it was actually Richard Wightman, not Nan, who "wrote the book." Wightman, head of the Bible Corporation of America, for whom Nan worked as a secretary, had helped Nan with the publication of her book. However, no proof is given of Wightman's supposed authorship.[11]

The general conviction of historians, on the other hand, uniformly follows the views of Allen, Russell, and Mencken that, as, Carl Anthony puts it, "Nan's account of her love affair with Warren might be romanticized but was generally accurate."[12] Even Ferrell accepts the content of The President's Daughter as wholly truthful, treating incidents he cites from it as apparently established facts. He, indeed, goes beyond what others have noted about the interim financial assistance Harding had given Nan, underscoring the fact that his regular payments of $300 to $400 (at times $500) were "quite generous for the times when annual incomes of $2,000 or less were common for professional people" (op. cit., 53).

In the final analysis, Nan was telling us what, after Harding's death, she alone could have known. In her account, as nowhere else, one finds Harding to be very believably captured in his most poignant emotional experiences seen at their high and low points, which brought on moments of dramatic intensity for the lovers and empathy from readers.

Nan had backing for those revelations, based on her having retained some letters from Harding (Payne, op. cit., 133). Although the few she preserved were lacking in anything intimate, they did show there was actual contact between Warren and Nan, and that they dealt with Harding's desire to get Nan a job, as described in her book.

Further evidence was obtainable from the Secret Service Agent, Jim Sloan (Slade in PD) who was one of the lovers' go-betweens for transporting the money Harding was sending Nan, along with the correspondence he was taking back and forth between them. Nan told of secret meetings she had had with Harding in the White House itself, in fact in an ante-room to the Oval Office, which, though seemingly hard to believe, were certified to have been true.

The head of the Secret Service detail assigned to the White House, Colonel Edward Starling, guarded as he was about official duties, did confirm that one of his agents there had, as Nan indicated, transmitted letters between Harding and a young lady from New York, whom he "supposed was Nan Britton" (Russell, "Four Mysteries," American Heritage [1963] p.83). Of comparable importance, Daisy Harding supported her belief in Nan's story by sending her periodic payments (until they were suspended, likely on pressure from brother George) and she at one point went out of her way to set up Nan and daughter in an apartment of their own.

There is additional confirmation for Nan's account of her affair with Warren, to which I return in appropriate contexts. But, for the moment, there is sufficient reason to recognize that the delicate information she imparts is immensely revelatory and had a credible basis. Needless to say, there was some audacity in Nan's spelling out an aspect of Harding's private life otherwise impossible to secure and best left private. However, necessity having pushed her to do this memoir, history has been a beneficiary of the result. She was, after all, writing about the love life of a man who became the Nation's Twenty-Ninth President.

Given the authenticity of Nan's account, it fills out an area of rather fantastic goings-on in Warren's life. Stressful as things were for him as a Presidential candidate who really didn't want to be one and got himself elected anyway on the pledge of a return to normalcy—indeed "serenity" (Murray, Era, 70)—there he was recklessly swinging between two women he loved, to whom he made equally strong commitments he couldn't keep.

As this dragged on, the first of his mistresses would be alternately reigniting their sex-inspired love and threatening to make a public exposure of it. Toward the end of their relationship, Harding feared ruination was looking him in the eye.

Meanwhile, as if that wasn't tension enough, Warren had been sharing a bedroom, but not a bed, with another woman, a homely and bossy type whom he did not love, but needed: his wife. She increased the profitability of his newspaper, got him started in politics, involved herself in White House affairs, censored his speeches, proved herself dependable, and made him dependent on her. Wise and helpful she was. Otherwise, however, she, as he said, made life hell for him (PD, 74) but wouldn't tolerate a separation.

How did Harding handle such a dilemma? Having largely made a muddle of it, he didn't try to. But that was his personal life. He was far more adept in the political arena, a model for how a non-entity becomes President of the United States. Staying on course for political advancement, he turned the tables on his wife and exploited her managerial skills to abet that advancement. It took a good politician to know one, a proof of which was her tolerance of this husband's dalliance. She knew it, felt hurt by it, and looked past it toward bigger issues, like running the country. Meanwhile, her husband-President needed the comfort that would help keep him in the game.

As for the bottom line on Nan Britton's Memoir, first, there are sufficient reasons to believe in the truth of what she tells us about her relationship with Warren Harding. Secondly, even if her story is questioned, that doesn't get us around the fact that Nan had indisputably had a child with Harding. Moreover, however truthful, what a young woman discloses about her affair with an adulterous President of the United States—assumedly taboo—is more than just flashy news. Her doing that is a fact in itself, and, as such, makes a place for itself in the overall biography. Welcome or not, it has to be dealt with.

CHAPTER 6

"He Loves Carrie; Contradictory Life-Style"

Difficult as it has been to learn much about Harding's relationship with Nan Britton outside of what she has told us, it has been equally difficult to get a good fix on his relationship with Carrie Phillips. Francis Russell, the one biographer who had, until rather recently, had the sole opportunity to read Harding's love letters to Carrie, was under court injunction not to publish quotation from them. Nonetheless, though superseded by a work by James Robenalt, to be considered in the next Chapter, there was much useful information Russell came up with.

For one thing, he noted that in some of his love letters to Carrie, Harding ran on for all of 40 pages, which corresponded to the size of letters Nan claimed that he had written to her. He used the same Senate stationary for both. Russell also showed that the clichéd romantic sentiments Nan attributed to Harding were, word for word, very similar to those he had used in letters to Carrie. In each case, he meant what he felt—sincerely. Having been head over heels in love with both, he had been equivalently smitten by each.

Although Russell's reading of those letters to Carrie has made him a valuable source for details regarding Harding's love life, until the letters themselves become publicly available (though parts had appeared in the Press in the mid-1960s) one has to tread carefully with the scenario Russell gave of Harding in love. Apparently writing largely from memory of what he had read, Russell was evidently careless sometimes about documenting his assertions.

Quite clear, however, was his showing the other side to the love triangle—i.e., the passion Carrie had for Warren. It was not just that "with Carrie his sensuality struck depths he was unaware of in himself," but Carrie was quite eager "to slip away with him to the nearest city [for] the anonymous intimacy of a hotel room" (Shadow, 169f.).

On the other hand, based on evidence from various biographical sources already out there—eminently including The President's Daughter along with thoughts Harding confided to Frank Scobey—enough information is accessible to put together a substantial picture of Harding's behind-the-scenes persona and one aspect of the character that he brought to the Presidency.

Proceeding from that base, one could better understand the psyche of this newspaper man turned politician, who became an accidental President. How, one might ask, does one put together the insanity of Warren Harding's personal life with the relative sanity of his Presidential life? If asked that way, the obvious answer is one can't. Except that it happened. This was but one of the inexplicable decisions Harding made about how he would live his life.

While the story of his personal life did not impinge on his political life, there were areas in which personal decisions had to be measured against political ones. Part, if not the nucleus, of that story resides in Harding's internal debate over whether he could pursue the passion he enjoyed with Carrie Phillips at the price of forgetting politics, or, whether it was better for him to stay on with the wife who guided his political career. Since he chose to maintain both relationships, there could not be smooth sailing with either. But sail he did.

In order to get a better understanding of Harding's contradictory life style I draw on two main sources of new information; as indicated, Harding's correspondence with Frank Edgar Scobey, and the untouched content of Nan Britton's Memoir of her love life with Harding. Surely, it is well past time to delve into Nan's Memoir and accept her credibility. It can only be enlightening. But, first, there is the recent publication of parts of Harding's correspondence with Carrie Phillips to be fitted into the picture.

CHAPTER 7

"Robenalt Vs Nan"

ALTHOUGH JAMES D. ROBENALT'S THE Harding Affair: Love and Espionage During the Great War was issued after I had written a large portion of this book, it wasn't difficult to get caught up on the basis for Robenalt's negative opinion of Nan Britton's President's Daughter. Robenalt based his criticism in part on such items as Nan's probable misdating the July, 1917 day on which, as she put it, she "became Mr. Harding's bride" (PD, 49). He also, for example, doubts Nan's account of her stay with Warren at the New Witherill hotel in Plattsburgh, NY, though Francis Russell and another Harding researcher have found that Nan and Warren had signed the register at that Hotel for the date in question, with her using a different, but identifiable, name, as she had done elsewhere.

Robenalt, at the outset, incredibly remarks: "In some ways, Warren G. Harding seemed like the most unlikely person to become enmeshed in an extramarital relationship" (Affair, 13). Based on Warren's prior history, he seems, on the contrary, quite likely to have become regularly enmeshed in adulterous sex. It wasn't simply the proximity of Carrie Phillips' beauty that got him started.

Aware of "a lawyer's demand for proof, " (Affair, 383) Robenalt makes the absurd assumption that Nan Britton, prior to 1927, had somehow had access to the Warren-Carrie love letters, which Carrie had kept hidden in a tightly packed shoe box secluded in a locked closet of her home. The letters were first discovered around 1957 and made known to Francis Russell in 1964 (Shadow, 330f.).

There is no way that Carrie, alive and well, before 1927, would have allowed anyone, least of all Nan Britton, to have free access to those shoe-box letters. No one beyond Carrie even knew of their existence.

Carrie's motive was obvious. She had at one point written Warren that she had, as indirectly noted by Robenalt, "been protective of their relationship in part to guard Florence from embarrassment" (Ibid., 259). Should any hint of the existence of Warren's love letters to Carrie have reached Florence, the blow-up would have been considerable.

The reason Robenalt speculates that Nan had had access to Warren's love letters to Carrie is interesting. Robenalt thinks that that was the only way Nan could have derived the truthful information in her Memoir which is confirmed by those love letters. But, plainly the fact that happenings which Nan described correspond to those which also appear in his letters to Carrie came about because Nan had independently experienced those happenings—not because she could possibly have sought out such information in letters that she did not know existed.

In fact, if Nan wrote of matters that were also covered in the Carrie letters, then those letters actually provide corroboration for the truth of what Nan wrote in The President's Daughter.

In the first place, there is no evidence whatsoever that Nan had laid her hands on those letters. Carrie not only kept the letters in that locked closet, but her house itself was securely locked. She, in fact, had at one point locked herself out and used a tire iron to pry open a window through which she could hoist herself in. Those disclosures were provided by a columnist for the Ohio Farmer, and cited by Robenalt himself in his "Epilogue" (Ibid., 345).

Clearly, no one in small town Marion would have failed to observe anyone trying to force a way into Carrie's house in her absence. Surely not Nan Britton, well enough known in town. Anyway, there is no evidence whatsoever that Nan had gotten her hands on Warren's love letters, unknown to Nan and secure in Carrie's possession.

Robenalt writes that his grandfather, Francis Durbin, had read Nan's book and that "he reported his sources in Marion thought the account was true." In addition to that, Durbin added, in writing to James Cox (Harding's opponent in the 1920 election) "there is no question but the facts in this book are absolutely true" (Ibid., 351).

Robenalt does concede that "since so many of [Nan's] dates and 'facts' are corroborated by the Phillips letters, her story could be true, though not as she has embellished it" (Ibid., 347). Despite his acquiescence on that point, Robenalt still has it that the truth of certain incidents in Nan's book had to have been derived from the "facts" she had stolen from Warren's love letters in Carrie Phillips' locked possession.

WHEN THE ONE Harding historian who has had privileged access to those letters goes out of his way to take a negative position on Nan's Memoir, one need not wonder why. It is obvious that any discussion of Nan from Robenalt comes with a caveat.

James Robenalt wanted the approval of Dr. Warren Harding III, the President's great-grand-nephew, for his use of the Carrie letters. Robenalt wanted that even though he had already had legal clearance for use of the letters, based on expiration of the copyright on the photocopy of the letters in possession of the Western Reserve Historical Society.

Dr. Harding was the one who decided on use of the President's papers with an eye to protecting his legacy. The idea presented to Dr. Harding by Dean and Robenalt was that suppression of the love-letters gave "the false impression that there was something hidden, when, in fact, there was much to be revealed that showed what a fine man, and able President, Harding had been" (John Dean's "Foreword," Affair, xvi).

Since the family's attorney had wanted "sensational" references in the letters to be suppressed, Robenalt, in return, showed that he had the family's sensitivities in mind. Among other things, he did indeed avoid, or tone down, where possible, anything of a sensational nature, such as Warren's explicit admiration of Carrie's sensual body.

Nan, by the way, essentially adhered to the same formula. She showed discretion, avoiding anything in bad taste, and, anything that might make Warren look bad, beyond the fact of their adulterous relationship itself. But for the Hardings, and Robenalt, that was bad enough.

A reason for Robenalt's put-down of Nan's account of her illicit relationship with Warren Harding is that he seemed to be guided by a silent bias to make Harding look good, subtlety indicated by Dean. For Robenalt, the very mention of Nan made Harding look bad. Nan was, of course, vulnerable. Although the Carrie-Warren relationship looked bad, there were reasons why that could be overlooked. Carrie and Warren were contemporaries, approximate equals in age and status in Marion, and their story was out.

On the other hand, Nan was thirty-one years younger than Warren, a mere child of sixteen when they first started corresponding, and just over twenty when they exchanged kisses, as a prelude to sex, which came two months later. It was unbecoming for a married man of fifty-six to be having a relationship with that young a girl. Worse yet, she would have a daughter with Warren, and petition the Harding family for money to raise her. For them to accede would have been to honor the truth of her Memoir, dishonor Warren; and cost them a goodly sum, to boot.

Since Carrie's leaving for Berlin in 1911, and the subsequent decline in her affair with Warren provided an opening for Nan, Robenalt's treatment of the reason for Carrie's departure makes it relevant. It also sets up a contrast between problems Warren had in his personal life and those he had in his political life. A key question on 1911 is whether or not Carrie's departure was due to Warren's failure to act on their plan that he divorce Florence so they could legitimatize their relationship.

Carl Anthony, for example, was among those who held that Warren was at fault. Carrie was leaving because she was exasperated with him over his failure to make good on his repeated promises to come through with his side of their bargain. Warren had, after all, written her "[if] you want me then I'm yours now, any time—for all time." But time dragged on, Warren kept stalling, and, as with his getting the two couples to take an economy trip to Bermuda, it seemed that he'd do anything to keep Carrie around.

He would make an impressive promise, and just as impressively fail to act on it. Carrie had had enough, and she left, daughter in hand (Florence, 92f.).

Set forth that way, the break-up makes Warren look bad. For Robenalt, it seems that the situation should preferably be turned around. His position is that Carrie was at fault. Warren was ready to proceed with their plan and Carrie was not. Robenalt starts out by noting that "few" of Harding's letters "tell the story of exactly what happened in 1911 that led to her decision to leave [for Germany]" (op. cit., 47). That makes for an open question as to which party was responsible for Carrie's departure.

Robenalt points out that Warren "continued to plainly state that he was ready to give up his marriage for her and that she was the one who was not ready." With blame for the break-up put on Carrie, Warren looks better than her. But not really

It is true that he did say he'd give up his marriage for Carrie, but, since he made no move to do so, it looks like that was the reason Carrie would not be ready to do so herself. Evidently, Warren was caught in a quandary: he couldn't leave Florence and didn't want to have Carrie leave him. His promises were empty, made worse by his piling on endearments. Carrie, at least, did act. She left her husband to go to Berlin.

Then, to the point, did she leave specifically because she was unready, or because he was? There is no supporting evidence for Robenalt's putting the blame on Carrie. None, that is, with a clear reference to the reason for her 1911 departure. Instead, what we are given is a quote from a Harding letter of 5 January, 1913, a year and a half later, in which he says she did "write and say [she] was not ready." But not ready for what?

Having been burned back in 1911, she in 1913 looks at their relationship from another perspective. She projects an imaginary situation, which is, to quote Robenalt, "their dream of becoming parents together." (81). Hence, it was a different year and a different subject, not a rehash of 1911.

Robenalt suggests this is a thought additional to Warren's stating "he was ready to give up his marriage for her and that she was the one who was not ready." This, however, is not a quote; it is a paraphrase of what Robenalt says Warren wrote.

When Robenalt does quote what Warren wrote to Carrie, the words are: "You write and say you are not ready." Then he goes on to quote the clarifying reference of what she was not ready for according to Warren. It is "for I's sake [Isabelle's, Carrie's daughter's] and for the sake of the one we hope for [a child], you do not wish to be mine until you can be in the acceptance of the world's requirements." (Ibid., 81).

In other words, 'first we must marry,' and, despite bold words, he had taken no action to make that possible. She, by contrast, had made a move, albeit in disgust. Acceptance will have to wait, and delay is what he had been wanting all along. As for Carrie's intent regarding "acceptance," she did not want an illegitimate child.

Again, this was the subject in 1913, when she was already gone, and it had nothing to do with 1911.

However, their hope of getting together upon acceptance was not a sure thing. For in that same letter of 5 January, 1913, Carrie reiterated what she had told Warren during their December tryst, a sexual epiphany—namely, that she was interested in another man.

Warren was not blind to the uncertainty of where he stood with Carrie. True, she was unkind to him, but, for his sake, that would help to account for the fervor with which he rushed into the arms of a young woman who was thoughtful of him. Warren had a knack for weaving his way through knotty problems, which often was not pretty. However, he could adapt, and did so more skillfully in his political life than his personal one.

In any event, Robenalt brings out Warren Harding at his best, for which he can very well be applauded. As much as possible, Robenalt exercised discretion in quoting from letters at his disposal, and left out, for example, part of one in which Warren recalled an orgasmic event with Carrie. Anthony had quoted that part of the letter (Florence, 87).

Overall, Robenalt shows Warren to have been stronger than how he was characterized by most others who had written about him. I totally agree with that part of his treatment of Warren, particularly in his role as President. Carrie, of course, would exploit her special dominion over Warren, prone as she was to take whimsical advantage of his love and make a fool of him because of it. But that is a tale unto itself.

An important outcome that one takes away from Harding's failure to divorce Florence in order to marry gorgeous Carrie is that, politically, it would have left him in ruinous default. How, then, could he have run for the Senate and how even think of running for President?

CHAPTER 8

"The Bad That Was Said, The Good Done"

To BEGIN, THEN, WITH THE initial negatives directed at the newly elected Warren G. Harding, Princetonian Woodrow Wilson, on taking in his incredible successor, would credit him with "a bungalow mind" (Murray, Era, 120). Wilson's additional comment that Harding "had nothing to think with" was echoed by members of his Cabinet, who joined in the game of poking fun at Harding. They reflected the open contempt that Washingtonians had for this low-brow Ohioan who was to assume the Office of his high-minded predecessor.[13]

On the face of it, the transfer seemed rather ludicrous. But much of the credit for perpetuating Harding's blighted reputation has been attributed to several of the early commentators on "Politics of the 1920s," like, for example, William Allen White, Mark Sullivan, Frederick Lewis Allen, and Samuel Hopkins Adams, with the last two of these, as indicated, having been particularly derisive. Robert Murray observed that what they had to say about Harding became "historical 'gospel,' rarely contested and widely accepted" (op.cit., 526).

Interestingly, negative as they had been in evaluating Harding, in time, most journalists, like White and Sullivan, would rethink their criticism and find it difficult to bypass the positives. Since what views they held depended on when they held them, we learn much about Harding from how their opinions of him varied, and, in fact, changed, when timed with unfolding events, which in the first two years of his Presidency favored Harding. Suddenly this new President became a revelation.

White, the one most widely respected of this group, was also the one personally closest to Harding. In addition to the roles they shared as fellow Republican Delegates to the notorious June, 1920 Nominating Convention, White also shared Harding's experience of arriving on the national scene from having been a small-town newspaper man with Middle-American roots. White had practically free access to Harding, at times coming on call, when Harding wanted someone he could comfortably talk to. In many respects, White not only mirrored popular opinion of Harding, but, given a political climate prone to volatility, he, in effect, also became its shifting barometer.

He traversed the spectrum from an original high, to a disapproving low, to an unexpected high again, that varied to a mixed high-low, and ultimately descended into disillusionment, followed by sorrow in fateful 1923. White's writings in themselves embody the good-bad syndrome that marked Harding's career.

Looking at Harding from the perspective of a Roosevelt Progressive, White initially regarded him as a backward conservative, in effect, a rank Reactionary, and he proclaimed that nomination of Harding would disgrace the Republican Party and bring shame upon the country.[14] Like other Progressives—and Democrats—he regarded Harding as a ridiculous candidate, mediocrity exemplified—prior to election "a third-rater," and surely beatable.[15] Needless to say, White was hardly alone in his original opinion of Harding.[16]

He not only saw Harding as falling short of presidential timber, he was also the only member of the Kansas delegation who would vote against him, even on the tenth ballot when Harding's second-choice status in a deadlocked Convention practically made his nomination a fait accompli (Autobiog. 586-588).

On principle, White's vote would go to Herbert Hoover (Ibid., 388). However, this was the same Harding whom White had found projecting an impressive presence as keynote speaker at the 1916 Republican Convention, and, in that role, visibly appearing to be a leader of some stature. He was "vigorous, self-contained almost to the point of self-repression" with the "calm, assured, gracious manner," of a "well-schooled senatorial orator," whose "clarion voice filled the hall." Harding all of a sudden seemed to be "eagerly," but discreetly "tiptoeing…into a national limelight" (Masks, 394f.).

Moreover, even if an undertone of subtle dismay lurked in this portrait (was that appearance all 'show,' an empty façade?) less than three months into the presidential campaign which White had wanted to deny Harding, he was writing him with some enthusiasm about his manner of campaigning. White praised Harding's modest, low-key style, finding it had high-road appeal, particularly when contrasted with the abrasiveness of his opponent, James M. Cox. He noted that Harding was "making a great impression on the American people," adding in very personal terms, "You have grown every moment since the day of the nomination. It seems to me that your sincerity, your sense of dignity and your steady thoughts have made themselves felt in the American heart."[17]

Early on in Harding's Presidency, White's regard for him would even exceed those prior expectations, as he found Harding rising above his backwater origins, as a "country printer," (Masks, 233) to creditably fulfill the demands of the Office which, because of those limitations, Harding was sincerely wanting to make himself worthy of.

Others did a similar turn-about from post-Nomination dismay to post-election praise of Harding, as can be traced in New York Times editorial comments.[18] The day after his nomination, Harding was looked upon as a "second class" politician with a "faint and colorless," record in the Senate. He "measures down" to the political stature of a Franklin Pierce, being the "perfect flower of the cowardice and imbecility of the Senatorial cabal" that had managed the Republican Convention (11 June, 1920, p.10).

Then, several months into his Presidency, the Times suddenly reversed itself, praising him on a number of issues: "It is inspiring news" that he has taken the initiative on the Disarmament Conference, giving the United States "the high distinction [of] leading in a noble work for civilization." Furthermore, Harding was "courageous" in opposing the Bonus Bill for WW I veterans, which had, after all, been sponsored by the American Legion.

He seemed to have an instinct for getting things right. Suddenly he was getting accolades for that. He wanted a reduction in war time taxes, among other laudable measures, and appealed to our "finer sympathies," in doing so, (14 July, 1921, p. 14). In his "easy smashing of the dishonest duty on oil," Harding again showed "that courage pays," and he displayed a great "capacity for leadership" (20 July, 1921, p. 14). It's as if the Times editors couldn't say enough good about him, after having three days earlier chided him for "benevolent impartiality" in failing to deal with the "distinct break-down of leadership within Congress" (8 July, 1921, p. 8).

Suddenly, President Harding was a revelation.

CHAPTER 9

"Behold: A Leader"

THOUGH TOTALLY UNEXPECTED, IT WAS no accident that WGH began to exert leadership. During that first year of his Presidency, and beyond, he went at the job with a will to serve and get things done. Far from slothful, a label often applied to him, Harding was actually working hard at the job, impressing reporters with the time he put in at the desk; indeed, by some accounts doing sixteen-hour days. This was the Harding nobody would recognize, not then, not now. Indeed, to point this out today would provoke disbelief—probably amusement.

But contrary to the prevalent opinion of Harding, Mark Sullivan took note that, "In the mere prosaic quality of capacity for hard work, Harding is extraordinary."[19] Since Harding was not exactly known as a workaholic by temperament or past political performance, one might be inclined to see this remark by Sullivan—a personal friend and fellow golfer—as hyperbole by virtue of friendship.

But, interestingly, during his last meeting with Nan Britton in January, 1923, in the midst of the ultimate crisis over the state of their relationship, Harding would propose "work" as an exigent solution that he had found to be productive for himself. Caught between a Presidency he described as "nerve-wrecking [and] energy-sapping," a chronically ailing wife, and an inability to make his relationship with Nan legitimate, that was what he offered Nan as the best stopgap antidote to their troubles: "Work, dearie, work!" (PD, 239).

"Toil" would be what he'd prescribe for himself to treat a

disappointment he had experienced with Carrie Phillips: "I can dissipate a lot of depression amid the engrossment of toil. It is my one relief" (Affair, 168). Robert Murray observed that, however exacting Harding's work load, a friend would point out, "there is no indication that Harding ever physically shirked his presidential duties" (op. cit., 123).

The long hours might have been compensation for Harding's self-expressed doubts about his ability to handle the awesome responsibilities of Chief Executive. But, whatever his immediate motivation, Harding was fully aware of how long a shot he had been, beginning with his unlikely Nomination. Assessing his near-miraculous luck, he suggested it could best be described in poker terms: "We drew to a pair of deuces and filled" (Shadow, 396).[20]

Harding's ability to poke fun at himself, not only made him likeable to the public, but it also betrayed an underlying confidence that, after all, he would be up to the job. The point is not so much that "good fellow" Harding didn't take himself too seriously, as that his 'lucky" election motivated him to meet the challenge before him, and prove his doubters wrong.

He knew perfectly well how little was expected of him by the Senate Cabal, a circumstance, alone, which—translated into a dare—would have prompted him to come to the Office primed for work. Since the Press was at the outset not just critical, but outright disdainful (using terms like "colorless and pliable," "fool," "brainless," "third-rater") it had to have been apparent to Harding that recovery from such treatment could only be achieved by dint of performance.

One trait that had much to do with his buckling down with a will to master the work at hand was a certain dogged determination he could summon when pressured, an attitude that emerged early in his campaign for the Nomination. Since he couldn't have been unaware of how the Press disparaged him, it was as if he felt he had something to prove, primarily to himself, as well as to the country. In fact, he settled into this attitude rather early, as with his undertaking the campaign for Nomination—not always happily—as a self-imposed obligation.

So, in January 1920, although he noted that "The call for speeches is quite beyond my capacity to meet," he nonetheless intended to do all that would be required of him, regardless of its being "a pretty absorbing task." No need for him to complain, because, as he put it, "I have undertaken this job and I have got to give it the best that I have in me."[21] Though not yet a candidate, whatever Harding lacked in other qualifications, when challenged, he was capable of bringing forth the typical underdog reflex of defiant grit.

Regarding Presidential efficiency—also not usually ascribed to Harding—Sullivan observed that Harding "has the valuable quality of dividing the business of the day into compartments. He waits until the matter in hand demands decision; he makes the decision, then passes on to the next thing" (The Great Adventure, 225). It sounds very much as if Sullivan, who in time could join in the late criticism of Harding, was writing this from first hand observation, as recalled. In other words, we are invited to view Harding in a way that does not correspond with the impression normally given of him by biographers, historians, and interested laymen.

Though he had not had much administrative experience, and the Times was not far off in calling attention to his limited background in leadership (13 June, 1920, p.1) he did have a sense for taking command. After the Times recognized that the new Harding had begun to exert his will on Congress, it ran a story about his activist attitude in, for example, proposing that all aircraft services of the government, both military and civilian, be placed under one central authority (16 July, 1921, p. 30). In itself, this was no great matter, but as a sign of his taking charge in making a demand for efficiency, these had not been seen as typically Harding traits.

Nor did he subsequently slacken off, despite impressions to the contrary. As late as February, 1923, when passage of the British Debt Agreement faced captious Senate opposition, Harding made a personal appearance before a joint session of Congress and set forth a persuasive argument for its passage, based on which he got it done—emphatically, with votes to spare. As reported on by Andrew Sinclair, "Harding stood in triumph in front of his discredited first Congress, which even Senator Lodge admitted had been 'more criticized and more fiercely attacked' [by Harding] than any other [President] he had known" (Available Man, 273).

Looking back, even after all of the devastating exposures had come out, Sullivan could still call attention to a positive side of Harding's term in Office, stressing a matter universally overlooked: "As a result of Harding's insistence on economy," Sullivan pointed out, "the fiscal condition of the government showed steady improvement almost from the day Harding took office." With little fanfare, Harding had made a "reduction of the public debt at the rate of almost one hundred million dollars monthly"[22] Not bad for a President remembered for his disgrace.

CHAPTER 10

"And He Has A Heart"

WHITE, HAVING VIEWED HARDING UP-CLOSE in the early stages of his Presidency, would come away with a favorable idea of his on-the-job character, something called into question often enough. Among such occasions was one on which the far from credulous White would find himself giving Harding considerable respect.

To wit, the newly elected President was being confronted by a group of social workers who wanted him to make good on his desire to propose a pardon for Eugene V. Debs (imprisoned under Wilson for his anti-war activities) and White saw Harding comport himself with "gentle dignity," while firmly resisting one woman's aggressive demand for an immediate 'yes or no' answer. Though he openly favored the pardon, the point was made that it would have to be done on his terms and at a time when he was ready to grant it, after having had it checked out by his Attorney General (Autobiog, p.623).

Unpopular as the pardon was with the public and not just with the super-patriot American Legion, but with the Press as well (e.g., the New York Times) Harding additionally faced the opposition of his strong-minded wife and his politically astute Attorney General. Even Herbert Hoover, who had a broader vision of the world than other advisors, thought it would be an unnecessary mistake.

Then, once Harding got Congressional ratification of the World War peace treaties, to which he affixed his signature in July, 1920, and declared November 11th a national holiday, he decided to act on

Debs' pardon, insisting that it was appropriate, as well as consistent with the spirit of reconciliation. It was also an act of kindness. Harding had Debs come to the Justice Department for a personal meeting. He greeted him warmly, with outstretched hand, and provided time for a friendly conversation. Harding wanted the pardon to be granted on Christmas Eve, so Debs could have Christmas dinner with his wife (Murray, Era, 168).

For good measure, Harding saw to it that twenty-three social radicals, considered political prisoners, were pardoned as well, with yet others similarly circumstanced to be quietly pardoned thereafter.[23] Even as President-elect, Harding had had Debs on his mind and had already wanted Daugherty to be looking into the matter of a pardon. For his role in getting it done, Daugherty, who was bitterly opposed to the idea, declared that he took quite a bit of heat—in fact, "scorn"—from The Nation and the New York World (Inside Story of the Harding Tragedy, Ibid.). It was actually Christmas Day that Debs left the Atlanta Penitentiary.[24]

On the other hand, when it came to Harding's vetoing so emotional an issue as the popular WW I Bonus Bill (a grant of $50 for each month of a veteran's service) on the common sense basis that we simply couldn't afford it, kindliness gave way to fiscal responsibility. Despite Congressional opposition, and despite the fact that it had been sponsored by the politically potent American Legion, Harding stood firmly behind his conviction, and, for this show of courage, he would subsequently win approval from the Press and the public at large.

Of course, it is also true that there were times enough when Harding could let things slide and avoid the fight for principle that he had shown himself to be capable of. There simply were some matters on which he had convictions and held fast to them, like the eight hour day for workers—when those in steel mills were doing twelve hour days, in seven day weeks—and naval disarmament, while there were other matters that he felt he could be flexible about, like prohibition and women's suffrage, preferring to go with popular sentiment on each (WGH to FES, 4 December, 1916, 13 September, 1917). Like every other President, he had a keen eye for the direction in which the political winds were blowing.

Himself a drinker, Harding couldn't see himself favoring prohibition, though he would, of course, have it enforced. Regarding women's suffrage, he saw no immediate urgency for it after decades of neglect and said he was as likely to vote for as against it. These were views that went back to his Senatorial days. On the other hand, following the presidential election and prior to his assuming office, he was eager to have a peace treaty with Germany enacted, to get the nation over residual bitterness aroused by the War.

This had led to a discussion with Nicholas Murray Butler which gave rise to his conviction about the need for a limitation on naval armaments, favored both as a deterrent to war and a means of promoting fiscal restraint.[25] To his credit, it was typical of Harding to consult with, and draw on the wisdom of, those of his advisors, like Butler and Hoover, who had the experience he lacked in international affairs.

Once Harding found himself comfortably installed in the Presidency and getting good things done, his essentially likeable personality blossomed. White reported that he had "a two years' honeymoon" with the Press, in which he was treated with "elaborate courtesy" and had the relaxed confidence with reporters of a "hail fellow well met." His warm reception went well beyond the greeting reporters would naturally give an ex-newspaper man turned President.

In 1923, two years into his Presidency—time enough for him to have taken his lumps politically—-Harding could always depend on finding a cordial group of well-wishers among the reporters who covered him. What they found, as White reported, was that "no one could have been more genuinely earnest in the manifestations of his public desire to be a good President." At his best, no politician of his day rivaled Harding in his relationship with the Press; and none had a more engaging style overall, which extended to his widening political affiliations.

As White continued, this was his portrait of President Warren G. Harding in prime form:

"He was frank in confessing his limitations, disarming in his candor to his friends, and even to casual acquaintances and always to newspaper men who crowded into his press conferences every Friday. He stood before them bland, charming, even jovial at times, but with an actor's quick sense of dignity; a fine, well set up figure of a man, clearly of the emotional type with the eager wistful lineaments of a friendly pup written on every flexible feature, with the warmth of a woman's cordial glow in his eyes."[26]

That was White capturing Harding at his appealing best, a virtual cynosure. Even if some might think him deceptively so, Harding was still quite self-assured. At the same time, however, unbeknownst to both the reporter and his subject, this image would also mark a watershed in Harding's career. Published in 1938, White's portrait was drawn from notes he had taken fifteen years earlier of a President he had observed prior to the disasters that were going to befall him in fateful 1923. To say nothing of the Damocles fallout from scandals yet to be heaped on him.

In spite of how congenially "Good Guy" Harding was received by reporters, White felt they also had a secret sense that trouble was brewing, as they actually "suspected more than they wrote, hoping that appearances were deceptive, that they were wrong in their surmises" (Ibid.). So underneath their overt approval, reporters, who knew more than the general public did, were having their apprehensions about what lay ahead for this President. For all of the ill wind that was blowing his way, they were smart enough to know that the Leader with a heart wasn't the man who should get picked on, certainly not the one to be isolated for blame.

CHAPTER 11

"The Bad That Became Worse"

UNFORTUNATELY, THAT WAS NOT THE way things looked after the Congressional investigations had finished laying waste to the Harding Administration. Though dead by that time, Harding himself was far from untouched, even if, by the record, he was the same decent man he'd been before. It's just that he was found to have been surrounded by crooks, and it was hard to believe he didn't know it.

Running the time-warp forward to 1938, when the derogatory verdict on Harding had been well established, William Allen White would render his own pejorative estimate of him. Reversing himself, White made a shallow person of the capable President he had formerly revered: His post-script was that Harding had been "one of those smilers and political masseurs who paw and pat their way out of difficulties" (Ibid.).

Considering that 1923 would become the year of a serious decline in Harding's health and, behind the scenes, signs of eroding confidence in his Presidency, White provided a version of the "smiler" Harding who was determined to stay up-beat before the public, despite the swarm of "difficulties" which lay in the offing. He wasn't sure he'd be able to swim his way through. It was remarkable enough that he managed to persevere for as long as he did. The stress had been mounting.

Since White had visited Harding in the winter of 1923, his unfavorable impression had to have emerged after the intimations of scandal got to Harding himself, culminating in the May 30th suicide of Jess Smith, Harry Daugherty's chief lieutenant. That was the watershed event.

In light of what he had heard about Smith, Harding had had to break the news to him that he was being scratched from the Alaska trip. There were several discomfiting reasons for Harding to be feeling bad that he had to do this. As boss, he was duty bound to tell Smith there were nothing less than criminal charges about to be brought down on him. Not alone a reflection on his Administration, this involved Harding himself. Personally, it also put him in the position of seeming to have influenced the suicide. That Jess had had an office but no official title in Justice, of all places, only made his suicide look that much worse.

Meanwhile, there was Harding preparing to leave Washington on 20 June for his well publicized trip to Alaska. He had no alternative but to pull himself together and pretend there was really nothing to be made of Smith's putting a bullet in his head.

The departure had been billed as a respite from the cares of Office, "A Journey of Understanding." The President was going out on a sort of Royal Progress to acquaint himself first hand with his country and his people. By the end of May, the trip had acquired a gala atmosphere. What Harding least needed was to have it overshadowed by just such cares as those originating from the Jess Smith affair. Coming not long after the exposure of scandal in the Veterans' Bureau, it didn't smell right, and raised suspicions that more of the same might be on the way.

Nor did it help matters that Harding had earlier had an emotional parting with Nan Britton. Was it over with Nan, after she had become the second true love of his life? Hence, it was by dint of a strenuous effort that Harding would maintain a felicitous pose during his trip west, which was to abruptly end in physical breakdown and, on 2 August, 1923, his untimely death.

Effort that it had been for him to have kept his trip going, worries notwithstanding, Harding persisted partly because he had no alternative and partly because he was infected by the exhilarating receptions given him at one stop after the other. Enthusiastic crowds were coming out eager to see their President. In person! There was also the uplift—however temporary—that he received from his contact with members of the Press along the way. Having been sympathetic toward Harding, they noticed signs of the growing strain on him.

As things proceeded, it became apparent that the underlying story of what caused that strain had to have been a fear that the worm of corruption was working its way through his Administration and showing signs that it was going to wriggle out into the open. Harding, it might be said, was among the first to recognize that there had been scandals afoot during his time in Office. This raised the bar for such stamina as would be exacted of him if he was to carry on despite his fears. Restless and unable to sleep at night, a victim of nervous energy which he couldn't shut off, it was as if Harding was trying to outrun his fate.

For explanation, one has to go back to Harding's having learned of Smith's improper conduct. There was a significant discrepancy between cause and effect in what Daugherty said that Harding had supposedly told him. Indeed, the truth is that there was much more to the circumstance with Smith than the trifling problems which Daugherty claimed that Harding said he had found out. This discrepancy has been missed by biographers, who literally accepted Daugherty's story of what Harding had supposedly said to him about Smith.[27] What Daugherty did was to provide a flimsy cover-up for Jess's nefarious activities, a story he made up to exonerate three persons at one stroke: himself, Jess, and Harding.

The fact that Harding was acutely aware of this had a lot to do with the massive depression that descended on him as he prepared for his trip west. It got worse as the overly long journey ran on, and would get worse yet.

Hoover, who had joined the journey at Tacoma, recalled that when he asked Harding about Dougherty's relation to the Smith affair, Harding had "abruptly dried up" (Hoover, Memoirs, II, 49). His memory of it continued to harass him. Dougherty, who was in constant contact with Harding couldn't have been providing cheerful word from Washington. Nonetheless, he had to keep Harding abreast of the latest. When a coded message expedited to reach Harding on shipboard practically exploded in his hands, its content collapsed him, and, incoherent when he came to, he was muttering something about false friends (Shadow , 587).

Already worn down to the breaking point, Harding did not need to be haunted by Smith's suicide. With the addition of secretive bad news from Daugherty, the person who knew 'where all the bodies lay,' things got to be too much for Harding. Jess Smith, a shadowy figure Harding never appointed, and didn't interact with, had apparently had something to do with what killed him.

CHAPTER 12

"Jess"

Tracing back to the point from which a deteriorating situation began its slide, let me explain what Daugherty's cover up was about. Daugherty said Harding told him that he, Harding, had been informed that Smith was "running with a gay crowd, attending all sorts of parties," and was "using the Attorney-General's car until all hours of the night" (Harding Tragedy, 248). But who could be so naïve as to believe that this was other than a fabrication, with Daugherty putting out a subterfuge to replace the raw information which had really been disclosed to Harding?

With all that Harding already knew about Smith's social activities (had he not been provisioning the White House with illegal booze?) the revelation of petty escapades, even if true, could not have been the basis for Smith's having been pushed to suicide. Backing off, Daugherty finally attributed that to Smith's having been despondent over his failing health—also flimsy grounds for the suicide. According to Dougherty, blubbery Jess had spent a month in the hospital, part of it "in a semi-conscious state caused by diabetes and absorption from the acute infection in the abdomen," etc. (Harding Tragedy, 247). But he did get well and had been up and about, sharing a paranoid obsession with his ex-wife Roxy Stinson. Cover-up deception came easily to Daugherty, however outlandish.

Daugherty was fully aware of the true information that came to Harding about Smith, who had been his co-conspirator in the easy-grafting Justice Department. Daugherty could not have written of Smith's corrupt practices without incriminating himself. It was, after all, in 1932 that Daugherty was publishing his account of the problem Harding had had with Smith, just four years after he himself had narrowly escaped conviction and imprisonment in two trials over the infamous American Metal case.

That had been a complicated affair, personally trying for Daugherty, which evolved from fraud in the Alien Property Custodian's Office. For his part in facilitating the disposition of German manufacturing properties to American Metal, at much less than market value, Smith, for example, was believed to have been nicely compensated, to the tune of over $200,000.

Next to this, talk of Smith's supposedly having had high times, attending parties and using the Attorney General's car, even if true, was sheer nonsense. Criminal charges for that? Not worth the time of day for the President, true or false. In either case, it would have merited no more than a reprimand from the Attorney General.

Under the circumstances, an actual irregularity should have raised a red flag. For Harding it did. It also raised the legitimate fears which Smith confessed to Roxy. She said that throughout May, 1923, Smith had been "living in mortal terror, could not bear being alone, constantly suspected that he was being followed...and repeated over and over, 'they are going to get me.'" (Murray, Era, 435).

Contrary to assumptions that, as a diabetic, Smith might have been suffering from the effects of his illness, what had actually been weighing on him was the growing "threat of exposure and arrest" (Giglio, 158). Over his head in boodle, Jess had been regularly receiving payment for obtaining permits from the corrupt Prohibition Bureau to withdraw liquor out of the government's bonded warehouses.

Ever active in finding ways to increase the reach of his influence peddling, Jess was able to get the dismissal of countless indictments against coal operators. He got himself so deeply into grafting schemes that, in order to convince prospective clients of his potential influence, he had set them up to observe him ushering Harding into his residence for a poker night (Florence, 285). So, in addition to his being in the pay of bootleggers, Jess was accepting bribes from shady characters made aware of his access to power, devious persons who wanted recommendations for pardon or immunity from prosecution.

However, in one case, facilitating Jess was unable to come through with the immunity promised a Cincinnati bootlegger, after he had been paid a cool quarter of a million to get that job done. He feared the bootlegger more than he feared Harding. Having made similar mistakes, Jess had reason to live in fear for his life (Shadow, 514). Jess Smith, incidentally, was a perfect example of the blood-sucking incompetents who had found their way into low level posts in the Harding Administration. No one questioned how Jess Smith, a former dry goods clerk, lacking in any knowledge of the law, landed an unofficial position in the Justice Department. He worked for Daugherty. Nothing else needed to be said.

Herbert Hoover recalled that after he joined the Alaska journey on 3 July, 1923, he found Harding "exceedingly nervous and distraught." This, Hoover attributed to such "ugly facts," as the suicide of Charles Cramer (of the corrupt Veteran's Bureau) followed by that of Jess.

Harding directly asked Hoover (in an incident to be given more attention further on) what he'd do if he "knew of a great scandal" in their Administration. For particulars, Harding went on to say: "he had received some rumors of irregularities, centering around Smith, in connection with cases in the Department of Justice." Coming from Justice, those cases very likely surrounded American Metal. Harding added that "he had followed the matter up and finally sent for Smith. After a painful session he told Smith that he would be arrested in the morning. Smith went home, burned all his papers, and committed suicide." As noted above, when asked about Daugherty, Harding "abruptly dried up and never raised the question again" (Hoover, Memoirs, II, 49).

Harding had to have had his suspicions aroused prior to his being informed of the particulars concerning Smith. His worry was not that well concealed, as indicated by a tense, near-confessional session Harding had had with Nicholas Murray Butler in early May, 1923 (also to be noticed further on). Unable to bring himself to a catharsis, Harding's suspicions festered, and could only grow from their contrast to the popular reception that highlighted his last journey. The emergence of his fears during the talk with Hoover had a cast of inevitability. This Harding directly admitted in negating Hoover's advice that the best way to handle such matters was to bring them out and get credit for doing so (Ibid.).

With his inner thoughts being checked by repression, Harding's situation was fraught with ironies. He was connecting so well with those crowds, that people obviously felt themselves seeing a President at the apex of his career, basking in their adulation. Meanwhile, with Harding's realization that Jess Smith's activities were not an isolated situation (hence the silence about Daugherty) he could, at the same time, foresee all of the good that he had done being suddenly washed away. Yet, doing his best to conquer discouragement, Harding followed through with his exhausting itinerary of speeches, receptions, tours, and banquets, plus all of the glad-handing and celebration of local events en route, until his health gave out.

One reason Harding couldn't have followed through on Hoover's argument for disclosure was that by July, 1923 it was too late. The reason he wouldn't have been able to do it sooner was his knowing that he couldn't have done so without incurring insurmountable consequences—a total blow-up of his Presidency. He could not put it that gravely to Hoover, instead making the brief understatement that such disclosure "might be politically dangerous" (Ibid.). Regarding politics, and everything else, it turned out that the danger was more for the Party Man than the Party.

Considering the serious issues that Harding had come to know about Jess Smith, it would have been ridiculous for him to concern himself with Jess's social life. Harry Daugherty, on the other hand, had no difficulty in making up that kind of concern, since he was putting words into Harding's mouth nine years after he had a chance to reject them.

CHAPTER 13

"Innocent, But Guilty Anyway"

It was self-evident that, however innocent Harding himself might have been of any malfeasance, if perpetrated by a member of his Administration, the responsibility would be charged to him. That, of course, is exactly what happened in the investigative frenzy that got underway after his death, eventuating in the parade of scandals being exposed which would sink his Presidency.

The good that he felt he had done evaporated in the blink of an eye; the suddenness took no more than the hearing of a Congressional Committee smelling political advantage. Recalled, among other things, was how he had been able to bully Congress, and gain public approval at their expense. Democrats were waiting to ambush him anyway. Harding had been able to foresee what might be done with the information he had gained, but, unable to counter it during his lifetime, he would get his name placed on the scandalous behavior of others.

While grafters like Charles R. Forbes, Charles S. Cramer, Jess Smith, and Albert Fall, as well as Harry Daugherty, profited handsomely from their chicanery, Harding died a debtor, deeply in the red to his brokerage firm to the tune of $90,000, which translates into a good deal more in today's dollars.[28]

Those in his Administration who knew the real story were helpless to exonerate Harding without getting impugned themselves. Hoover did make a laudable try at it. In his dedication of the Harding

Memorial, he deliberately made it a point to assert that the crimes of his associates "never touched the character of Warren Harding." Hoover's argument had no force to clear the late President, not after his name had been dragged in the mud.

Ignored as well, was the obvious rebuke that Hoover gave to Harry Daugherty. Too late to do Harding any good, Hoover was also too late in getting at his Chief Lawyer, who, adroit at escaping the Law, had, with Jess, originated much of the illegal mischief that muddied Harding's name.

Hoover did, however, duly note how Harding had suffered from his mistaken estimate of friends he had appointed to positions of power. However disillusioned others might have become with him, when Harding finally seemed to have gotten "a dim realization that he had been betrayed by a few of the men whom he had trusted, men whom he had believed were his devoted friends" he was in himself "a man whose soul was being seared by a great disillusionment" (Times, 17 June, 1931, p. 2; Hoover's Memoirs , II 53, 52).

Not that Harding did not have his faults. None of those who really knew him could have been more aware of his being personally flawed than Harding was himself. But, typically, there were also flaws he could not see, or saw too late. He had more than once confided that it was not his enemies, but his friends, who had him walking the floor at night.

Harding spoke to William Allen White very openly about this lament, when White came to the White House on call for that visit "in the midwinter of 1923." Some friends from Ohio that Harding said he had known for thirty years were about to be indicted, and he expected them to be asking him to dismiss the indictments, which he absolutely could not do. "My God, this is a hell of a job!" he said and went on to add, in remarks often quoted, "I have no trouble with my enemies. I can take care of my enemies all right. But my damn friends,...my God-damn friends, White, they're the ones that keep me walking the floor nights." He accented the irony of the situation by expressing his mention of those "damn friends," with, as White noticed, "a sort of serio-comic petulance."[29]

That Harding's trusting nature had been taken advantage of was no secret. Jim Sloan, Nan Britton's go-between for messages to and from Harding (including cash) told Nan he had warned the "boss" that "even his closest friends [in the Administration] were double-crossing him at every turn." But Harding wouldn't believe it, he being "adamant where his trust in his friends was concerned." (PD, 314).

Mark Sullivan, White's peer in covering Harding, would, during the aftermath, become equally disillusioned, after having at first been surprised at how well Harding was working out as President, good at getting things done and winning public approval. Ironically, there was a reverse side to the "unique" equanimity for which Sullivan saw Harding laudably "assuaging [the war-time] rancor" still abroad in the country.

His calming approach was that part of Harding's demeanor which Sullivan praised for his being free of "worry" and "fret," about what went on around him. He was fixated on his own role, needing to live up to it. Self-evidently, those were precisely the traits which made him heedless of what his associates might have been up to, and which contributed to the fated demise of his reputation (Our Times, VI, 180-182. The Great Adventure at Washington, 225).

Though somewhat too sanguine, Sullivan's early assessment does not fall all that short of the mark, when Harding's accomplishments are compared with those of Presidents who did not receive so prevalently low a ranking. One need only consider what it means to place Harding—prior to the current ranking—below the sequential triad of pale non-entities preceding Lincoln: the undistinguished likes of Millard Fillmore, Franklin Pierce and James Buchanan, who left little imprint on the annals of the Country's Presidency. Yet, among his bitterest critics, those on the New York World would nonetheless have considered Harding the least qualified candidate since Buchanan (Dean, 67)—a position Harding would clearly reverse as President.

Not an intellectual, Harding was also not as weak minded as H.L. Mencken made him out to be. And well aware of the low opinion that sage columnists had of him, Harding, in light of his popular approval, could well retort: "Mencken and those wiseacre pundits play me for a damned fool but the joke's on them." Harding would make a similar response to the local Marionite who thought that, as he lacked educational credentials, his political rise was due to the superficial appeal of an engaging personality (PD, 83).

Harding could justly rest his case on achievements, independent of his being considered a welcome successor to Wilsonian internationalism, which the public had become leery of. Still, the opinions of a Mencken prevailed. But they tended to be largely personal, mostly subjective, and often had more to do with how Harding might mangle the English language than how he ran the Government. However, that was the least of it, for what has been most remembered is not the wrong-doing of Daugherty and others, but the taint of corruption which they bestowed on Harding.

He may have been justly praised for the good things wrought by key members of his Administration—e.g., men of the caliber of Charles Evans Hughes—they being appointments suggested by the "Best Minds" he consulted. However, it was only natural that Harding would share in the shame created by the malfeasance of others he had chosen. As sensation naturally trumps decency, it was his fate that the acts of the latter would outweigh those of former.

CHAPTER 14

"Solid Accomplishment"

AS OPPOSED TO WHAT HARDING didn't do, what then of the good that he did do as President? Since that has been as much forgotten as the bad has been remembered, it is worth recalling that, measured by objective standards, Warren Harding's record was one of considerable accomplishment. And the record would have stood the test of time, were it not to be drowned by the ruinous tide of scandal exposed. Several years ago, I was asked to write a piece for the Marion Star, to commemorate the 86th anniversary of Harding's Inauguration, including the Inaugural Ball he didn't get.[30]

In that piece I instanced several of his achievements, citing, for example: his getting Congress to create the Bureau of the Budget, his convening the Disarmament Conference, and having Congress ratify the Four Nation Treaty to reduce naval armament and head off an expensive arms race. Less well known, but equally important was his authorizing our participation in the League of Nations' humanitarian Committees, in line with which he here at home recommended establishment of a Department of Public Welfare, and got the Sheppard-Towner Bill passed, which provided funding for the medical care to be given women and their infants.

Also, contrary to conservative opposition, he was a strong advocate for the World Court, which, though undercut by linkage to the League of Nations, was a worthy idea useful for mediating international conflict. Facing the same opposition in an area where he could exert executive authority, he was able to remove our troops from the Dominican Republic and secured ratification of the Columbian Treaty whereby, minus the "Regret" clause, Columbia would be indemnified for the loss of Panama. Both of these moves improved our standing with the region and abetted trade relations there.

Creation of the Bureau of the Budget—a matter that had languished under Wilson—was a master accomplishment, and a lasting one. Designed to promote control of federal spending, and hence rein in the national debt, it could be undermined, but it also restrained budgets from getting any worse. Though Harding favored tax reductions, he, in fairness, would not support further reduction of the sur-tax, mostly favoring the wealthy, unless there were comparable reductions for the rest of the populace as well.

Harding, having been assisted in his successful endeavors by the "best minds" in his Administration (e.g., Charles Evans Hughes, at State, Herbert Hoover at Commerce, and Charles G. Dawes as Director of the Bureau of the Budget) not the least of his accomplishments (as noted) was his effectively urging Congress, in July, 1921, to pass a resolution declaring the War with Germany and Austria at an end. So he finally gave the nation closure on that War, three years after the Treaty of Versailles had been signed. He had wanted people to put reminders of war-time gloom behind them and partake of the spirit of "Normalcy" that he pledged to promote, for uplifting the national mood.

Harding circumvented the divisive dispute over the League of Nations, which prompted the Senate to reject ratification of the Treaty of Versailles (among other things hung up on Article X). No need for him to roil the waters by pushing his interest in a World Court, with minimal expectation of its acceptance. But he did get his way in the successful Conference on the Reduction of Naval Armament.

As already observed, the Press was much impressed with Harding. His getting the Declaration of Peace passed occurred around the time that he would be praised in a New York Times' story headlined: "Harding Assumes Real Leadership as Congress Lags," with the sub-head: "Likely to Have His Way in Respect to Foreign Affairs" (18 July, 1921, p. 1).

This was followed in two days by an article which could not have been more laudatory on his "smashing of the dishonest duty on oil." "It is fortunate that [Harding] has the common sense, the energy, the capacity for leadership that are not too visible among the disorganized and wrangling Republicans of Congress." The result was that he both saved the Party and benefited the Country (20 July, 1921, p. 14). Coming across as a President in command, Harding, during his break-in year, would encounter little head-wind from Congress.

Rather quickly trashed was the idea that Harding was going to be controlled by the Cabal of Senators who were said to have been responsible for making him the compromise candidate for President. The praiseworthy initiatives he undertook were all the more to Harding's credit for their having been achieved despite the pressures available to the Cabal, a group of sixteen Senators that included thirteen who, until that last ballot, had opposed Harding's nomination (Murray, Era, 38f.).

Nor were they the only pressure group he had to deal with, as White reminded him that the Progressive wing of the Party was not "going to be easy to handle after the election." They didn't want a "McKinley type" President and were "going to have their say" about that (White, Selected Letters, 205-206). Walter Johnson pointed out that "Immediately after the election, [White] tried to bring sentiment to scare Harding into being progressive" (Ibid., 11). Harding is not given much credit for having forged his own way and emerging victorious over pressure groups to the left and right.

Meanwhile, also on the home front, he strenuously pressed Congress to pass anti-lynching legislation, despite resistance from Southern Senators. Unable to get such legislation passed, he nonetheless made it a national issue. Just seven months in office, Harding would bluntly confront the South on the issue of suffrage for Blacks. Though he made no secret of the fact that his motive was political (if enfranchised, southern Blacks would likely vote Republican) it was unheard of for a President to make such a forthright plea in, of all places, Birmingham,

Alabama, and, of all times, on the city's semi-centennial. On top of that, his plea was couched in Lincolnesque diction, with him asking "[to] let the black man vote when he is fit to vote; [and] prohibit the white man from voting when he is unfit to vote"[31]

Other social initiatives include his putting pressure on Judge Elbert Gary of U.S. Steel to lower the twelve hour work day to eight and reduce the seven day week to six—the former actually done a day before Harding's death. Despite his being pro-business and considered anti-labor, as, in the case of violence, he was, he ideally wanted to be neutral in labor disputes, preferring arbitration. He not only sympathized with the strikers in the Pullman Strike, he had also supported the strike of Ohio coal miners, denouncing the owners for their refusal to pay a living wage.

He wanted Congress to pass new legislation abolishing child labor, a prior law having been rejected by the Supreme Court. During that fateful trip to Alaska in 1923, on which he promised appealing goodies to various constituencies along the way, politician that he was, Harding went so far as to indicate that he felt workers had the right to join unions and, if need be, strike. Finally, although Marion, Ohio was a non-union town, Harding ran a union shop at his Star newspaper and joined the Printers' Union himself.

The point is that up to the time of his death, Harding had validly been regarded as a good President—not the absolute best, but far from the worst—and he might have retained that status except for all that came to light in the aftermath. In spite of that, there was still much to be said to his credit, including the record just cited, a worthy performance for his shortened tenure, and, if not overpowering, impressive enough when measured by most Presidential standards.

Nonetheless, if one wants to know who the real Harding was, chances are this view would not be the one that fits the commonly accepted identity given him—not after the ridicule he sustained in a popular novel (Adams' Revelry) that came out in 1926 and went through three editions in three weeks, to be followed by a play entitled "The Vegetable" which, though short-lived, openly mocked him.

Moreover, noted historians, polled in 1962, concurred in the opinion that Harding was a dismal failure as President (Murray, Era, 515).

Defects Harding did have—serious ones—and these will be dealt with. But, for all his faults, the facts show that he was far from the shallow nitwit that the satirists depicted him as, and far from a failure, when strictly evaluated as President. As indicated, his personal life, also trampled upon, was another matter, and, unfortunately, not exactly a state secret.

Obviously, just as a President could be blamed for bad things that happened during his time in office, for which he happened to be blameless, it follows that he could also be praised for good things for which he was not directly deserving of praise. Importantly, it so happens that Harding's Presidency would win high approval from as rigorous a "Revisionist" historian as Ellis W. Hawley, who adopted a new perspective from which to make an appropriately distanced re-evaluation of what had been achieved by the Harding Administration.

A tough-minded analyst, Hawley pointed out that, while "historians have long looked upon the Presidency of Warren G. Harding as a major debacle," that was not the whole story. On the contrary, what is "often missing from their accounts," Hawley observed, "is the fact that the Harding era came close to combining full employment and rising living standards with stable prices and international peace."

Moreover, Hawley went on to give the Harding Administration credit for presiding over "a series of developments that made the American economy the envy of much of the world." This is a kind of political nirvana that seems wholly incompatible with attributes connected to the Harding name. According to Hawley it was not so much the accomplishments per se that gave Harding a successful Presidency. Rather, it was by virtue of the practical instrumentality employed by key Cabinet Members that those accomplishments were realized. If he could be tarred with the corruption of certain appointees, it follows that he should be credited with the achievement of others.

As Hawley evaluated political success in relation to the Harding Administration, he held it was derived from the application of "new managerial designs reflecting the continuing search for a 'new liberalism' and foreshadowing the 'modern capitalism' of a later era."[32] In other words, good governance followed from little noticed changes in how members of Harding's Administration used managerial control for the achievement of their respective goals.

As Hawley sees it, the key to Harding's getting this done was by his willingness "to delegate economic and diplomatic policy making to the 'superior minds' who understood such matters." Counterbalancing the cabinet members who contributed to the debacle-side of his Administration (Albert B. Fall and Harry M. Daugherty) Harding gave a free hand to "four of the strongest cabinet-level officers in the nation's history" (Ibid., 59).

These, according to Hawley were respectively Andrew Mellon heading Treasury, Charles Evans Hughes, State, Herbert Hoover, Commerce, and Henry C. Wallace, Agriculture. As a group, they were able "to lend credibility to claims that permanent peace and prosperity were in train and that ways had been found to realize the dreams of the progressive era while avoiding the evils feared by conservatives."

More specifically, Mellon, for example, a "master of corporate finance," was able to bring "business methods to public finance," which resulted in a "new budget and accounting system." By their collective efforts, Hughes and Hoover, "through conferences and negotiations...set out to reduce political obstacles to enlightened private development." Their efforts had much to do with the success of the Conference on Naval Disarmament, and, as cited above, they undertook measures leading to improved relationships with Columbia, Mexico, and Latin-America in general.

Among a variety of unheralded administrative improvements were Henry Wallace's ability to get legislation passed that enabled the Agriculture Department to establish farm credit institutions, and regulate the activities of agricultural middlemen (Ibid., 60, 66, 68, et passim). What this group of Cabinet Members collectively did was to make government work effectively. This had been done so smoothly, and, above all, un-hampered that it was scarcely noticed, back then, or subsequently.

Harding made his individual contribution in the areas cited, which, together with those of his central appointees, enabled him to make the most of his Presidency. At the Disarmament Conference, for example, he sought advice from Secretary Hughes and, being a natural arbitrator, he successfully put it across. Unfortunately, the freedom given his top appointees was too liberally granted to others less deserving.

The latitude given Harry Daugherty and Jess Smith resulted in the thievery that would become glued to the President who gave it to them, while the acumen of Secretaries Hughes and Mellon, for example, would go by unrecognized, as would their contribution to the good governance given their President.

Though it may seem that Harding was being given credit for favorable activity on the part of his major Cabinet members, that was how all Presidents were judged, just as he had to take the blame for the unfavorable activity of other Cabinet members. In Harding's case, he had more of a hand in work done by the former, than he had in work done by the latter. Unfortunately for this President, it was the latter that would outshine the former. In terms of reputation, everyone knew the latter, and nobody knew the former.

The easy management style, for which Harding had been criticized—justly—was based on misplaced trust in those who deserved it least, while, according to Hawley, that trust worked wonders for those who deserved it most.

PART II:

IT TURNS AGAINST HIM; FROM GOOD TO BAD

CHAPTER 15

"And There Were Scandals"

THERE WAS MUCH ADVERSITY AWAITING Harding's reputation, the majority of it post-mortem. When the scandals broke, none of his esteemed success mattered. Harding's fall from grace was swift and precipitous, the blow to his reputation being particularly exacerbated by how long the protracted exposures kept coming. The Congressional Investigation and subsequent prosecution of those involved in Teapot Dome, for example, would be strung out for all of six years, traced from its beginnings with the initial Senatorial Investigation begun in October, 1923 (less than three months after Harding's death) to October, 1929, when Albert Fall was found guilty of accepting a bribe from Edward L. Doheny.

With experienced legal representation, Doheny, along with fellow corporate oilman Harry Sinclair, would both win acquittals, despite the fact that they had been the ones who, in the first place, had offered the criminal bribes. As each case of hidden skullduggery was brought to light, between the ballyhoo excited by the Press and the jockeying for political advantage in Congress, it was beginning to seem like there had to be more of that kind, and, in the circus that followed, those expectations were not disappointed.

Only in rare instances did any of the scandals touch Harding personally, and when they did, the connection was tangential, occurring through relatives, or close associates, like his Attorney General, to whom he was obligated for achieving his Nomination and Election.

In 1924-25 there was the trial and conviction of Charles R. Forbes, head of the Veterans' Bureau (newly centralized for efficiency) on the discovery that he profited from selling hospital supplies at outrageously low prices (new sheets, e.g., sold at salvage value) and getting kickbacks for that, as well as from firms contracted to build veterans' hospitals. Favored were contractors from whom Forbes had "borrowed" large sums of money.

It turned out that Forbes' appointment had initially been favored by Florence Harding, who had been charmed by flirtatious Charley during her activities on behalf of veterans' welfare. Adding to the embarrassment was knowledge that Warren's sister, Carolyn Votaw, was persuaded to work for Forbes. So word of the Bureau's notoriously lavish social life rubbed off on her, scarcely a participant. Moreover, it was found that Carolyn's husband Heber Votaw, the Seventh-Day-Adventist minister, who was appointed Superintendent of Prisons, had covered up a drug scandal at the Atlanta Penitentiary. As a family favor, Harding had facilitated Heber's job, by removing his Office from Civil Service restrictions.

The idea that Harding's Administration was riddled with scandal yet to be uncovered was abetted when Charles F. Cramer, General Counsel for the Veterans' Bureau, and the person in charge during Forbes' absence, resigned once an investigation was begun. And—out of the blue—Cramer committed suicide in, of all places, Harding's former Wyoming Street residence. Other seamy details came to light as a result of Forbes' having seduced the wife of Elias Mortimer, his associate in graft, which prompted Mortimer's angry testimony about Forbes' activities.

Meanwhile, Attorney General Harry Daugherty and his Alien Property Custodian, Colonel Thomas W. Miller, were being indicted for conspiracy. Daugherty had failed to prosecute fraudulent transactions in the disposition of the assets appropriated from German companies after the War. These were matters in which Daugherty himself had participated and from which he had allegedly profited. It was thought that for selling off those assets at bargain prices he had presumably received under the table remuneration. As indicated, Jess Smith had also had a hand in facilitating those sales. Miller, who negotiated deals for which he was rewarded, one specifically for selling German chemical patents at a discount, would be convicted of conspiracy to defraud the government.

The scandals having been abundantly covered by Harding's biographers and other chroniclers of the 1920s, they need not be more fully rehearsed here. Some generally known snap-shots, however, deserve mention, as a reminder of all the wrongs extraneously heaped on Harding, responsibility for which, he'd be blamed, regardless of his personal distance from them, and often because of that distance.—As, how could he not have known? And, if so, why not?

In essence, the implicit criticism would be that, if the President was unaware, he shouldn't have been, an omission on his part that, true enough, might be seen as constituting indirect responsibility via negligence, though nonetheless a miscue blown out of proportion to its innocuous source.

Then, there was the example of the ever-voluble prevaricator Gaston Means, himself a small time swindler getting to be a large one, and relishing his day in the national spotlight. Means was all too eager to oblige a Congressional Committee with the dirt that Members wanted to hear. He slyly let it be known that he had worked for Daugherty's unappointed assistant, influence-peddling Jess Smith, who along with his boss, had, among other pursuits, garnered some quarter of a million, at a shot, in graft, kickbacks, and the like. Means' testimony was that they had been allegedly selling permits for the illegal withdrawal of liquor from government warehouses.

Adding further spice to the Congressional Hearings, was the revenge testimony of Roxy Stinson, Jess Smith's divorced wife, who said she had inside information from Smith about surreptitious big-time money deals conducted at the infamous "Little Green House on K Street," favorite meeting place of "the Ohio Gang." In one of his bigger transactions, Smith had apparently also received a cool quarter of a million from a famed Chicago bootlegger in exchange for providing him with immunity from prosecution.

On the other hand, Andrew W. Mellon, Secretary of the Treasury, ranked as one the most upright of Harding's Cabinet Members, was, as head of the Prohibition Commission, known to have hypocritically had private distillery holdings, in addition to which he was said have been implicated in the illegal issuance of the "B" liquor permits purportedly granted for medical reasons.

Moreover, with Prohibition in full force and strengthened by the Volstead Act, which Harding endorsed enforcement of, for those liquor permits which Means had Smith purportedly selling to bootleggers in New York, he had had the collaboration of Daugherty. The profits were considerable, and so were the indictments.

Specifically, one Congressman wanted Daugherty impeached for using his office for personal gain, as well as for failure to enforce anti-trust laws. While a Senate Committee had found Daugherty guilty of malpractice on a variety of counts, he would eventually escape conviction on criminal charges. But the suspicions he excited, most well grounded, would not go away, and they got legs. Substantiated were grounds that the government's Head Lawyer was crooked, and was getting away with it.

As if a sampling of unsavory goings-on by members of Harding's Administration was not sufficient condemnation, particularly when exposed under the glare of drawn-out Congressional Hearings and endlessly trumpeted in the Press, there was yet the Teapot Dome Affair. That, more than anything else, would make Harding's name indelibly synonymous with the corruption-by-association bestowed on him by his appointees, one a close personal friend, Albert B. Fall.

It was Fall who headed the negotiation for the oil leases, in which Harding had played no part and from which he derived no benefit. Obviously, politics were involved, as Congressional Democrats pounced on the opportunity to come down hard on Harding in retaliation for his having been hard on them in 1923 regarding legislative work left undone. Interestingly, Teapot, political curse that it was, did not hinder Republicans from capturing the White House in the proximal elections of 1924 and 1928, encompassing the span of Teapot Dome investigations and active court proceedings.

Nonetheless, in the public eye, Teapot Dome would remain the identifying shibboleth of corruption, being, as described by a political analyst for the Baltimore Sun, "the worst scandal in the Government in many decades" (Noggle, 87). For the Harding Administration, and even more so for Harding personally, it would become an abiding albatross—abidingly unearned.

CHAPTER 16

"But How Bad Was Teapot?"

As with Harding's record, which showed he was not as bad as he was reputed to have been, somewhat the same could be said of Teapot Dome, on several counts, one based on the rationale offered for the oil leases.[33] Both Harding and Teapot Dome were considered good at the outset and bad, veering on disastrous, towards the end, the latter greatly exaggerated.

Though it did not mitigate the damage done by the granting of leases, the idea of setting up the reserves had, in itself, predated the Harding Administration. Naval Oil Reserves Numbers 1 and 2 in California had originally been created by the Taft Administration, and Number 3, the Teapot Dome tract in Wyoming, had been created by the Wilson Administration. When Harding took Office, he was about to be stuck with both.

The proposal for transferring jurisdiction of the reserves at Elk Hills and Buena Vista in California and Teapot Dome in Natrona County, Wyoming from the Department of the Navy under Edwin N. Denby to Albert B. Fall in the Interior Department was put forth as having a worthy objective. For one thing, it countered unauthorized drainage from those reserves by adjacent commercial interests.

By selling leases to the oil companies of Edward L. Doheny and Harry Sinclair, the Navy would in exchange get valuable storage tanks at Pearl Harbor and pipelines, along with docks, wharfs, and other facilities for fueling the fleet—all of this over and above the up to 50% in royalties to be realized by the Government. Meanwhile, the oil would be efficiently refined and made readily available to the Navy. Oilmen, naturally interested in cultivating a good image, made the valid argument that it was better to have the oil stored above ground and ready for use than to have it subject to drainage while underground.

For Oil Reserve Number 1 in California, it was thought that there had been open and competitive bidding and that drainage had been substantial. Reserve Number 3, Teapot Dome in Wyoming, was another matter. The trouble was that, for arranging a deal highly lucrative to the leasing company—without competitive bidding—Secretary Fall had received substantial "loans," finally totaling all of $409,000, most of it in Liberty Bonds secretly given by bountiful Sinclair.

In addition to his receiving other emoluments from the oilmen, Fall had lied about an initial $100,000 "loan" from Doheny, while keeping dark the payments from Sinclair. Nor was it disclosed at the time that Fall had done legal work for Harry Sinclair. His connection with Doheny went back to Fall's early prospecting days, when Doheny had been his adventuresome "Pard" out on the Southwest frontier.

There were, of course, problems with the Teapot Dome leases, beyond the pay-offs and beyond the concerns raised by conservationists, who objected to the exploitation of our natural resources. Although Harding's Secretary of the Navy, Denby, could justifiably claim that leases to Edward Doheny's Pan-American Company for off-set wells would counter the illicit drainage, the same could not be positively said of the lease which went out to Harry Sinclair's Mammoth Oil Company, since drainage was said to be a geological non-factor in the Teapot Dome basin, and no oil companies were located at its rim.

Moreover, the lease went out unannounced on 7 April, 1921, a little over a month after Harding's inauguration; and, suspiciously, it wasn't made known publicly until a week beyond that in a Wall Street Journal front page story. Formal announcement was not forthcoming till four days later, and put out by an obscure acting Secretary of the Interior.

With the power at Fall's disposal exciting both his covetous instinct and his anti-Conservationist bias, he had acted rather quickly in setting up the lease program. However, word of the first step, Harding's granting the transfer of the Navy Department's reserves to Interior, wasn't publicly announced until 1 June, over a month after the lease had gone out to Sinclair. Harding had depended on the professional recommendation of Secretaries Denby and Fall for his signing the transfer order, practically sight unseen, as the document was too long, detailed, and complicated for him to make any sense of the thing, had he delved into it.

Favorable to Denby's argument was the fact that in the instance of California, it was estimated that the government had already lost about twenty-two million barrels of oil due to the failure to drill off-set wells there during the Wilson Administration. This had happened because it was thought to have been a good idea to save in the ground the oil that was still contained in the Reserves, which, of course, overlooked the potential for drainage and its extent.

In any event, Harding must have given some thought to conservationist concerns, pushed by the outrage of head conservationist, Gifford Pinchot, for he subsequently did not approve Fall's request to have the Forestry Service transferred from the Agriculture Department to Interior. Had that been done, it would have given Fall the opportunity to allow private exploitation of Alaska's natural resources—mainly, timber and pulp for paper—by private companies, something strongly opposed by the Conservation Lobby.

The Lobby had gotten to Senator Robert M. La Follette, a progressive Republican, who, becoming suspicious of Fall's activities, decided that there should be an investigation of Teapot Dome. He was joined by two Democratic Senators, John B. Kendrick of Wyoming and Thomas J. Walsh of Montana, the latter to become the lead investigator, who would gain credit for bringing out the questionable practices surrounding the leases. Kendrick had been receiving questions from his constituents, and when, on contacting Interior, he was told no contract had actually been issued for a lease, he suspected deception.

Not the least of the complications faced by the Senate Investigating

Committees was the contradictory evidence that was presented to them regarding drainage. Countering Senator Kendrick's charge which disputed the claim of drainage from Teapot Dome was the testimony of geologists. They indicated that, while Teapot Dome was said to have contained 135,000,000 barrels of oil, the reserve actually contained less than 70 percent of that amount, with the existing reserve still draining into adjacent areas. Meanwhile, a disgusted Harry Sinclair put out word that he had spent about $25,000,000 on Teapot Dome and would be happy to relinquish the lease in exchange for reimbursement of that expense.

This, plus the geologists' testimony, temporarily dampened the interest in Teapot Dome, only to have it come roaring back to life when Fall's claim that he had received the infamous $100,000 loan from millionaire Edward McLean (spendthrift owner of the Washington Post and Cincinnati Enquirer) was shown to have been false, on Doheny's testimony that he, not McLean, had actually given Fall the loan back in 1921. Adding a neat little sensational image to the investigation, Doheny revealed that his son had carried the $100,000 cash loan to Fall's office in a "little black bag."

Additionally damaging to Fall was his having suddenly come into visible affluence, presumed to be beyond his means, money which would provide the wherewithal for substantial improvements made to his Three Rivers Ranch in New Mexico. The infectious nature of the scandal was such that, as respected a personage as Harding's Secretary of State, Charles Evans Hughes—no friend of Fall's—felt obliged to point out in January, 1924, that the leases "were never brought before the Cabinet for its decision" (Noggle, 83). In the following month, the Senate passed a resolution to investigate Daugherty for his having failed to prosecute Fall, Sinclair, and Doheny, along with a variety of additional grafters in the Harding Administration.

As part of the eventual fall-out from Teapot Dome, Secretary Denby resigned in February, 1924. Although President Coolidge was at first reluctant to accept Daugherty's resignation, considering how it would reflect on Harding, a month later, he decided to go ahead and ask for it anyway. In March, 1927, Coolidge would at last revoke

Harding's executive order that had transferred the naval oil reserves to the Interior Department. In the following year, the Supreme Court finally did mercifully nullify the oil leases themselves, effectively closing the book on a scandal that had grown tedious, and was, in itself, hardly scandalous.

As for Albert Fall himself, after being found guilty, in October, 1929, of having accepted a bribe from Doheny, and lying about it, he went to prison on 30 July, 1931. A broken man, Fall served less than ten months, and most of that time was spent in the prison hospital.

In itself, Teapot was vastly over-rated. It was as distant from Harding as Wyoming was. The publicity which made Harding the fall-guy was bogus. Nonetheless, once he got tagged with it, it stuck. The residual effect of scandals is that they hang on, justifiably or not, particularly if they make a big splash, as had been the case with Teapot. But there are exceptions, as with Secretary Fall. The payments to him were forgotten. By serving his jail time he got closure. That left Harding's name hanging out there. His involvement with Albert Fall? Misplaced trust.

CHAPTER 17

"Forgotten: He Was A Good President"

THOUGH HARDING HAD NOTHING TO do with the scandal that did great damage to his reputation, it was symptomatic of a career that ended with him taking his lumps for other scandals generally beyond his control. That was the case with the smoke emanating from Congressional Committees, and with the Press that would perpetuate ill-fame that did not get interred with the man. It was difficult to remember that during his time in Office, he had been a good President, officially well regarded, and, outright loved by the people. Just as Teapot was not really as bad as it was made out to have been, the same was true of Harding himself. By looking back, some commentators would reconsider the conventional judgment of him.

In the wake of the scandals, William Allen White came down hard on the President he had formerly praised so highly. In fact, his condemnation was overly hard, and, as such, indicated the level of White's disillusionment. It also implied regret, which, for decently inclined White, was as much as to say he wished it weren't so. Wholly set aside was White's admiration for such matters as Harding's having shown himself to be an effective political tactician, persuasive even with Democrats, so that using "good sense and tact...he [did] bring home the bacon," as White put it.

Trailing Harding's reputation, for example, was a remembrance of how he could effectively mold a recalcitrant Congress to his will, as shown by his getting the slow moving Senate to ratify his Disarmament Treaty.[34] These reminiscences of White's came out fourteen years after Harding's death, derived from his looking back for perspective.

For all that there was on the negative side of the ledger, during his lifetime and not long thereafter, Harding's name would withstand isolated challenges. Ill-fame did not immediately close down on him. In fact, he emerged looking lots better than the plucked goose which the scandals had made of him. There were reminders that he had a knack not only for mastering the art of politics, but for cultivating popular appeal without consciously seeming to do so. He did not need to play at being a good guy, because he was one. There were a host of negatives that, on reconsideration, simply would not stick. Some had to be worked through.

For example, when Brand Whitlock in 1926 wrote White that he ought to do a book about Harding, it is said that White responded in disgust, responding that "the story of Babylon is a Sunday School story compared with the story of Washington from June 1919, until July 1923. … If ever there was a man who was a he-harlot, it was this same Warren G. Harding." Actually, taken in context, White acknowledged that his comment went considerably overboard in suggesting that Harding's wrongs would account for wide-spread profligacy in the era of his Presidency.

Indeed, White distinctly admitted exactly that when he went on to say: "It isn't Harding's story; it is the story of his times, the story of the Prodigal Son, our democracy that turned away from the things of the spirit, got its share of the patrimony ruthlessly and went out and lived riotously and ended it by feeding among the swine" (Selected Letters, 260).

So what most offended White was much more the overall permissive spirit of the times than the supposedly ruinous example of Harding, to whom it was nominally tied, and who thereby could be unjustly seen as ushering in the—for White—morally decadent atmosphere of the "Roaring Twenties." One can't say Harding was totally blameless, but, his sexual misdeeds were not part of the public record. With the popular need for an identifying figure, it has always been easier to disparage a coincidental Leader than the sins of the Era when he happened to have had that role.

Thus, it is the "he-harlot' reference, minus White's qualifiers, that is picked up and perpetuated as epitomizing Harding's time in office. Andrew Sinclair takes it a little far in suggesting that White's making this criticism of Harding "set or shaped the fashion of nearly all historians and journalists" who have in concert created the generalized defamation of President Harding (The Available Man, 297). But, in any case, the record of corrupt practices and its perpetrators was there for everyone to see, and make judgment on, which would conveniently—if not necessarily—fall on Harding's head.

The ridicule heaped on Harding by H. L. Mencken and Samuel Hopkins Adams did much to accelerate the downward slide, as did young Nan Britton's book disclosing in embarrassing (and morally disgraceful) detail a prolonged extra-marital affair that would produce an illegitimate daughter.

In addition to ignoring his record of accomplishments, the damning of Harding's Presidency also overlooks the fact that, to the end, he retained one redeeming virtue: he was not only likeable, but genuinely liked by the people. They felt he was one of them. His approval rested on the perception that, as Robert K. Murray has put it, "Next to Lincoln, Harding was probably the most human man to occupy the presidential office" (op. cit., 115). Mention of Harding in connection with Lincoln in a number of instances may have had something to do with his having given a moving speech in dedicating the Lincoln Memorial on 30 May, 1922.

Harding's humble beginnings as a farm boy in rural Ohio were not unlike Lincoln's origins. At a practical level, Congressional awareness that Harding had popular support translated into political leverage for legislation he favored, as well as for legislation he would veto, as was the case with the improvident, but politically appealing Veterans' Bonus Bill.

When it came to a matter of fiscal responsibility, Harding could staunchly assert himself, an asset that lent credibility to his Presidency, and was a virtue easily overlooked. Yet, as Ellis Hawley has pointed out, the fact that Harding presided over good times was attributable to his stewardship. He had the right men in influential positions doing good things for the country's economy.

However, it was scarcely vindicating for Harding to be placed in the same category with Lincoln, when his generosity at heart in dealing with people would become obscured by such things as a reputation for womanizing. In his breezy satiric novel, Revelry, Samuel Hopkins Adams had also made the comparison to Lincoln, which, being part of the undeserved praise heaped on his caricatured President, comes off as ridicule in disguise.

On the other hand, the lugubrious death scene Adams depicted turns out to have been more than a truth written in jest. For the sympathetic outpouring of love which Adams had sweeping the country on word that the fictive President was "gravely ill," had actually come about not on Harding's final illness, but instantly following his death. So, the account that there had been such a reaction was essentially true.

As Adams put it in his misdated summation, "The President, who was more of the people than any president since Lincoln, more simply human in his frailties and deficiencies as well as in his kindly virtues, was in danger, and the heart of America went out to him."[35]

Regardless of exaggeration, the popular affection was there, which Harding first acquired during his Candidacy, and it was sustained on his winning the Presidency by an impressive plurality of over seven million votes. He had indeed received the highest percentage of the popular vote since James Monroe. Not to be discounted is the fact that, to his day, he had been the first sitting Senator to have ascended to the Presidency, a sign that his support was nation-wide.

The popular affection re-emerged, even after the first disclosure of wrong-doing became known, when, also reminiscent of Lincoln, on Harding's pre-mature death, grieving crowds came out to see the funeral train. Ribboned in purple and black crepe, the train was solemnly carrying the fallen President cross-country from California back to Washington.

To some extent, Harding's appeal rested on his impressive

appearance. It could, of course, be deceptive, and critics of Harding felt it was. But it did have its affect. In addition to his receiving popular approval, he had the right official bearing. Having by habit taken on a rather solemn expression, he looked like a President and bore himself like one. The influential Senator Boies Penrose, according to White, "the original Harding discoverer," had seen him, a year in advance of the Nomination, as having the very appearance of another "McKinley type of candidate" (A Puritan in Babylon, 204).

Mark Sullivan observed that Harding presided over state business with an "unruffled serenity" along with "a sense of assurance and confidence" which created the "spirit and atmosphere" that had "much to do with the success" of the Four Power Disarmament Conference, and gained him the admiration of reporters (Great Adventure at Washington, 223).

Early on, Sir Charles Sykes, a British MP, reported, after a visit to the White House, that he was "very much impressed by the President's personality, which convinced him that the destinies of the United States were in strong capable hands" (New York Times, 29 July, 1921, p. 2). Spoken like a diplomat, of course, but perceptions of this kind were not inconsequential, and they counted, having had an effect that went beyond foreign relations.

Also bolstering the perception Harding gave of a man who maintained a befitting Presidential bearing was his gift of oratory. Notoriously windy as it might have been, and prime material for the derision of Mencken and others, it nonetheless made the requisite impression of a Head of State.

In his verbose Inaugural Address, for example, (almost seven printed pages long) he sounded the tone of high resolve needed to gain public confidence that he knew the matters of post-war economic stability which needed to be addressed, like tax reduction and tariff adjustment. He had a sense of national purpose that he hoped to fulfill, harking back to the original Washingtonian policy of "non-involvement in Old World affairs" (well received in the country's post-war mood) and he concluded with an aspiration to make the Government mindful of serving the "popular will," something he very much wanted to do.[36]

He spoke with a conviction that would inspire the public to believe in him. On assuming the Presidency, he took on a sense of command. He didn't hesitate to use the weight of Office to urge action on the part of a fractious Congress unable to pass controversial legislation, on matters, for example, affecting international relations (like those of Naval Disarmament).

It was pointed out in the New York Times that, while Congress didn't "appear to know its own mind" on, among other things, the tariff bill (8 July, 1921, p.8), Harding, by contrast, was taking action on such substantive issues as disarmament, and in so doing overcame "a vast inertia" on Capital Hill (11 July, 1921, p.10).

Harding right off gave notice that he had a clear sense of the pressure available to him, particularly in dealing with Congress, with whose workings he was roundly familiar. For most of his term in office, he projected the image of political mastery. The people were comfortable with him, and he was confident of having their confidence.

Of course, there was another side to this equation. By the end of the decade of the '20s, all of that confidence would be forgotten, gone with the wind. The friends who had thought well of Harding would have second thoughts, much as they might have wanted to bring back the good feeling he had given the country.

CHAPTER 18

"Despite The Good, Where Did He Go Wrong?"

Post-mortem appraisals of Harding's term in Office, by those who knew him personally (e.g., White and Nicholas Murray Butler) were generally ambivalent, balancing the perception that, while well-intentioned, he was ill-equipped for the role he had to fulfill. For one thing, he lacked the will to impose vigilance on subordinates. It wasn't his style. He'd been an underdog himself. That attitude, as indicated, made it easy for him to be taken advantage of by members of his Administration who were encouraged to free lance, unafraid that shady deals might not go unnoticed. Charles Forbes, made Director of the Veterans' Bureau, would be a perfect example of the type.

As a sign of how difficult it was to regard Harding in other than ambiguous terms, White would picturesquely write of a Harding who had been "created...out of the red Ohio mud," only to dramatically became "Fate's tragic manikin." White had it that, whereas Harding "could summon the indomitable strength of the humble," he "could not grapple with the men who made him—with the Daughertys [sic] and the Falls" (Masks, 388, 419). Nicholas Murray Butler, in offering a similar appraisal, felt that "Harding was one of the kindest men who ever lived, but he was without any serious qualifications for the Presidency" (Across the Years, I, 410).

Butler's appraisal was typical of how, on the look back, friends felt that they had to adjust their view of him to assimilate the weakness revealed by scandals. As previously noted, later biographers (Murray, Downes, Sinclair, Russell, et al.) aiming for a balanced view, instead tilted from an objectively mixed to a subtlety adversarial stance.

The thing to be noticed in this ambivalence, is not just that the bad seems to outweigh the good, but that praise for Harding, post mortem, has usually been qualified, and mostly rare. When mentioned, the better side of the equation is usually predicated on his having been a good man, not on his successful achievements—some of which, like the Bureau of the Budget were important and long-lasting.

Suddenly, it seemed that all of the good that Harding had done was swept away. Maligned as he had been, most of his friends could, with exceptions, make no great effort to restore reminders of his accomplishments in Office. Post-mortem it didn't matter.

It takes no great insight on the part of biographers (or anyone else) to observe, that, self-evidently, being loved and regarded as a good man do not a good President make. The superficial compliments of a Butler were flattering, but they did not reflect a Harding who, as President, would grow qualifications. Objectively considered, Harding exceeded expectations, and he certainly wasn't as bad a President as the one classified as our worst. He might not be characterized as a strong President. But it was also be true that while Harding's strength did not lie in being strong, there were matters in which self-assertion on his part, above all greater self-scrutiny, would surely have been helpful. And that in itself spelled trouble.

With hindsight, it is easy enough to point up reasons for Harding's late difficulties as President. But there were certain markers from the years leading up to his Presidency, along with his early years in the White House, that paint an informative picture of him antecedent to his coming into those difficulties, some of which helped to mature him on the job—and one for which there was no cure.

To a significant degree, Harding brought his troubles onto himself. There are certain of those early experiences from which this can be traced. First of all, there was his initial fear of becoming President and insecurity when he got it. Secondly, he had a disinclination to deal with essential parts of his job, one in particular being patronage. Third, he suffered not alone from his unchecked loyalty in trusting members of his Administration, but from a defective sense of the mettle of some men that he appointed.

A key to Harding's ultimate debacle can be traced to his admiration for one such appointee, Albert B. Fall, who engineered Teapot. All else aside, Harding's whole-hearted trust in Fall epitomizes the most glaring problem he brought upon himself. Most knowledgeable politicians, except Harding, saw Fall as an opportunistic conniver. Obvious as this was, one can't under-rate how delusional was Harding's blindness to it. He had at one time considered appointing Fall Secretary of State, narrowly based on the impression he had made on Harding as a very knowledgeable colleague when they jointly served on the Senate Foreign Relations Committee.

Additionally, following Fall's resignation as Secretary of the Interior in March, 1923 (announced on January 2nd), Harding, having dismissed suspicions regarding his departure, gave thought to offering Fall an appointment to the Supreme Court.

Regarding the other two points, they indicated that Harding really didn't want the job of President, and when he got it, there were times when he said so. He had once told a friend who was a Judge, "I don't think I'm big enough for the Presidency." He had also unashamedly confessed to a newspaper columnist, "Oftentimes, as I sit here, I don't seem to grasp that I am President" (Shadow, 452).

Together, all three points do not suggest there was much oversight on Harding's part. Justice was the one area of government where, with staunch supporter Daugherty in charge, Harding's attitude was pretty much hands off. Since he wasn't a lawyer, he was glad he had one. With anonymous Jess Smith being given an unchecked free hand, a time-bomb was ticking. Until it exploded, the big irony regarding drawbacks is that Harding did do rather well, despite danger signals.

Point three encompassed another time-bomb that was equally explosive: Albert Fall, who deserves more attention. Incredible to those who knew something of his background, Fall was a frontier type who rose to prominence in his home state on the slimmest credentials.

Having had no formal schooling in law, he became a self-educated lawyer who would get himself elevated to a New Mexican judgeship, and would allegedly have bought votes to get himself elected to the Senate. Fall impressed important personages that he put himself in contact with, and was prestigiously regarded by colleagues in the Senate, who knew little of his background.

Frank Scobey, a true friend for Harding, had tried to warn him about his friendship with Fall. From the time of Harding's initially considering Fall for a cabinet post, Scobey had bluntly reported he had word from a reliable source that his friend was involved in remunerative negotiations to gain American recognition of the newly installed Mexican President, Alvaro Obregon. But Harding dismissed that as, on the face of it, so much "bunk."

He just couldn't believe Fall would have had anything to do "with the political situation down there," and he told Scobey that, not only couldn't he think ill of Fall, he indeed regarded him as "a star of a fellow." He had convinced himself that Fall was "very much on the square and…a very dependable friend,"[37] Nonetheless, contrary to Harding's opinion, Fall did have lots to do "with the political situation down there." More particulars of Harding's reaction to Fall's scheme to get diplomatic recognition of Obregon's regime are to be considered shortly.

Fall, more than any other figure, was the poster-boy for Harding's fall by virtue of friendship. For example, so sure was Fall of Harding's support that he felt he could resign free of suspicion that he was leaving to escape exposure for conspiracy to commit fraud because he knew he'd be protected by Harding's bias in his favor. The truth is Harding's trust in Fall was unqualified.

And, therein lies an indication of how liable Harding was to hurt himself. It was perhaps due to Fall's shrewd ability to size up fellow politicians that he could foresee trouble for Harding in the very trust that was accorded him by his protector. Was it by smelling trouble for himself—never mind Harding—that Fall was prompted to leave office before questions could be raised about the rationale for Teapot and his "loan" from Doheny? Self-seeking, he knew he could find greener pastures elsewhere, and he did, based on the connections he had made with important personages in the oil industry.

Vis-à-vis Harding, however, Fall's damage had been done. That Harding could not pick up on Fall's self-seeking attitude, resulted from the fact that he wouldn't. Blind to the cost of all-out trust, he paid the price.

CHAPTER 19

"Some Faults Overcome, Some Not"

Because he allowed himself to be led astray by the value he placed on loyalty, one cannot say that that in itself added up to Harding's coming across as weaker than he was. What it does suggest is that a large part of the demise of his reputation rested on self-deception. He couldn't back down from the trust he expected from members of his Administration, notably Fall and Daugherty, blandly disposing of the questions raised about them.

In the case of Fall, Harding would reject evidence of a secret deal for financial reward that he couldn't believe possible because it didn't fit his preconceived impression of Fall's character. True, Fall's scheme did not pan out, but with Harding's out of hand rejection of Scobey's warning, it was as if he was saying, 'my mind is made up; don't confuse me with the facts.'

Nonetheless, were it not for the scandals that were bruited about after his death, most of the negatives—however consequential—would easily have been outweighed. They would, in fact, have been eclipsed by the record of achievements and steady leadership which Harding had proven himself capable of. The country was at peace; the economy was healthy. What politician would not be esteemed for that, however badly he did otherwise, short of thievery? All else aside, for the moment, particularly Harding's hectic personal life, he could act effectively, particularly at using the power of the Presidency to get things done.

Based on his inside knowledge of the workings of the United States Senate, one of Harding's strengths, as I've indicated, was that he knew how to work his will on Congress to have necessary legislation passed. While his expectation of loyalty could work against him, there were situations where it worked for him, which is why he abided by it. It was not enough for him to gain the upper hand over an indecisive Congress.

Beyond that, it helped that during his time in the Senate he had ingratiated himself with fellow Republicans to the extent that, by their awareness of his gift for diplomacy, they felt he could smooth out the intra-party strife of Progressives vs. Conservatives. He made a reputation for himself as Party Harmonizer. Satisfaction on that front got him approval from important people in the political world. In a word, though loyalty to friends got him in trouble; loyalty to the Party got him in the White House.

So ingrained was his loyalty to Party that, despite the intense emotionalism of his final meeting with Nan Britton, in the midst of their travail, out comes a plea for saving the Party from harm. Harding, weakened by the flu, his heart-felt relationship with his sweet young mistress about to fall apart, despondent that he "can do no more," generally depressed, despairing, remorseful, filled with self-hatred, and needing to prepare for the Alaska trip, what does he come up with but a plea for Nan's help that could not have been more malapropos: "Nan, darling, you must help me; our secret must not come out. Why, I would rather die than disappoint my party!"

Nan suggests that he fairly shouted this out in a tone of desperation. Save the Party at all costs! Nan was left to wonder what that would do to mend the breach in their relationship (PD, 240).

Despite his having cultivated a mood of contentment in the country at large, typified by the Prohibition-flaunting '20s, Harding was not very content with himself. And some part of it was political. Not only did he make his share of mistakes, but there were some he was too myopic to recognize. With Fall, for example, it went beyond the loyalty factor. As Nicholas Murray Butler, for instance, pointed out, Harding would consider Fall to be "the best-posted man of the whole lot" for State, and had to be talked out of appointing him to that position (based on a trail of corruption he had left in Colorado) instead of rightly choosing Charles Evans Hughes (Across the Years, I, 402-403). While many difficulties for Harding stemmed from some of the conniving men who surrounded him, crucial are those faults that could be attributed to him personally. For what troubled Harding as a person also troubled him as President.

It was his nature to be trustful, but it was doubtless his lack of self-assurance that had him feeling it was best to trust those whom he felt should have competence for the jobs assigned to them. Unfortunately, that didn't make them immune to temptation. In situations where he gave up responsibility, Harding lost authority.

This applied in a significant way to the authority he was willing to relinquish to his overbearing wife, who wanted to be President more than he did. Florence being a woman to whom he allowed himself to be umbilically tied, he accepted her help because she was going to give it, whether asked for or not. Since she had the political smarts and made careful decisions for him, he relied on her judgment, which, on average, was wise, though not always best.

Despite all of the things that could have derailed his Presidency, once he got himself into the job, Harding was encouraged by his successes, and grew confidence in what he did well. But, just as he was hampered by the faults of others, it is also true that what he had most to overcome to reach the confidence that William Allen White recognized in 1923 was none other than himself. For he had to go through a personal 'slough of despond' in looking with fear, doubt, and wavering certainty at the prospect of his running for, and then of actually assuming, the role of President.

He was filled with apprehension upon his unpredictably winning the Nomination, and, intimidated, he instinctively looked around for support. But his mastering the Office, once there, turned out to have been a personal triumph. In fact, a double triumph, for by conquering his dubious self, he made a commendable record for himself by also conquering the demands of the Office. That gained him two important areas of support: the affection of the people and the approval of the Press.

This is not to say he was wholly transformed, as faults continued to plague him. But one can best appreciate Harding's Presidency as a success story, by taking into account the self-imposed problems he faced leading up to that result, some overcome and some overcoming him. En route, one can see the foundation of shortcomings that persisted, and in some measure led to his undoing. While those shortcomings point to what he failed to do, they have permanently obscured all that he did do, rather well, in fact, and free of scandal. To appreciate how far he went as President, one has to consider how far he had to go in order to conquer his fear of becoming one.

Under-appreciated then as President, Harding is also unappreciated for certain personal victories he achieved: one in overcoming that inordinate fear of becoming President, and another in his overcoming a desire to avoid Presidential duties like patronage. Likewise unassessed is the degree to which his undoing was tied to a purblind estimate of subordinates, Albert Fall in particular. First, the fear.

PART III:

ESSENTIAL PROBLEMS; THE ESSENTIAL HARDING

CHAPTER 20

"Fearing He'd—God-forbid— Become President!"

RETURNING TO THE MATTER OF appearance, the idea that Harding 'looked like a President,' obviously meant that his appearance mirrored leadership, self-assurance and the like. Some high ranking politicians came by it naturally, and some seemed to. In Harding's case, "naturally" as the Presidential look became him, those in the Press who knew him thought he'd be unlikely to give it substance.

However, his getting elected made a difference. As family friend Evalyn McLean saw it, Harding appeared ready to grow into being the President he was supposed to be. An idea she attributed to him was "that when a man was elected to the presidency, his wits, by some automatic mental chemistry, were increased to fit the stature of his office" (Shadow, 421).

Whether or not Harding literally believed in this transformation, hidden behind it was an internal reality that contradicted his stereotypic appearance. The truth is that whatever the doubts others had regarding his qualification to become President, he intimately shared those doubts, even before he decided to become a candidate, at which point they became accentuated.

That was characteristic of essential problems Harding confronted, typically self-imposed. Additionally typical was the manner in which the essential Harding dealt with them, or failed to.

As William Allen White looked at his candidacy, in a view widely shared, Harry Daugherty "had to drag Harding into the Presidential race by the ears, protesting" (Puritan In Babylon, 178). The pulling had indeed been preceded by some notorious pushing. As Daugherty had earlier described getting his man to run for the Senate: "I found him like a turtle sunning himself on a log, and I pushed him into the water" (Florence, 109).

Jumping ahead to the end result of his Presidential Candidacy, when Harding received word from the Convention floor that he had astonishingly won the Nomination, his first response was incredulity. His second, a desire for support from friends randomly accompanying him at the moment of victory, Frank Lowden and Nicholas Murray Butler, whom he told: "I shall need all the help that you two friends can give" (Puritan, 211n.).

Not given to false modesty, he had no difficulty in letting anyone reasonably close know his feeling of insufficiency. In between agreeing to run for the Presidential Nomination and getting it, he had to swim through an ocean of doubt.

This was reinforced when the doubts recurred in Harding's Presidential campaign, during which they sometimes exceeded those of his doubters. But both pre- and post-election, there were times when Harding not only regretted being a Candidate, he also despaired of being able to handle all that he saw awaiting him. He gave the impression that his reluctance would become a burden on his Presidency. It didn't help that, in anticipation of a poor showing, his fear seemed to project a self-fulfilling prophecy. Thus, for an assessment of his favorable performance as President, one has to take into account the obstacles that lay in his way, big ones, again of his own making.

A sidelight of this is that there is no known instance of a Presidential Candidate who went through the self-imposed ordeal that afflicted Harding. He didn't have much time to straighten himself out, and he needed the ability to get it done. But, remarkably, he did do it. In fact, if one looks at his election as a blue-print for redemption, Harding's affirming the view of doubters, and then rising up to make a worthy record as President recapitulates a favorite American story: that of the 'come-back kid,' who became the underdog triumphant. His earning that goal was preceded by a bewildering cycle of wanting, not wanting, then dubiously wanting again to take the first step toward going for the Nomination and then the Presidency.

Considering that cycle, he had good reason, at any point, to have given up the chase. And he would have done so had the Nomination not been handed to him by a Convention of delegates exhausted by their own tedious proceedings on those hot June nights in 1920 Chicago. That had been a highly unanticipated event, by Harding no less than by the Convention.

Up to 25 November, 1919, when he wrote Scobey he was surprised (more likely alarmed) at seeing a newspaper report that Harry Daugherty said he was already in the race for President, Harding had been struggling with the idea of it. There he was, oscillating between a changeable 'yea,' an ambivalent 'maybe,' and a staunch 'nay,' while still subject to being swayed in favor of going for it. To get him to the latter fortuitous point, a situation as improbable to him as to others, took some doing.

Daugherty, as he had started to lay the ground work for pushing Harding into the race, was confiding to George B. Christian, Sr., Harding's Marion neighbor and long time friend, that Harding was the last person to know what they were up to. Preferably, he should think the opposite. "We need say no more [than] that he would not be a candidate for the Presidency." Daugherty's idea was to do a "canvas," and to do it "without Harding knowing about it." (Downes, 312; my ital.). This was contemplated on 2 November, 1919, three weeks before Daugherty made his surprise announcement to the Press that Harding was in the running.

Once the word was out, Harding's "fitness" was questioned from all sides. There was a remark to that effect from the well-known Conservationist, and soon to be Governor of Pennsylvania, Gifford Pinchot. Having been fired by staunchly conservative President Taft, Pinchot held out the uncertain hope that support for his movement might yet be forthcoming from Harding.[38]

The thinking was that Harding had shown he had a weak streak, which made him malleable. As noted, William Allen White had had much the same opinion, and it was exactly what was assumed by the "cabal" of Senators who claimed credit for getting unlikely Harding the Nomination. Scobey, fully aware of the weakness factor, had wanted to prod his friend along with the stark suggestion that "if we are going into this fight, let us go in to win, and in order to win we have to commence now to make an aggressive campaign, especially through the press, as the time is getting short and it takes quite a while to organize a campaign of this magnitude" (op. cit., Warren G. Harding Papers, 8 December, 1919).

The more Harding showed signs of worry, the more Daugherty and Scobey persisted in getting him focused. He had to be put in high campaign mode, and quickly. For a while, it seemed like Scobey would have made a better candidate than Harding. But he lacked "appearance," and ambition. Harding had both, but also symptoms of wavering, which showed. This was big-time politics. It was a question of whether Harding could be persuaded to see what it would look like for him to win in that arena.

Despite his effort to keep it under wraps, Harding's fear was obvious enough to persons who knew him, like Malcolm Mac Jennings, his former campaign manager in his run for Governor. The idea apparently was that the fear simply had to play out while his two active sponsors forged ahead on his behalf. He never forthrightly told them to forget it.

CHAPTER 21

"How The Fear Played Out"

It is hard to say how widely Harding's fear of running for President was suspected, but it couldn't have been totally hidden from those outside his circle of friends. A crusty old Texas politician and National Committeeman, H. F. MacGregor, had gathered a sufficient impression of Harding to tell Daugherty, during the primary season, that "the country at this time is not looking for a candidate that is afraid."[39]

Neo-Texan Frank Edgar Scobey, Harding's most ardent supporter, knew he had a problem in prepping his candidate for the Nomination. He had contacted Daugherty on the subject and rejoined, "Leave this situation to me and if you can show at the Chicago Convention that our candidate has some strength, I am satisfied that we can work this thing out all right" (Ibid.). The truth is his working it out was to be done on the fly.

Scobey felt he and Daugherty had to account for a strength Harding had yet to show. What came across as a consequence of Harding's fear was the lack of a "fighting aggressive spirit," which was observed by friends who knew him best—for instance, Mac Jennings.[40] This perception was not lost on Harding himself. When he went out of his way to claim Daugherty did not own him in any respect, adding that he was "under no spell in [his] relationship with him," Harding would arouse the suspicion that he did protest too much.[41] Daugherty's ownership was all too obvious, and was at one point spelled out by Jennings.

It is no accident that in the same letter that Harding denied Daugherty's ownership, his awareness of the perception that he was lacking in spine came out in an interesting circumstance. He was envious that Henry H. Timken, the Canton, Ohio industrialist, would "worship" Senator Hiram Johnson as a "red blooded leader," even after he had voted against Timken's economic interest on a Naval Appropriations Bill (approving a "Rider" Timken opposed) whereas, even after Harding had voted Timken's way, Harding lamented that Timken, "continues to look upon me as a complacent chap without either courage or capacity" (Ibid.).

All the while that Daugherty was secretly preparing to make Harding President—on his part a matter of professional pride, for which his principal was the pawn—Harding, beset by his Prufrockean Angst—had been hoping he wouldn't get drawn into campaigning, to say nothing of assuming the burden of becoming President. Looking for excuses, he told Scobey (even prior to his getting into the race) that he worried about the utter bothersomeness of incurring political debts which would have to be repaid.[42]

This would become a significant qualifier. A month later, and a short two weeks after he does get into the race, Harding is saying he doesn't want a campaign that will require "extravagant money," and, if that should become necessary, he would "not want the thing at all."[43]

He had, after all, obtained his nomination to the Senate on less than $4,000, and rather cherished that good old-time kind of political expenditure. Considering the money that was backing Leonard Wood, Harding noted, "I think there is wholesome strength in being free from the big financial interests of the country" (Ibid.).

So, while he thought the economic well-being of the nation was tied to an environment in which businessmen could thrive, Harding wouldn't want their money to put them in a position to dictate policy. But then, as his doubts began to mount, out of the torment comes a climactic confession, again made just two weeks after he had already decided to go for the Nomination: "The only thing I really worry about is that I am sometimes afraid very much I am going to be nominated and elected. That's an awful thing to contemplate."[44]

So, while he made no bones about being afraid of getting the Presidency, as he suddenly began to contemplate its accomplishment, he was caught in a dilemma. He didn't really want to go after that role, but, since he had just put himself in contention, he lacked the spirit to decisively pull himself out of it. This repeats a consistent ambivalence that went back to his earliest thoughts about running for President about two months after he had declared for the race. His desire to avoid the "annoyances and worries"[45] of a campaign imposed a psychological barrier. He wasn't naïve enough to think there weren't worries, almost always about money, but there was more to it than that.

In connection with Harding's affair with Nan Britton, January, 1919 had been a time when their relationship reached a high point. It was also the month from which she dated the conception of their child. The feelings they experienced also had an impact on how Harding would regard the then dismal idea of his becoming a candidate for President, as that would stand in the way of their ambition to have a future together. Euphoric possibilities were dancing before their eyes, and the Presidency was not one of them.

That sentiment probably had something to do with the letter to Scobey on 14 January, 1919, in which Harding was more than ever doubtful that he wanted to make a run for the political position he, at that point, had no great enthusiasm for, and little prospect of attaining. He would have to go for it at the cost of sacrificing the near-sacred closeness he was enjoying with Nan, which could continue unhampered if he just retained the permissive life-style afforded by the Senate. The same secret attitude doubtless had a bearing on his Lincoln Day meeting in February, 1919, (when Nan's pregnancy had been confirmed) which had him wanting to dampen any thought of his running for the Presidential Nomination.

In the end, his desire to run would outlast his desire not to. The decision to move on from a tempting life-style would be driven by another temptation: not just politics, but a chance to be posted at the top of the political food chain.

CHAPTER 22

"Doubt Persists, But He Wants It"

FROM THE TIME OF HIS election to the Senate in 1914, Harding had had the temptation for Presidential Candidacy bouncing around in the back of his mind. His impressive 100,000 vote plurality almost instantly put him in contention, which Scobey was quick to point out less than a week later. Having churned about between nays and yeas for six years, there Harding was, ending up in story book fashion, with the Convention having placed the ultimate prize in sight. Looking toward it became intimidating, but temporarily it was as if he couldn't resist wanting to take a bite out of that luscious plum.

Harding campaigned not so much with a conviction that he was the man to run for President, as by his seizing a once-in-a-lifetime chance considered unavailable to him. Prior anxieties were suddenly cast aside, making way for a rise in that old political blood which had lain stagnating in the Senate.

But there were realities that had to be taken into account. As observed, Harding's fortuitously getting the Nomination resulted from the willingness of weary delegates to accept a secondary, and obviously lesser, alternative to Leonard Wood or Frank Lowden. Harding was assumed to be pliable enough, within reach—namely, controllable—and not too strong a leader. Nicholas Murray Butler offered the belittling verdict that, "a group of Senators put their heads together to nominate a man who, as one of them cynically said, would, when elected, sign whatever bills the Senate sent him and not send bills to the Senate to pass" (Across the Busy Years, I, 279).

In effect, what Harding had claimed he didn't want was given to him by delegates who themselves didn't especially want him. The negativity was strongest with Harding, as, even before he arrived at the Nomination, his downer train of thought had been predominating, sustained during the Convention by the low vote total he was getting at first. Eventually, delegate frustration would set in, and there was an unexpected movement to accept the non-threatening compromise.

Having suffered through ten burdensome ballots during the hottest of June nights Conventioners were eager to have it over with. Never mind what non-entity they had finally selected. He'd be a tool manipulated by seasoned politicians in the Senate

The tortuous course of doubt that Harding traversed in order to get there was as exhausting as the Convention itself. Little as the delegates knew of their obscure Nominee, there was lots it was just as well they didn't know. A big void was how often he had expressed disqualifying doubts. For example, a couple of weeks after telling Scobey of his fear of being nominated (14 January, 1919) Harding came up with a reason for not wanting to be.

It was an idle thought which candidly reflected the slack side of his nature. He felt that, as President, he'd not have "any real enjoyment in life" on losing the leisure he had been enjoying as Senator.[46] This objection came eight short days after the death of Teddy Roosevelt had left the field wide open for Harding to run, and deprived him of a rationalization for not wanting to.

As big a reason as any other for his holding back (aside from his delicate situation with Nan Britton) was the objection of his wife, the Duchess, who had been aroused by a portent of her husband's demise provided by her psychic, Madam Marcia. That brought forth the opposition Florence reiterated at the Nominating Convention, from which, not unlike the Candidate, she could, as if by contagion, suddenly reverse herself. Evidently, that didn't muddy the waters for the delegates. They needed any reason that came to hand for closing out the Convention, and Harding would do.

Meanwhile, he had much to live down. In February, 1919, at the Lincoln Day celebration, which involved a significant—and intimidating—confab for Harding, he had cringed at the suggestion that he should run for the Nomination. It was an attitude, as indicated, he had just written Scobey about. He would insistently tell Charles E. Hard, Secretary of the Ohio Republican Executive Committee, he wanted no part of the Nomination. And Hard, no great supporter in the first place, placated him by coming up with three good reasons for him not to change his mind (Downs, 306).

One of the reasons Hard offered was that, first of all, Harding "did not feel that he was big enough to fill the office of President. There were many Republicans much better qualified" (Ibid.). As William Allen White had pointed out, Harding could be quite candid about his limitations, and wasn't inclined to deceive himself about them. He certainly couldn't deceive fellow Republicans in Ohio. Moreover, as he thought things over, he didn't relish the stress and expense of going for it.

This went counter to what his friends had been pressing, dating from 1914. A month after Harding had won the Senate seat, Scobey was telling Mac Jennings that he concurred with Mac's view of Harding's prospects. According to both, he would do well enough in the Senator to become a credible candidate for the Presidency. Harding himself told Scobey that he believed he "would make as good a President as a great many men who are talked of for that position," indirectly including "the man who [then] occupied the White House." But Harding had, at the same time, opened up about why he really didn't want to try "winning such an undertaking." Thoughts of the run for President having been kicked around for five years, he wrote his chief advocate:

"Really, my dear Scobey… [it] is not worth the work and anxiety involved. I do not mean by this that I am utterly lazy and unwilling to shoulder my share of the burden, but I can not for the life of me see why any body would deliberately shoulder the annoyances and worries and incessant trials incident to a campaign for nomination and election to the presidency." That was in February, 1919, when he also acknowledged that he'd get "cordial support" from his home state.

The best he could make of that was to prefer waiting "until public support [was] more thoroughly crystallized." Having told Scobey on 14 January that he knew his "own insufficiency," less than a month later he wanted to add an exclamation point. [47]

Further evidence of the persistence of Harding's self-doubt arose in various ways. One particularly revealing instance involved an interesting sequence of events, pre-Nomination. On 16 December, 1919, Harding wrote Scobey, "I have decided to take the plunge and play the big game." And he added, "You know how reluctant I was to take this step, but it looked like I needed to do so to preserve my political life and influence in Ohio."[48] In this instance, the reluctance was forced upon him, but it added up to the perception of doubt anyway.

James Robenalt has provided the background motive here, pointing out that when Leonard Wood received support from the soap king, William Procter, Wood backers threatened to take over the Ohio Party, and that made it necessary for Harding to protect his base by declaring his candidacy for President (Affair, 342).

Skipped over here, unfortunately, is something that lay behind this move; namely, an insulting proposition which Harding had rejected With Procter having placed his money behind Wood, he proposed that Harding should put himself up as Favorite Son to lock up the Ohio delegation, and then throw the delegation to Wood.

Harding was being forced to take his plunge, not just because he wanted to, but as a matter of political self-preservation, motivation enough for his pride as committed politician. However, once he was compelled to hit the campaign trail and begin to actively work for his Nomination, the idea of its achievement made him think of some uncomfortable sacrifices awaiting him.

Flattered as he was over being backed for the Candidacy, Harding nonetheless felt it would rob him of the good life. "I should be unhappy every hour from the time I entered the race until the thing were settled, and I am sure I should never have any more fun or real enjoyment in life if I should be so politically fortunate to win a nomination and election" (op.cit; n. 46).

By March, 1920, he knew he couldn't pull out and realized as well that he had to pledge himself to do all he "reasonably [could] to bring [the campaign] to a successful conclusion." As a reminder, he went on to assert what he really wanted. "I am sure, however, that I will be vastly more happy, if it turns out in a manner to bring about my political retirement; than [sic] I can pursue my own way in life and assume an attitude of telling everybody whom I do not like to go jump in the river."[49]

Again, the plunge metaphor, used as a kind of abstract revenge against the forces with which he had cooperated to put himself into a race he disliked for an unwanted position that promised to rob him of the "way in life" he liked. He mentioned golf on this occasion as one pleasure to be denied him. There were also poker, fishing, and relaxation times with his old cronies. Mainly, however, it was the women who gave him the relaxation he most enjoyed. At the time—1920—there was one in particular whom he was not willing to leave simply because he might get nominated to run for President.

Interestingly, the sense of reluctance he felt in the run-up to his campaign and in the campaign itself, would return when, as President, he became frustrated over how to sort out his responsibilities. An instance of one such situation had to do with the provincial innocence of his trying to personally tackle the huge stack of letters that came in from the public—to say the least, a misapplication of conscientiousness. Nicholas Murray Butler, coming upon him at such a moment, was astounded by his naiveté (Across the Busy Years, I, 410).

That unanswered stack of letters left him feeling overwhelmed by the job, and he bleakly declared, "I am not fit for this office and should never have been here" (Ibid., 411). He yet again used the criterion of "fitness," as a negative marker. How could he deal with more important duties, if those letters would consume so much of his time? It was much like the local Editor in him wanting to keep in touch with his readership.

As President, Harding was honest enough to admit there were times when he felt unable to handle all that was demanded of him. But, as with the over-load of letter-writing, this arose not so much out of laziness as from his being awed by the impossibility of being as good about serving the public as he ideally would like to be. In point of fact, this pathetic awareness made him all the more conscientious about applying himself to the job, something noticed by reporters who covered him; for instance, Mark Sullivan.

Harding's trepidations about becoming President fairly well evaporated when he got down to the business of being President. His natural political instincts took over, and William Allen White reported on how they worked for him. As White would put it in a different connection, "When Harding came to the White House, surely something happened to him" (Masks, 412). White, imagining the green President to have been abashed by thoughts of what lay in waiting for him, likened him to "Moses before the burning bush" (Ibid.). Fright made him doubt he could do the job, but it also gave him the incentive to get it done.

As Herbert Hoover observed, once Harding took over the Office, "The responsibilities of the White House gave him a real spiritual lift. He deeply wanted to make a name as President" (Memoirs II, 47).

CHAPTER 23

"The Party Harmonizer Hated Patronage"

PATRONAGE ISOLATED TWO CONDITIONS WHICH had made Harding leery of running for President: money and influence. However, patronage would become a little known enterprise that Harding got himself involved in, and it also became an area in which he polished his political instincts to get just the effect he wanted.

Patronage was looked upon as a thorny process, and it seemed a laborious one, which Harding preferred to avoid. On being prodded to get himself into it, Harding held off at first. But, in giving behind the scenes help to appease Scobey, he relied on a tactic that was effective for him in political situations: Make everybody happy. He could bend a local rule, but Party rules being hard and fast, he could slough off the follow-through on Scobey. When Robert Murray remarked that "only in the matter of patronage could [Harding] be held culpable," (Era, 403) he was referring to race relations, but Harding's distaste for patronage was universal.

Once he was elected President, the weight of Office raised expectations that he would use it for preferred appointments. He did get busy with the major ones. But beyond that, his lack of interest in patronage at large was faulted by friend Scobey. Unfortunately, however, Scobey wanted him to become occupied with gritty local politics, where the efforts to be mounted by a President would be misplaced.

First, a look at how monumental an issue patronage could be for the incoming President. Arriving after eight years of dominance by Democrats, the new Republican Administration had the daunting task of replacing a multitude of appointees, totaling as many as a quarter of a million. Usually, the method of rewarding supporters was handled by political operatives, headed in Harding's case by Harry Daugherty and Party Chairman Will Hays, who both assigned much of it—the low level appointments, to their respective staffs. As any President would know, delegation went down, never up.

Since there still were far more applicants than positions, Harding welcomed assistance from all quarters, including, appropriately enough, his wife and Administrative Partner par excellance. Florence Harding was indeed quite eager to delve into the mountain of incoming requests for jobs and make suggestions on the important ones. She went so far as to canvass suggestions from knowledgeable supporters. In the end, however, it was customary for appointments to follow the money.

But dealing with appointments at the state and county levels scarcely ever reached consideration in Washington, and they were even less likely to land on the President's desk. For example, there were some 13,000 postmasterships alone to be filled, a position that was removed from the civil service protection granted by the Wilson Administration—a Jacksonian-type move. Among the unsolicited appeals for jobs, there suddenly appeared requests from Hardings all over the country, claiming a clannish relationship. As Harding wrote George Harvey, "I never knew how many Hardings there were until I was elected to the Presidency" (Shadow, 457).

In the face of his being deluged with petitions for an assortment of posts—those of immediate significance, plus the thousands out on the hustings—Harding would be expected to systematically distance himself from those thousands as he prepared to take on the Presidency itself. Surely there was no good reason for him to become involved in the scrap over patronage in Texas, scarcely a critical State in comparison with Oklahoma, whose oil-rich Jake Hamon had come through with financial support as well as important votes at the National Convention.

Absurd as it was, Harding nonetheless did allow himself to be drawn into the situation down there in Texas. How else but by submitting to the demands of friendship? Harding had made such a fetish of friendship that when he spoke of having been betrayed by the corrupt members of his Administration, he still referred to them as friends—albeit ironically. Scobey was a good friend, and the advice he offered was based on his wanting to be of service to Harding by letting him know what was happening with the dispensation of jobs, and who was doing the dispensing, and in non-critical Texas, of all places.

Scobey was in high dudgeon over Harding's indifference to those who had supported him in Texas, and he felt his friend needed to know the consequence of his neglect. Scobey, for example, listed the number of key appointments that had been promoted by his arch rival H. F. MacGregor (all of six), while not one of the Harding's supporters had received an appointment.

Once Harding had been sworn in, this, to Scobey's chagrin, was a sorry state of affairs. Condescendingly he scolded, "You'll agree that competency, standing and other things being equal, the men who made the fight and stood by the game when the outlook was gloomy should have the preference instead of favoring those who opposed you." As for why Texas, interestingly, one backdoor reason for Republican interest there was that, according to Daugherty, it was a state where money raised for the Harding campaign could be used to carry doubtful states. Daugherty had made the point that if those interested people in Texas would back "the nomination of a man who will win," the expectation of a reward would "create more substantial and lasting obligations."[50]

On that basis alone, Texas patronage was worthy of concern; and also in need of work. Exasperated that he had to educate his friend on the subject, Scobey had a point to make. Since the status of the Party in the hinterlands had a bearing on the larger picture, patronage out there couldn't be ignored. Unless Harding had supportive people placed in key local positions and avoided such placement for those who had opposed him, the authority he could exert would be diminished.

However, a mere month after his election, Harding had to remind Scobey that he had priorities.

If six appointees in Texas were not worthy of Presidential concern, Scobey felt he could get somewhere by alerting Harding to his upcoming appointment of Albert Fall as Interior Secretary. Scobey pointed out that Fall had earlier worked against Harding's interest, and was indeed involving himself—as indicated—in a potentially lucrative arrangement with high-stakes Mexican politics. Considering appointees who had been with him, as opposed to those who had been against him, perhaps Harding was unaware that Fall had been a Democrat, and in 1906 had opportunistically become a Republican, but not by conviction.

More importantly, Harding had no idea that, as Scobey heatedly told him, Fall had never gotten any votes for Harding in Texas or New Mexico, in addition to his having managed the campaign of Congressman Wurzbach, who also never did anything good for Harding and opposed most of his supporters. Scobey, who had a lot to unload concerning Fall, went so far as to contend that, at the Nominating Convention, Fall had joined the forces of Leonard Wood, whose "crowd" had conspired against Harding in the Ohio Primary.[51]

With Fall, Scobey, of course, was on to something. But, as he had been riding Harding so hard on minor issues, he had to be reminded by Harding that larger ones needed to be attended to in Washington. Harding had already written Scobey, two weeks prior to Scobey's missive on Fall, that it was "futile" for him to become involved with the Texas patronage which preoccupied Scobey. "My immediate task," he declared, "is the big job and lesser matters will have to wait [for] my convenience and time"[52]

Besides getting himself apprised of Presidential affairs, Harding had to have an evaluation of candidates suggested to him for major administrative posts, where he could suffer from wrong choices. Above all, he had to avoid time consuming side-issues, as he mulled over the composition of his Cabinet. With he and Scobey being driven in different directions—local versus federal—Harding would ignore the warning on Albert Fall that fell in the midst of Scobey's concern over low-level nuisance appointments.

As Harding directly put it to Scobey, when R. B. "Gus" Creager, Scobey's ally, came to see him about their local patronage issue, he couldn't give Gus "a lot of time," pleading that he was "painfully busy"[53] That was what Harding would write Scobey some two weeks after receiving his letter related to Fall, in between which came bothersome difficulties with Texas Congressman Wurzbach that had to be deferred. All that Scobey and Creager were waiting for was an ad hoc direction from Harding for the patronage problem they were going to lay before him.

As a sign of Harding's feeling that he needed to avoid distraction, Creager was actually a person he had come to like after meeting him a year earlier. He had gone so far as to tell Scobey, "Creager is a really great companion and I rejoice to think he thinks kindly of me. …he really strikes me as one of the best fellows that I ever came to know."[54] Harding surely should have wanted to make time for the likes of Gus. He wasn't exactly a non-entity. In time, Harding saw a way to give him leeway, if for no other reason than to unload responsibility he didn't need.

This came together with pressure from Scobey, who was emphasizing that, given authority, he could "build a real party in Texas." [55] The side of this that would have caught Harding's attention was Daugherty's point that Texas money could be used where it might be beneficially spent elsewhere.

Meanwhile, as things moved along, Creager had been unanimously elected Chairman of the State Republican Committee, and had brought in as Vice-Chairman Eugene Nolte, a man objected to by their enemy, MacGregor, whose influence had suddenly dwindled to his commanding just six of the thirty-one votes on the Committee.

That much accomplished, Scobey could write Harding that he and Creager had a plan which had been hatched to relieve him of further annoyance over Texas patronage. The idea was to set up a three man Referee Committee composed of Creager, H.F. MacGregor, and Scobey, with all patronage to be decided by a majority of the

Committee. MacGregor, would get a vote, but be outvoted. Scobey had been nervously hoping their "suggestions" for a Referee Committee would "meet with [Harding's] approval."

He got some relief from Harding's response that "it is useless to think of naming a triumvirate down there to referee matters of patronage down there, but... I will take a chance on letting him [Creager] settle matters to the best possible advantage" [56]

For the time being, that smoothed things out, but issues remained. The reason Harding considered it "useless" to grant Creager-Scobey such freedom is that all appointments had to conform to pre-established rules having to do with geography, the prerogative of local congressmen, and civil service regulations. Harding was apparently suspicious that locals ruling on locals might put grievances (like Scobey's) ahead of underlying Party rules.

CHAPTER 24

"It Gets More Complicated"

The problems Scobey was focused on would not go away. One went back to December, 1920. Harding had rejected an appointment Scobey wanted to have made on the basis of who had backed Harding's Nomination when it was needed. However, Harding gave patronage precedence to none other than Congressman, Harry M. Wurzbach, of whom Scobey had precisely complained on grounds that he had never done anything for Harding and opposed "most of Harding's leading people."[57]

Among other defenses, like the rules of location (an appointee had to live in the region where he was to be given an appointment) Harding relied on the dictates of Party Discipline. He, in fact, fell back on a policy urged by members of the Republican National Committee (led by the influential Senator Boies Penrose) and that was likewise called for by self-aggrandizing MacGregor. The idea was to uphold the principle of "standing by the organization," in making appointments, the importance of which Harding would precisely spell out for Scobey (cited above, WGH to FES, 20 April, 1921). But what that meant for Scobey was giving preference to antagonistic Harry Wurzbach.

From the earliest days of his political career, Harding was known as the solid "organization man," so labeled during the first time he wanted to make himself a candidate for Governor of Ohio in 1903, years before his ill fated run for that position in 1910. With Harding being seen as so "thoroughly [an] organization man" by a reporter for the Cincinnati Enquirer, it was noted that "because of this attitude [he] ha[d] the confidence of the political leaders in various parts of the state" (Shadow, 148). Throughout his political career this kind of dependability served him well, and—practically ingrained—Harding depended on it to do that for him.

So strong an asset was it for him to be the very symbol of Party Harmony that when Teddy Roosevelt in 1918 seemed the certain Presidential Nominee for 1920, he saw Harding as a good fit for Vice President, just the man who could offset the breach between Progressives and Conservatives. If the role as Harmonizer carried that far for Harding, adherence to Party simply had to take precedence—even over so strongly personal a tie as friendship, hard as it was for him to go against Scobey's wishes.

A corollary of this attitude was his unwavering sense of loyalty. It might be impossible to think of Harding as fanatical about anything, but Party Loyalty would be the notable exception. As he had to choose between Party and friendship, the habitual Harmonizer wanted to accommodate both.

Meanwhile, with Scobey, on his own, doing what he could to get appointments for people friendly to Harding, and to disqualify those who had been unfriendly, he was doing just what Harding would expect of his man on the scene. But Scobey remained increasingly put out with Harding for his reluctance to get himself more closely involved with the patronage process. Worse yet, from Scobey's perspective, he was displeased with Harding for his failing to give heed to what his strongest advocate was telling him, and acceding by default to those who contested Scobey's choices for appointment.

Scobey wrote that he found himself in the awkward position of having to defend himself against surreptitious attacks that he believed had reached Harding from political enemies making false accusations about him. Scobey assumed the attacks had likely come from the Wurzbach camp. Indignant over the free hand given Wurzbach to make appointments, Scobey used every argument he could muster for Harding to recognize how bad a decision that was. At one point, he went so far as to point out: "The Congressman is supporting a man who was considered pro-German during the war and is backed by all that element."[58]

As for the assumption that surreptitious attacks had been unfairly directed against him, Scobey felt he had had to write Harding very directly about his disappointment: "It is incomprehensive [sic] to me that I have to defend myself to you against attacks and statements by enemies of mine who undoubtedly have misrepresented and lied about me."[59]

Moreover, Scobey had to bring up the embarrassment that, pre-election, Harding had indicated he would "look to no one in Texas but Creager and Scobey," only to turn around post-election and favor MacGregar and Wurzbach along with other "outside influences." Together, that group, Scobey claimed, was going "to oppose a number of your and our friends who had helped to make the fight."

Walking the tight-rope of pleasing both sides, Harding came up with a consolation. "I do think," he wrote, "that under the Executive Order [which overruled geography] we may be able to work it out to name your man when the case comes up for consideration." To this, Harding added the reassuring sweetener, "I think I know a way of helping without cheating."[60]

On the other hand, in accord with what Harding called the Party's "organizational situation," there really were inescapable reasons for courting Wurzbach. From the time of Reconstruction, he was one of the few Texas Republicans who would win a seat in Congress. Under those circumstances, and also going safely by the book, Harding allowed that Wurzbach's preference for appointments in his 14th District had to be honored.

Harding had to tell Scobey, point blank, that it would be a violation of his own "conviction of political propriety and decency…[to] go over the head of a Congressman" in making local appointments.[61] It simply was not done; certainly wouldn't be by him. Harding was holding to the larger issue of the consistency with Party policy that members were expected to abide by—a rule, in relation to which Scobey's view tended to be parochial.

As indicated in the letter of 12 May on "helping without cheating,"

Harding had clearly spelled out specific reasons, beyond Party prerogatives, for denying Scobey preferences; namely, that he couldn't appoint Scobey's candidate for Internal Revenue Commissioner, for example, because that post had to be filled by a person who resided in the District in question, which was not the case with the man Scobey wanted, J. W. Bass, whose appointment also happened to have been objected to by MacGregor.

Harding likewise couldn't come through with Scobey's candidate to be San Antonio Post Master because that position required a Civil Service Exam, and the appointee had to be chosen from among the three persons scoring highest on the Exam.

After the difficulty Scobey had had in reconciling Harding's broader view with his own close scrutiny of Texas patronage, Scobey's disappointment would linger and almost lead to a falling out of the two fast friends. In March, 1922, Scobey on his way to Washington from Chicago, wrote that, since Harding indicated he might be out of town when Scobey and his wife were coming to Washington, they could put themselves up at a hotel. Harding, aware of Scobey's hurt, answered that he thought he would be back in Washington on the 17th to treat Scobey "with proper courtesy when he arrives."[62] This came shortly after Harding had sent the Senate his nomination of Scobey to be head of the U.S. Mint.

On the other hand, also mindful of friendship, Harding did actually help to get things balanced out with frustrated Scobey by facilitating the selection of a number of appointments that Scobey favored. One was the appointment of his friend Roy Campbell to the Internal Revenue Collectorship. But for any future patronage issues, Harding would make sure to add the bedeviling qualifier of responsibility to Party. "You can expect me to do the best that a friend can do without taking such a course as tends to result in party wreck."[63]

In the end, one thing that Harding's point of view accomplished was to activate the local maneuvering of Scobey and Creager to get preferred appointments made by means of the Referee Committee of Three. Scobey was pleased to be able to tell Harding that this plan would follow his original desire to be relieved of involvement in

Texas patronage, but Scobey wanted it made known to MacGregor and Wurzbach that Harding backed the Referee Committee.[64] Harding did follow through on his promise to do that, enabling Scobey and Greager to savor their victory over a nemesis.

But the treatment of MacGregor had a history. There had to have been a reason why he would accept a minority role on the Referee Committee.

CHAPTER 25

"He Actually Prepared The Way"

THE TEXAS VICTORY DIDN'T MEAN that Harding disliked patronage any less. It remained an extension of the money side of politics. Prior to his Candidacy for President, he had indeed cited just that as a major reason for his wanting to beg off. As previously indicated, what had originally inhibited him from wanting to run for President was the fear of incurring political debts that had to be repaid. This was underscored in his letter to Scobey of 25 November, 1919, the date when Harding learned that Daugherty had, unasked, announced his Candidacy to the Press.

The rivalry over patronage in Texas replayed Harding's problem, lessened when taken over by Scobey. From the beginning, a key obstructionist for Scobey had been F.L. MacGregor, the aged National Committeeman, who coveted his own role for making appointments. In place of Scobey's man, for example, MacGregor had favored giving the appointment of Collector of Internal Revenue to C. J. McDowell, a previously registered Democrat and incompetent under investigation for a fraudulent stock deal.

Though it would have been easy enough for Harding to step in and, on the face of it, prevent the appointment himself, he instead assured Scobey the appointment "will not take place. Daugherty will be glad to join in working things out the way you want it." This was the concluding pat on the back that Harding gave Scobey in the previously cited letter of 2 May, 1921.

Patronage for Harding was not only a distasteful issue, it was also a fuzzy one, and what attention he did give to it was, for Scobey, at best, fuzzier yet. For example, in early January, 1921, being preoccupied with mulling over Cabinet appointments, Harding had shown himself to be so detached from anything having to do with local appointments that he seemed temporarily oblivious of the fact that Daugherty, was already "contemplat[ing] the distribution of patronage." Harding was aware that he had "some responsibilities of this job," but awareness did not translate into more than minimal involvement.

Rather, as patronage surely did need attention, Harding, off-hand, would keep pointing out, as in the letter to Scobey of 2 May, 1921, that Daugherty in his role of enforcer would cooperate with Scobey and Creager, as much as was needed.

This was nothing new. The best Harding could do to answer Scobey's concern in early January, 1921 was to offer the succinct, but vague, assurance, "I know he [Daugherty] will want to do what I wish"[65] This could still have left Scobey wondering whether Daugherty would necessarily do what Scobey felt was best from his perspective, since Harding's "wish" did not always coincide with his own.

But, it was all a matter of timing. As opposed to post-election time, it was a different story in Harding's pre-Nomination days. Harding back then had had no compunctions about mixing it up with the local politicos. He knew what it would take in 1919 to summon grass-roots support for his Nomination, in particular in Texas and indeed from MacGregor, empowered at that point, and known to be difficult. No slouch, Harding knew exactly how to exert himself, when he had to. Importantly, what he did was to soften up Scobey's chief opponent, and make him amenable to accepting the downgrade to low man on the Referee Committee.

Harding's manner of dealing with MacGregor, then, was by a typical show of affable consideration, above all an avoidance of the confrontation this National Committeeman deserved. In mid-December, 1919, Harding wrote Scobey of his having met MacGregor and finding him, not only "friendly," but agreeing to have Harding come to Texas for a series of speeches. This came up in the same letter in which Harding informed Scobey that he had actually made the decision "to take the plunge" and go for the Presidential Nomination, Daugherty having announced it a month earlier.

Word of Harding's being in the race was greeted warmly in Ohio and the East, but it needed to be bolstered elsewhere. Thus, when he encountered MacGregor, Harding had seemed pretty much a long-shot for the Nomination, in want of support from all quarters, including the one represented by National Committeeman MacGregor. Daugherty had specifically assured him that Harding would not neglect his friends. To such an approach MacGregor would indeed be quite responsive, which, he clearly did not need to be prior to Harding's getting the Nomination, especially with the Party credentials MacGregor had.

Harding's finding that MacGregor seemed "friendly" to him was an attitude he simply had a talent for cultivating, especially on a face-to-face basis. Writing Scobey on 12 January, 1920, Harding began by stating his confidence on this point: "I have not been in doubt about the reasonably friendly attitude of MacGregor." He based this on an intuition that MacGregor wished to keep his options open.

With his campaign for the Nomination in need of gaining traction, Harding made known his understanding of MacGregor's motivation: "I am not finding fault about it." He knew that this fellow just wanted "to make sure that we are going to make a good showing else he will look down the highway for an approaching band-wagon [of someone else]." Having reached MacGregor prior to his having made a "showing," Harding saw how his face to face understanding paid off.

In fact, so strongly did he win this Committeeman's support—still thought to have been dubious—that MacGregor went out of his way to tell Scobey of his warm support when Harding undertook his speaking tour of Texas in February, 1920. MacGregor wrote that, should Daugherty think people would talk more freely if he did not go along, he would gladly absent himself. He was indeed very much in favor of Harding being "in good shape."[66]

No one knew the political Harding better than Daugherty, who, having seen him in action, noted that Harding's "method was always one of conciliation," which he employed on the basis that, given a chance, he "believed he could convert and win his enemies," a sentiment precisely echoed by Florence Harding (Inside Story, 12, 38).

As for Daugherty himself, back in early December, 1919, he had anticipated that he'd be compelled to work with MacGregor. In so doing, he had likely prepared the way for Harding's meeting with that fellow, preparation made in accordance with Daugherty's plain spoken manner of dealing with recalcitrants out in the field. In fact, MacGregor was just the kind of challenge Daugherty delighted in confronting. As he told Scobey, "don't worry about my being able to talk to MacGregor in the language that Americans, Republicans and practical politicians have to be talked to [in]."[67]

Making sure MacGregor got the message, Daugherty and Harding, working in tandem, decided the old fella could be manipulated. With Harding following Daugherty's tough approach by employing a soft one, MacGregor was brought in line. So, it turned out that, even though Harding had a kind of left-handed interest in what was going on in politics at the local level, on finding that he had to become involved with it, he knew the most expeditious approach for getting things done his way. Daugherty may have loosened MacGregor up, but Harding won him over.

This typified Harding's modus operandi. Regarding the difficulties brought out by Scobey, for example, when caught between the primacy of Party and the preservation of friendship, Harding would be adaptable Harding. Good guy that he was, he wanted both, and, as noted, found a way to have both. When pressed to become serious enough about addressing such problems, Harding showed he had the political skills to deal with them. This was not so, however, with a course of action he refused to see as detrimental, that being the case with the unmerited loyalty given certain of his close associates.

This becomes all the more ironic when compared with the savvy skills Harding could bring to bear on Texas politics, in which, as President-elect he had had minimal interest, but which, back in his nascent Candidacy, he was confident to employ. As politician, Harding was peerless. Andrew Sinclair's calling him "a formidable opponent in an election" (op.cit., 298) wasn't hyperbolic. Harding knew how to reach people. Herbert Hoover was neither the first nor the last to point out how unfortunate, how unnecessary, it was that, in Office, Harding should lose his way, by trusting the untrustworthy whom he brought into his Administration.

Had he taken heed of the lessons in patronage that Scobey wanted to press upon him, he might have acquired an ability to understand the necessity, in politics, of more often extending the barb of toughness than the balm of harmony. But that wouldn't have been Harding, and wouldn't have produced the things he was good at in establishing a creditable record for himself as President.

It seems that, in an evaluation of Harding's strengths, there were some issues, on which those strengths could become the face side of a coin that bore corresponding weaknesses on its verso. There was one instance, in particular, where this would be culminating, and that was in Harding's relationship with Albert B. Fall.

Minus Fall, Harding would not have had the curse of Teapot Dome to blight his reputation, overshadowing the fact that as President he had made an enviable record of accomplishments, earned in less than a full term in Office.

If Albert Fall became the bête noir of the Harding Administration, Harry Daugherty ran him a close second.

CHAPTER 26

"Indebted to Daugherty"

Clearly, Harding's good nature was not a work liability. For one thing, adaptability being a counterpart of his congeniality, Harding's first year as President revealed him to have been an on-the-job fast learner. Yet along with his congeniality came laxity, and, because of it, he remained in some respects the easy-going Harmonizer that he had been before becoming conscientious and effective. Fully dominant, like the Roosevelt who preceded him, Harding was not.

Among deficiencies that persisted, one that seriously worked against him was the lapse of judgment shown in some of his appointments. He brought in a socially smooth operator like Charlie Forbes, whose flagrant corruption was so out in the open, Harding should have been alerted to it long before the particulars came to his attention.

That was the kind of problem which Harding would usually be loath to look into very closely until it stared him in the face. Sufficiently provoked, he finally did heatedly confront Forbes, calling him a "double-crossing bastard" while grabbing him at the neck, and all but choking him. However, typically, he would allow this crook, who had done him dirt, to silently resign and quietly slip away to Europe.

In the case of Daugherty, Harding couldn't have not known about the shady dealings of the man who had practically handed him his career, after it had fallen flat following his loss of the 1910 race for Governor. Daugherty re-started him by inducing his run for the

Senate in 1914. If there were allegations afloat that some of his activities were highly suspect, these had to be dismissed by Harding. He was too deeply indebted to the man so instrumental in getting him both miraculously nominated, and convincingly elected President.

It mattered little that Congress had brought forth evidence for Daugherty's indictment. He seemed fully capable of taking care of himself, and hence, there being no outright proof of guilt obtained in a court of law, he was, to the end, a facile lawyer enough to dodge conviction. However, Daugherty, being a known conniver, became controversial enough to raise questions about the probity of Harding's Administration.

As Harding's close friend, Mac Jennings, pointed out to Scobey, the low opinion of Daugherty was wide-spread and especially great among the "rank and file of both parties" who regarded him as a "political adventurer with a shady past as a lobbiest [sic]." [68] There had actually been a previous caveat registered against Daugherty by a member of the Ohio Legislature, who communicated it to Scobey on 15 December, 1919, the day before Harding wrote that he had made his critical decision to "play the big game."

The anonymous Legislator told Scobey that Harding himself had never been a favorite of important county leaders, and it was implied that his association with Daugherty did not improve matters. Daugherty was looked upon as both a help and a hindrance. He had "as many enemies as any man in Ohio politics," though he earned some respect for being "resourceful and cunning."[69]

Jennings had at the same time been offering Scobey his opinion of the relationship between Harding and Daugherty. "You know and I know that he [Harding] did not pick H.M.D., but he permitted D. to pick himself and was unwilling to take the trouble to make his own organization or to assert himself in a way which would minimize the hostility to D."[70] A less dependent and more forceful President might have had Daugherty resign, outright.

Apparently, Harding never considered that. Regardless of what was thought of the man, Daugherty was far more instrumental in abetting Harding's effectiveness, than otherwise. That he would retain

Daugherty might be seen as a sign of weakness, but it was also a sound decision, pragmatically wise, and a sign of Harding's instinct for being clear-headed when it came to political necessities that touched him personally. His retention of Daugherty fit yet another aspect of the essential Harding.

What else touched him personally with Daugherty was gratitude. So there arose the loyalty factor—to a fault. Harding, as I have intimated, had that one major fault which couldn't be corrected because he wouldn't recognize it as such, embracing it instead as a virtue. As Harmonizer, Harding didn't duck a challenge. Shrewd as he was as a political animal, compromising when necessary to get things done, what he, on the other hand, saw as an unalterable virtue—blind loyalty—misled him more gravely than any other fault.

For example, he wrote Scobey, that, while he knew that people in Ohio who backed him were hostile to Harry Daugherty, "If a fellow has to sacrifice those he believes to be his friends in order to win other friends he had better not venture on the undertaking at all. I simply won't do it."[71] Significantly, this statement occurred in the same letter in which Harding said he was going to make a run for the Presidential Nomination, a decision which Daugherty had pushed him into, after Harding had expressed the strongest doubts over whether he really wanted to take that step.

In any event, his emphasis on the value of friendships was Harding's pre-Nomination view. It remained unchanged post-election, even though he had reason enough to dismiss an indictable Daugherty, who, sly as a fox, kept skirting the edges of legality. Harding's tolerance of an allegedly law-breaking Chief Lawman being known, it would affect the responsibility that was due him from others, like the Lawman's chief henchman, free-wheeling Jess Smith, in bed with the bootleggers and otherwise engaged in seven-figure graft.

Loyalty, above all other considerations, was so much a rock solid principle for Harding that he reiterated several variations of it, as in his telling Scobey, with whom he shared his inner thoughts, that Scobey knew him well enough "to believe that [he] would rather go into a fight with [his] friends and lose than be guilty of deserting them."[72]

Harding was by nature a conciliator. He had made a reputation for it in the Ohio Legislature. If he could garner a friendly response from those who opposed him, as with the likes of H. F. MacGregor, he was understandably hesitant to change his mind about a friend to whom he felt indebted, based on activities it was inexpedient for him to question. For Harding, loyalty was the measure of friendship, and it was all one with his desire to bring the country back to Normalcy after the Big War. He wanted to get good things done for the Party, the people, and the Country. All at once, if possible, and predicable from a politician unique in his tribute to friendship.

William Allen White, keen observer of the political scene that he was, pointed out that what Harding's friends "saw and felt was … the reaction of a kindly heart to a crushing sense of responsibility" (Masks, 413).

It was particularly when weighed down by this crushing sense that Harding appreciated the help of knowledgeable associates, as when he had sought help with conflicting economic assessments. Going back to the beginning of his odyssey, a small time newspaperman who found himself out of his depth in a big time job, Warren Harding did not forget who got him there. When he ignored what was known about a devious Attorney-General, one reason he did so was linked to the effort Daugherty had made to raise the money—some his own—to get him, an unknown, nominated for the highest office in the land. It was unprecedented. On Daugherty's side, a matter of pride, on Harding's, obligation for access to the impossible.

CHAPTER 27

"Albert Fall Trusted, Despite Mexican Scheme"

WHAT HARDING GAINED IN HIS relationship with Daugherty, he lost in his friendship with Fall. It wasn't that Harding had not been warned about Fall. Indeed, that made it all the more necessary for him to reinforce his defense of Fall. This prevailed even after Scobey produced a post-election letter (of 31 December, 1920) that described how Fall concocted a prospective influence peddling scheme, whereby, in exchange for gaining American recognition of the new Mexican regime under General Alvaro Obregon, Fall and his associates were to be handsomely remunerated.

In response, Scobey encountered nothing but blind trust. He had had information communicated to him by Fall's liaison man, Captain William C. Hansen, that it was Fall personally who was "going to see that he and his friends [were properly] rewarded."[73] Harding dismissed out of hand, as "bunk," this very credible accusation corroborated by a reliable source, H. L. Beach, who for ten years had been the Western Superintendent for the Associated Press, based in Chicago.

As justification for his response, Harding added, "I do not think [Fall] is even interested, and I know he would not seek to have done that which would not be in harmony with the wishes of my friends."[74] His <u>friends?</u> For emphasis, Harding apparently wanted his point to be all-embracing.

Though his carte blanche approval was based on no more than conjecture, specifically on his feeling that he knew his man, it was an attitude Harding would adhere to despite grounds for suspicion. It never occurred to him to question why Fall, accompanied by an Obregon representative had been very quick about getting to meet Harding in Brownsville, Texas, just days after he had been elected, ostensibly in hopes of setting up a meeting between Harding and Obregon, the two new Heads of State.

But, for the moment, to appreciate the consequence of Harding's blind loyalty to Fall, one need only consider what was spelled out for him in H. L. Beach's letter. Fall's plot was put forth as a corrupt proceeding on an international scale, which should at least have been checked out, but wouldn't be, because Harding didn't want to have to rethink his estimate of an established friend. To evaluate the substance of what Beach had written Scobey on New Year's Eve, 31 December, 1920, one didn't have to have great powers of insight.

In sum, Beach began by pointing out that, since the Obregon government had not been recognized by the previous, Democratic Administration, a movement was underway to obtain recognition through the new Republican Administration as quickly as possible after Harding's inauguration, and before its implications could be looked into. Included in the plot was an effort to obtain the appointment of Colonel F.A. Chapa as Minister to Mexico, he being a Mexican born in San Antonio and, as a member of Texas Governor William Hobby's staff, well-connected. Chapa would presumably help facilitate the plot.

Other participants were Colonel William C. Hansen (attaché of Fall's Foreign Relations Committee) Fall himself, and Frank G. Huntress, Editor of the San Antonio Express, all of whom would collectively obtain from the Mexican Government a very large sum of money, once President Harding, acting on Fall's persuasion, gained recognition for the Obregon Government.[75]

An interesting addition to this picture was Beach's idea that, amazingly, neither Obregon, nor former President De La Huerta were thought to have been a party to this scheme, and, so far as Beach knew, they might have had no concurrent knowledge of it (Ibid.). Quite a revelation this, of what a behind-the-scenes and out-of-sight operation the scheme was in its conception. Since the way Fall customarily operated was to brusquely take charge, seeing to it that things fell his way, it would seem possible that he was going to play this one opportunistically, improvising as he went along, so well did he know Mexican politics.

The question arises, however, as to how a substantial payment could be forthcoming, if Principals in the new Mexican regime had no knowledge of what Fall was up to. Perhaps that had something to do with Harding's dismissive attitude, though his trust in Fall would have been primary.

In any event, the problem regarding the apparent non-involvement of the Principals should have been worthy of mention, but it does not appear in Harding's strange follow-up response: "I am glad to have the information which comes from Beach. I do not consider it important because there is nothing to the story with which I am in any way acquainted, and any intrigue of the character indicated would fail because I would have nothing to do with it. Nevertheless, I am glad to have the information."[76]

True, that Harding would obviously not have been informed of the scheme (certainly not of the pay-off), and true, as well, that it was not the sort of thing he would get himself involved with. But it seems incredible that he would make nothing of the fact that, on information from a reliable source, Fall was said to have been actively promoting a backdoor operation in search of financial gain.

For that, there was additional reason for suspicion, since, shortly after Harding's election, Fall, as indicated, did swiftly try to get going on an initiative for the recognition of Obregon's regime. But, while the plan didn't go through for a number of reasons, one being the absence of a proviso prohibiting Mexican appropriation of American properties, the very fact of Fall's wanting to find a way to put it through for a big payoff certainly should have set off an alarm bell regarding the ethics of Harding's friend and how they might reflect on his Administration.

As seen, Harding's reply to Scobey for sending him this letter was a dug-in, head in the sand refusal to consider what it should have told him about Fall, regardless of what <u>he</u> himself would have done. The least of Harding's problems would have been embarrassment should the advancement of such a plan have come about by a rigorously underhanded pursuit—not beyond Fall's skills, and not beyond those of his Mexican contacts.

Since consummation of Fall's plan would have had to finally go through Harding, however skeptical he might have been, Fall had to have been counting on the fact that he had Harding's ear, and on his knowing how highly Harding valued his advice.

Fall was an especially favored guest for Harding, under almost any circumstances. So greatly did Harding prize his advice and counsel, based on Fall's quick mind and sound knowledge, particularly with regard to Mexican affairs (extending as well to Colombia, and to South America in general) that he had asked Fall to be a campaign advisor shortly after he got the Nomination, in which role Fall was to be helpful in speech writing and providing information on foreign policy.

And, after his election, Harding wanted Fall close by as an official advisor, meaning his certain placement in a Cabinet post—at one point, the likelihood of State, though, finally, Interior. Clearly, Harding had fallen under the spell of a valued consultant, whose personality Daugherty described as "distinctly dominating to say nothing of domineering" (Harding Tragedy, 77). As further evidence of Fall's Mexican connections, the representative he brought to meet Harding was Elias L. Torres, an experienced diplomat, who, from his important post in Mexico's Washington mission, had worked for the Foreign Minister of the previous Carranza regime as well as for Obregon, obviously a diplomat who could shift with the direction of the wind.

In other words, Fall knew whereof he spoke, based on inside knowledge. As a first step in the putative plan for recognition, it was hoped that an arrangement could be made for President-elect Harding to have a personal meeting with Obregon, barring which, Fall would go as his representative. Evidently that effort did get underway, and might have made some headway for Spanish-speaking Fall, had it not fallen short when Fall was abruptly stopped at the El Paso border.

Regardless of the credibility of Beach's charge, seconded by Fall's own Captain Hansen, complications lay in the way of the overall plan beyond those of its having been foiled in El Paso, which was one sign that it could not have been smoothly executed—certainly not instantly. Though the proposed meeting of Harding and Obregon would have facilitated the process, it first would have had to take place, and prospects for a meeting did not seem bright. Beyond that, the recognition being sought could not have actually been put in play until after Harding had been sworn in, and, thereafter, not until it was, in due time, looked into by the State Department.

Chances are, that once it got to Secretary Hughes' desk in State, it would have remained unfulfilled, as indeed it was, in face of the stipulation that American properties, principally those of oil companies, would initially have had to be protected from expropriation, the same reason that recognition had been denied by the Wilson administration.

Ironically, it was just that provision, which none other than Fall himself had scrupulously written into the proposal for recognition during the Wilson Administration, that had doomed its acceptance then, since iron-clad Mexican assurance could not be obtained for immunity from expropriation. Harding, at the time of his dismissing the accusation against Fall, could not have known how the State Department would rule on Obregon's recognition, though he would come to know that Hughes was no friend of Fall's. But that the very idea of Fall's involvement in such a scheme was to Harding unbelievable, is itself unbelievable, when it should at least have been subject to suspicion.

Militating against suspicion, was Fall's impressive status in the Senate, where he had gained the respect and approval of leaders, like Henry Cabot Lodge and William E. Borah, with both of whom he stood on a friendly, first-name basis. His fellow Senators admired him for the same reasons Harding did, as an intelligent, probing, and hard-working colleague. As a sign of the mark Fall made, he was equally esteemed by those who opposed him on some issues. This was the case with the respect he had gotten from the strongly Progressive Bronson Cutting, who thought Fall had a mind sharp enough to get to the bottom of a complicated document due to his astonishing capacity for insight.[77]

As regards the matter of support for Harding's Presidential Nomination, it is quite likely that Scobey was right in pointing out that Fall had not exactly been keen for Harding. With Fall having been a member of the Rough Riders, there is a strong likelihood that his comrade-in-arms preference would primarily have been for the General, Leonard Wood. As things turned out, he may have liked Harding, while still leaning toward Wood, and then, like others, he would have turned around to get on board with the winner before the train left the station.

More significantly, Fall was so influential, so thoroughly knowledgeable about true conditions south of the border, that he had written the plank on Mexico which would go into the Republican Platform at the 1920 Convention. Since part of his plank included a proviso that recognition should be withheld until Mexico agreed to protect American lives and property, that may have had something to do with Harding's refusal to accept Beach's report of a surreptitious attempt at recognition promoted for financial reward.

It didn't seem to fit, unless one was aware of how ruthless Fall could be in getting what he wanted. Aware mainly of Fall's great knowledge and prestige, Harding would likely have felt that his loyalty to Fall was based on fact and judgment, and was not blind. It was well known that no other Senator had as deep an understanding of Mexico's laws, history, and culture; certainly none knew Spanish as fluently, and none had made the connections with Mexican politicians and businessmen that Fall had.

On that basis, and on the basis of what he knew about the immunity proviso, Fall also had to have known of a way to negotiate that problem, or his supposed scheme would have made no sense on the face of it. And, sure enough, the problem—well known to State—would indeed get properly taken care of, so that recognition would, at last, be put into diplomatic effect, not long after Fall's resignation and less than a month after Harding's death.

The net effect of this rigmarole was that Fall's plan slipped short of execution and slipped completely by Harding. That Fall had been capable of it made no dent in Harding's trust of a friend whose probity he had been thoroughly convinced of beforehand.

CHAPTER 28

"Scobey Offers Reason For Doubt"

For Harding friendship, after all, was friendship, which made it unquestioned. The Press saw Fall as "closer to Harding, socially and politically than any other [Senator]" (Stratton, Tempest, 196). One key reason for this closeness came about because Harding needed help with foreign policy, and he had witnessed Fall's expertise in the area.

When the subject came up, Harding went so far as to ask Fall to speak to the Press on his behalf. One instance of this occurred in home-town Marion, Ohio in December, 1920, when the two men came out to see reporters walking arm in arm. (The cozying up to one another, by the way, came about at the time when Scobey was receiving those warnings about Fall's Mexican scheme.) Fall had strong views on the Versailles Treaty, which was anathema for Republicans opposed to Wilson, and no one could have articulated the objections better than Fall, which Harding was glad to have him do. The Versailles Treaty was not a subject Harding had made very much of during his Presidential campaign, no doubt as he harbored a muted interest in the establishment of a World Court.

Harding, a month after his election, would have been tired of being pressed by reporters to clarify his stand on the Versailles Treaty. As Randolph Downes, succinctly put it, the stand was that, "Harding did not like the United States to be subject to the whims and fancies of 'insignificant nations' trying to get us to pull chestnuts out of the fire for them." Harding, in his own words, feared that "a goodly number of [those insignificant nations] are looking anxiously to a draft upon American resources in wealth and man-power to settle their problems" (Downes, 343).

For that sort of thing, Fall seemed an excellent choice to publicly identify Harding's position. So Fall came to be regarded as Harding's spokesman on foreign policy, and Harding appreciated his assuming the role. Among other things, it communicated to Fall the leeway Harding was prone to give him.

Smoothly confident as Fall was for taking on authority that he could sink his teeth into, it followed that he could run to extreme measures, some reckless. Nothing new, this was evidenced by his having been so antagonistic to Conservationists that in his maiden speech in the Senate in 1915, he ironically expressed the fervent hope that Congress would abolish the Interior Department (Tempest, 113). His platform plank carried a demand for the use of arms as a potential means of enforcing the clause protecting American lives and property in Mexico.

Moreover, when his appointment to Interior was delayed, Fall, wanting action, had sent Harding a telegram, under Daugherty's name (without getting Daugherty's permission to do so) asking that Harding announce his appointment to Interior prior to March 4th, 1921, so that Fall might have leverage in determining his successor when he resigned his position in the Senate.[78] Daugherty had reason to attribute a "tyrannical temperament" to Fall (Harding Tragedy, 198). If he wanted something badly enough, Fall could be as head-strong as he was strong-minded. He had been schooled in intimidation as an unspoken article of the code of the West, to be exercised pistol in hand, if need be. This tended more to impress than to caution Harding, who was glad to have strong man Fall at his side.

Additionally, it did not matter to Harding that Scobey had information that Fall might have conspired with Wood forces to take pre-Convention votes away from him in Texas and New Mexico. Hoping Harding would see the light, Scobey proceeded to pile up the adversarial actions of Fall's "crowd," apparently led by Fall's associate in the Obregon negotiations, Captain William C. Hansen. As it came to

Scobey, Fall's people had circulated reports in Ohio that Harding was "Lily White," a canard backed by Wood money, which cost Harding 20,000 "Negro" votes in the Ohio primary, as well as 57,000 votes in Texas due to other false rumors.[79]

Furthermore, as Scobey piled up the indictment, he disclosed that Fall had managed Congressman-elect Harry Wurzbach's campaign, a man who, according to Scobey, never did a thing for Harding and was against most of Harding's leading friends in Texas. Scobey put Fall's cohorts in the same category with MacGregor, a person who, despite his position with the National Committee, had no desire, as Scobey saw it, to build up the Party. Rather, MacGregor's main objective had been to control patronage, and, even on the eighth ballot in Chicago, he was making an appeal to line up delegates for Lowden, obviously believing he was the probable winner (Ibid.).

To Scobey's chagrin, all of that slid off Harding's back. His good opinion of Fall was not to be compromised, by anything. Certainly not by the lucrative plot that he was being apprised of. There was much more to the Harding-Fall story, none of it complimentary to either man. Fall did Harding more harm than any other one person, and it compounded the difficulty of resurrecting a positive reading of Harding's Presidency. Nor was not all.

All else aside, Harding didn't actually know a great deal about Albert Fall. Chances are, for example, that Harding did not know (or care, if he did know) that Fall had substantial land holdings and mining interests in Mexico, making him an interested party in its political upheaval, contrary to Harding's belief that Fall wouldn't have anything to do "with the political situation down there." Nor would he have been aware that Fall had violated a limitation on sheep grazing rights near his New Mexico ranch, to the tune of 2,000 unauthorized sheep, which he wanted to be counted independently as his son's flock.

Had Harding taken the trouble to inquire about Fall's background before appointing him to head Interior, he might have learned that Fall had been accused of bribery, along with other irregularities, in getting himself elected to the U.S. Senate in 1912 by the New Mexico Legislature. Once Harding had convinced himself that Fall was "a star of a fellow," and more importantly a "very dependable friend" as well, that was it; there was nothing that could change his mind.[80] A year prior to Scobey's ponderous indictment, Harding, in comparing Fall to Senator Ellison D. Smith of South Carolina, said he thought that "Senator Smith is a delightful chap…but he is not made of the same kind of stuff which constitutes the make-up of Albert Fall" (Ibid.). It was true that mild natured Ellison was no match for aggressive Albert.

As with his regard for Daugherty, Harding was evidently impressed by Fall's toughness. He had, as noted, been a member of Roosevelt's Rough Riders. Harding's respect for a man with Fall's rugged frontier background ("a fighter who took and gave hard blows") was likely compensation for something he himself lacked and would liked to have had from somebody (a "gun") working for him.

David H. Stratton in his brief biography mentioned an instance in which Fall physically struck a member of the New Mexico Territorial Legislature in the midst of a heated debate. Characterized as "an epitomized Westerner," Fall followed the code "of the frontier and of frontier politics." It was rumored that "he always carried a gun and was not afraid to use it." The background he brought to Interior was that of "a prospector, practical miner, mining investor, farmer, and rancher for almost forty years."[81]

Concerning those notorious oil leases in California and Wyoming, Stratton observed that Fall didn't need to be bribed to get them done. Rather, "with his belief in the unrestrained and immediate disposition of the [Country's] natural resources, and for that reason alone, he [Fall] no doubt would have turned over the reserves [anyway] to Sinclair and Doheny, or to some other representatives of private enterprise" (Memoirs of Albert B. Fall, 8).

If one sought a single fault that more than others brought Harding's reputation to the sorry end that posterity assigned him as our "worst" President, this same blind loyalty would have been that fault. And the one figure to whom Harding was blindly loyal, who became linked to the consequent downfall of his reputation, was, appropriately enough, Fall himself, the person most responsible for Teapot Dome, that being the by-word used to identify what was supposedly the most damning instance of corruption to be coupled with Warren G. Harding's name. That in itself dimmed much of the good that might objectively have been assigned to his Presidency.

Why Fall, when Harding was probably more blindly loyal to Harry Daugherty, by far his closest associate, and, as leader of the "Ohio Gang," responsible for some shady developments linked to Harding's political career? The loyalty Harding gave Daugherty was returned, and it paid off handsomely, for Daugherty's success was both tied to, and dependent on, Harding's success. The good outcome he wanted for Harding benefited both of them.

Not so the relationship of Fall to Harding, which was self-seeking. Fall was egregiously underhanded in his ambition to use his Cabinet position for financial enhancement, treating his influential office as a money making proposition. Conservationists were in despair over Fall's wanting to turn over the nation's natural resources to business interests for their exploitation. Fall was committed to the belief that "the land, timber, and minerals of the Western states should be used for the immediate development of that section" (Stratton, Memoirs, 7).

One reason for Harding's unwavering loyalty to Fall would stem from a feeling that, once he gave whole-heartedly support to a certain colleague, he wouldn't allow himself to rethink it. He didn't want to be proven wrong with Fall because he was going on a strong personal hunch, derived from a very favorable initial impression that turned into an emotional commitment. The insecurity that would bring Harding to that pass had its own source, which reappeared in other relationships.

Nicholas Murray Butler, a highly reliable friend, had warned Harding, strongly and explicitly, against appointing Fall Secretary of State, pointing out that his "reputation in Pueblo before he ever left Colorado for New Mexico was such that you must not think of him for [a] Cabinet office." Harding responded that he had listened to rumors circulated by jealous enemies of Fall's, but, implicitly considering their source, he felt they could be dismissed. The primary reason for Harding's good opinion of Fall was based on the fact that "[He] sat with him on the Committee on Foreign Relations and [knew] he

[was] the best-posted man of the whole lot, particularly as to all Latin American matters" (Across the Busy Years, I, 402-403).

Harding, as a matter of fact, sat right next to Fall on the Committee, and had observed first hand how knowledgeable he was about Mexico, based on his having been an ambitious frontiersman, who had at an early age made himself completely fluent in Spanish. Harding would also be inclined to look up to Fall as a prestigious Senator, who was serving his second term, when Harding arrived for his first.

Of course, Harding turned to Charles Evans Hughes for State. He might also have been temporarily deterred by Butler from giving Fall further consideration, as he waited till the first of March, three days prior to his Inauguration before announcing Fall was to be appointed Secretary of the Interior. Fall had joined Harding in Florida on a two day fishing trip in February, 1921, after which Fall wrote his wife Emma that Harding had made him the direct tender of an appointment to be Secretary of the Interior. He wanted Fall close by in the Cabinet where he could have him as "one of his official advisors" (Shadow, 431).

Since there was about a month and a half gap between the time that Fall saw Harding on the Obregon matter and Scobey's presenting Harding with Beach's assessment, and then another month's gap before Harding would make the tender to Fall, followed by yet one more month's gap before he actually came out with a direct appointment of Fall to Interior, one wonders if Harding may have had second thoughts to address, before he could finalize the appointment.

Fall had, of course, preferred State, to which prominent Senators were said to have raised strong objection. On that basis, whatever hesitancy Harding might have had about bringing Fall into his Cabinet as an official advisor—and evidently there was some—it could not have been long lasting. For he was able to disregard whatever else he had been told about the man.

Since, in his public announcement of Cabinet appointees, Harding mentioned Fall first, one wonders whether he may have been trying to allay the uneasiness that Fall made known to Harding about his delay in coming out with an announcement of his appointment—politically of first importance to Fall. As Fall would defensively put a spin on his getting a post lesser than State, William Allen White notes that he would recount "with pride that [alas] he went into the Interior Department only under pressure" (Puritan in Babylon, 228).

There is enormous irony in what Fall wrote his wife on Harding's offering him Interior in January, 1921, to which, since Fall really wanted State, he reconciled himself on the basis of Harding's telling him that that post was second only to State. Fall wrote that, regarding Interior, Harding felt "there is more opportunity for graft and scandal connected with the disposition of public lands etc., than there could be in any other Department and he wants a man who is thoroughly familiar with the business and one he can rely upon as thoroughly honest, etc etc." Fall thought it over for three days, then said he was "trying to look upon the bright side and see the compensations which may offer themselves in that position" (Tempest, 197). Imagine!

CHAPTER 29

"With Fall No End Of Ironies"

IN A RELATIONSHIP FRAUGHT WITH ironies, there were yet others. One reason that there had been an initial delay in Harding's committing to Fall for Interior was that there had been another strong—and possibly prior—candidate for the position, that being Jake Hamon, the flamboyant millionaire Oklahoma oilman. Jake had made a notable move by throwing his Oklahoma votes to Harding in the late balloting at the Nominating Convention.

During October of his Presidential Campaign, Harding made a stop in Oklahoma City, for which Jake had arranged a huge demonstration, complete with banquet, followed by a torchlight parade to the fairgrounds. Harding's speech there was greeted with boisterous acclaim, making it, as reported in the press, the "noisiest" of days that the Republican Party had known in Democratic Oklahoma.

On that occasion, Jake had been given a warm greeting by Florence, who happened to have been his cousin by marriage. A friend of Jake's reported that Jake, known for a connection with Standard Oil, had, in return for spending a cool million on Harding's Nomination, received a promise from Will Hays that he would be made Interior Secretary. Unfortunately, shortly after Harding's presidential victory, he had been informed that his millionaire supporter had been shot and killed in a quarrel with his mistress.

Harding, in tears, exclaimed "What a wonderful fellow he was!" To which, with not a trace of irony, he added, "Too bad he had that one fault—that admiration for women" (Shadow, 393, 411f., 621, 422). Since free spending Jake liked to be recompensed, he could very well have claimed precedence over Fall. Though Jake was more like a loose cannon than a negotiator, who knows what trouble he might have caused with the eye he had for exploiting Mexican oil?

As a way to reconcile Fall to Interior, there was a plan to have the very reputable Charles Evans Hughes installed at State on a temporary basis, and, thereafter, when an opening occurred on the Supreme Court (possibly within a few years) Hughes could be moved to the Court, supposedly a move up. Thereby, Fall, already making a mark for himself in Interior, could be shifted to State.

Fall had demonstrated his foreign policy stature by virtue of the spade work he had done for Harding on the Colombian Treaty. It so happened that when an opening on the Court did occur, with the death of Chief Justice Edward D. White in May 1921, Hughes objected to being made his replacement, as he felt that that would be a sign of 'no confidence.' Additionally, Hughes wanted Fall to have a significantly reduced role in Mexican relations, holding that such matters should go through normal diplomatic channels, rather than self-appointed intermediaries.

How Harding could have remained so staunch a supporter of Fall, on the ironic terms that Fall would describe to his wife Emma, once there was evidence that Fall might go back on the trust given him, remains one of the true mysteries of Harding's Presidency. Also difficult to fathom, Florence supposedly came up with the after-thought that Harding had received word of scandal afoot in the Teapot lease, but, luckily, died before Congressional investigators got going on it.

In any event, the carte blanche trust Harding had given Fall ran contrary to his otherwise political smarts, which got lost when personal impressions interfered with practical decisions. As he'd said, if he got into a fight with a friend, he'd rather lose. In the case of Fall, he lost without a fight.

The situation got complicated when two incompatible friendships were at stake. With Scobey on one side and Fall on the other, Harding was left with the predicament of wanting to appease both, a tactic that had worked for him elsewhere in finessing the conflict between his twin loyalties to Party and friendship. In this case, however, Harding let the conflict run its course. Meanwhile, the Congressional Committees were years long in their investigations, prolonging the adversity heaped on a defenseless President. Just as well late was recognition of the Obregon regime, accomplished on 31 August, 1923, the appropriate protections in place.

Nicholas Murray Butler, looking back on Harding's career from his last sorrowful meeting with him in May, 1923, made a summary observation on the President who desperately wanted the presence of a friend to whom he could unburden himself of his problems. Regarding Harding's relations with his friends, Butler felt "he was good-natured, lazy and weak when pressure was put on him by a will stronger than his own, which happened to be that of a friend" (Across the Busy Years, I, 410). Unfortunately, Harding couldn't sufficiently distinguish those of his friends who were unselfish and reliable, from those who weren't.

Equally unfortunate was Harding's allowing Fall to intimidate him, that being a tactic Fall had used as part of frontier life. Ruthlessness being alien to Harding's make-up, he didn't look for a way of coping with it. Obviously, that was to his credit, as, in what came naturally to Harding, the soft approach to problems would generally be more productive for him than a harsh one might have been. On the other hand, politics being a rough game, when it gave way to the leniency of friendship, that would become a source of the most unmanageable trouble which would plague Harding's Presidency.

This was no secret. Widely recognized by friend and foe alike, it was even taken up by Samuel Hopkins Adams, who made clear note of the consequences that had followed from Harding's upholding the pernicious obligations of friendship. In the ending of Revelry, Adams allowed Senator Peter Thorne, a political insider, "wise, cynical [and] tolerant, to speak the final word" on his version of the Harding debacle by offering the observation that "Friendship in politics undermines more principles than fraud, and gratitude is a worse poison than graft" (318).

There was no need to specify Fall. It was as if the satirist in Adams could be sufficiently objective to show understanding for Harding's seemingly innocuous failure to see friendship as a form of sentimentality that had no business in politics. What well-meaning Harding wanted most was to be liked, which he was—nationally—but at the hazard of limiting his ability to make hard, unsentimental decisions, particularly on personnel.

In the first place—and last—it took too long for Harding to finally realize that he'd been naïve. When Nan Britton relayed to him the inside view of their Secret-Service go-between, Jim Sloan, that Harding was being regularly double-crossed by his own people, who were "putting it over" on him, he insisted it couldn't be, because "he was surrounded by friends" (PD,196f.).

CHAPTER 30

"Post-Script"

One of the little known ironies of Harding's relationship with Fall is that Florence Harding, who, while so reliable in the judgment she gave Harding on appointments, had her own sentimentalities, one of which was her great partiality for Albert Fall. He happened to have been one Cabinet Member who was especially deferential to Florence, prompt in answering her requests, with the promise of their receiving priority attention.

Easily susceptible to male flattery, as had been the case with the wiles practiced on her by Charlie Forbes, Florence was greatly disturbed by word that this same Fall, who was so accommodating to her, somehow wanted to resign. She had, after all, been counting on his being put up for an appointment to the Supreme Court.

Indeed, on being told that Fall really did want out, Harding himself counseled Fall to talk to Florence first, and, above all, to let her talk to him. On 4 January, 1922, a day after Fall's decision to depart went into effect, Florence wrote to Fall's wife Emma expressing her regret over his leaving. Evidently, Florence had mentioned that Fall was greatly needed, based on how loyal a friend he had been to Harding. It was a letter Emma would read to friends in her eagerness to show there were no derogatory issues attached to Fall's resignation and that the Hardings truly wanted him to remain a member of their team.

But, could it be that disclosure of connivance on the part of good friend Fall contributed to the growing worries that wore Harding down during the final weeks of his life? Florence, in an unexpected change of mind, seems to have thought so. With Jess Smith's suicide and the concurrent revelation of his covert activities, prior to the Alaskan trip, that shocking news raised expectations that other things would come to light, but none were yet tied to Teapot.

Still, it is interesting that in the aftermath of Harding's death, Florence would strangely surmise that he had been informed, pre-departure, of suspicions regarding the legitimacy of Teapot, which, in her view, was what had weighed so heavily on Warren that he became a "crushed man." Her source for this would be hard to find.

Florence, in fact, believed he had been, "crushed…so completely" by a disclosure about Teapot that that was the reason she feared throughout the trip "he could not survive the disaster." Somewhat disoriented after the loss of Warren, Florence, in a rush to judgment, was the only one close to him who would connect Fall and Teapot to Harding's late depression. The Senate investigation of Teapot, did not get underway until October, 1923, two months after Harding's death and well in advance of the revelation of Fall's having received the incriminating $100,000 loan/bribe that did him in.

Since Florence in the end convinced herself that she had been wrong in her estimate of Fall, that was probably her reason for omitting his name from the list of Warren's "warm friends and admirers" to be offered permanent membership in the Harding Memorial Association (Florence, 395, 415, 503). Historian Ellis Hawley had offered good reason for Harding to be fittingly remembered, especially since he wasn't. Unfortunately, the positive result Harding derived from delegating authority to knowledgeable upper level appointees—for which Hawley praised him—didn't outweigh his problem-delegations in Justice and Interior.

As for the man himself, it would be futile to speculate on how Harding might have been able to survive the sequel to his ironically called Journey of Understanding. But he had cultivated a sympathetic following among the people, and, as an instinctive politician, he knew how to sustain their good will.

So, in closing the book on Warren G. Harding's Presidency, one might pause to consider the grounds he had on which to fight back against the disclosure of scandals, a case that would begin with his having been personally innocent of them. As for friends leeching on him, there had been some chummy Buckeyes, friends of thirty years, whose expectation of his dismissing indictments would be fervently denied. But Harding would have needed a lawyer, and the most available one had to look out for himself.

Hurt to the core, he would have had every reason to summon anger against injustice and to stand up for himself. He could have set a precedent for that. After all, the fact that little had been thought of his ability to become much of a President was a lot of what inspired him to make himself a far better one than has been perceived.

PART IV:

THEN THERE WERE THE WOMEN

CHAPTER 31

"They Weren't Made For One Another"

IF HE HAD DIFFICULTY WITH friendships, an examination of Harding's relationships with the major women in his life produced yet greater problems for him. For a time, these were briefly allayed when, after ending a turbulent affiliation with Carrie Phillips, Harding found opportunistic sex awaiting him with Nan Britton, that hometown girl whose adoration was publicly known in town. As lust grew to love—a duplication of what had evolved with Carrie—this suddenly became an experience of emotional depth for Harding. However, euphoric as their relationship became, it finally could not be matched up with reality.

As recorded by Nan, the drama of ardent lovers hitting a wall elicited a sympathetic response from readers of her Memoir, particularly those who saw Harding revealed in his vulnerable humanity, craving the unattainable, his disappointment becoming a factor in his declining health and death.

The scandalous activity of Albert Fall may not have been recognized by Harding for what it was. But one is left to wonder whether anxiety over the scandalous doings suddenly unloaded on him, when topped by the possibility of an end to his ill-omened romance with Nan, may have become part of the mix that hastened Harding's unanticipated demise.

Whereas, prior to the Jess Smith disclosures, Harding had been able to ride out mistakes made in his political life, he was denied a resolution of mistakes made in matters of the heart. Rewarding as Harding's experience may have been with each of his two long-term mistresses, neither of those relationships ended well. In each case, the prolongation of love in the shadows did not bode well for a satisfactory outcome. The most that could be said on Harding's behalf is that his adultery was compensation for the physical void in his married life, from which the impossibility of his leaving Florence—attributable as much to him as to her—would double the strain.

While responsibility for their dilemma might be shared, it would seem that moral indictment was wholly one-sided. However, when traced back to its origin, the issue of blame actually falls as much on Florence. She sought Warren out; he didn't seek her. When she courted Warren, Florence, it seems, was not primarily taken up with the male attractiveness that excited the imagination of other women.

In her eagerness to land him, Florence made the inexcusable mistake of foisting marriage on a known ladies' man, when she herself actually had no interest in sex, already made repugnant to her by a nettlesome marriage—evidently forced—with ne'er do well Pete DeWolfe.

Thus, the core problem of Florence's second marriage was that she couldn't refrained from pressuring Warren into one she sought mostly out of pride, and more for prestige than romance. That being the case, and with her knowing of his legendary pursuit of women, she should have understood that he'd find a solution to what he lacked at home.

Of course, he should have had backbone enough to resist her pressure in the first place, but his being so easily persuaded encouraged Florence to ensnare him. Once married, her persistence in holding onto Warren, despite his unhappiness with de facto celibacy, meant the principals were locked into troubles of their own making—which, on top of similar troubles in his political life, sounds like Warren was destined to be a marked man. Physical distance was apparent in the couples' choice of separate beds, a superficial item perhaps, but indicative of how they lived their married lives, minus togetherness at bed time.

With Florence being far from blind to Warren's inclination to rove, her resolution of that, as Carl Anthony saw it, was a compact, revealed during the Presidential campaign when Warren spoke of Florence as being "a good scout who knows all my faults and yet has stuck with me all the way" (Florence, 204). Added to this is a strange comment Florence committed to her calendar diary, apparently after Warren's slap-in-the-face affair with Susan Hodder: "There is no devotion like a husband's provided he is far enough out of his wife's sight to do as he pleases" (Ibid., 62).

It is hard to know whether Florence really believed what she had written, unless that is to be taken as solace, since she was determined to hold onto her husband at all costs, which was an admission of futility. Assuming it was, as well, a concession to reality, what this comes down to is that she could tolerate his tendency to wander, provided he'd be considerate enough to keep it dark.

Whatever else one can make of it, the record shows that, unable to change Warren, Florence certainly did her best to intercede with, and, when possible, try to prevent his adultery, hoping he would repay her loyalty with restraint—the emphasis being on hope. If true, Warren's side of the compact was honored more in the breach than the observance.

Whereas in his political life one views the 'essential Harding,' in that part of his private life which was driven by sexual compulsion it might be said that we see an unrestrained persona, the quintessential Harding.

CHAPTER 32

"His Relationship With Carrie In Keeping With The Times"

Put in perspective with the treatment given his political life, where Harding's fall from grace was inversely proportional to his former rise in grace, faults in his personal life were another matter. Once the posthumous revelations of political corruption began to pile up, one on top of the other, the fall in his reputation was precipitous, unrelieved, and decidedly final. In the long view, what did much to abet the slide to finality were the questions of morality raised by revelations of a lurid sex life, as these would have to have been taken seriously by historians who judged him our 'Worst' President. Though the moral issue did not carry much weight in Harding's lifetime, considering the atmosphere of the Twenties, what had been known in some quarters and continued to be dismissed for a time, was the fact that Harding's most objectionable conduct was decidedly private rather than official, and also fairly well hidden from public view prior to his death.

For that reason more than others, once the secret details began coming to light, thanks largely to his beloved mistresses, astonishment among the public at large turned to disillusionment. With his reputation being fairly well demolished, who would believe he could have nonetheless made a pretty good record for himself as President?

Carl Anthony has unearthed numerous instances of Harding's blatant adulteries—some cited below—and many of these could not have remained unknown. What, then, were the ramifications of Harding's obsession with sex? To begin with, a large part of this story is that, while it was assumed not to have been known, it very much was—in Washington circles, no less than in Marion, Ohio. In fact, though Harding could be looked upon as practically a libertine, in his lifetime no one seemed to think anything should have been made of it—not in the Jazz Age.

Whatever may have gotten out, Harding did not have to fear being scorned because of it. He remained very popular with the people, and needed no more favorable verdict on his person as Leader of his Country. America was at peace and prosperous. In and of themselves, the illicit affairs of high officials did not necessarily make them subject to prosecution, Presidents never. Brought up to date, at least nearly so. The possibility of recriminations mostly silenced opposing politicians.

The kind of talk usually bruited about regarding Harding's sexual adventures could easily be exaggerated for purposes of humor—actually, an insulating factor—particularly when treated as the stuff of satire. Rumors were, of course, common among White House staffers, and became grist for the Washington gossip mill. On the other hand, some details of those adventures, including the ladies involved, were no secret among people in the know; principally among associates like Harry Daugherty for example, who, for his own sake, had to keep an eye on the man he'd made President. Regarding those associates who knew, they being professional, male, and hardened by the political wars, their attitude was typically cynical.

Harding was being disloyal to his wife with a number of women, but consistently with two vastly different ones, to each of whom he independently professed his love, one the wife of a local merchant, Jim Phillips, who in company with his adulterous wife, Carrie, accompanied the Hardings on several pleasure trips. The traveling companionship of the two couples indicated how close they were, which was also rather amazing for its being so, considering the ulterior motives of Carrie and Warren, each of whom had instigated one of those trips.

There had been a three month tour of Europe in 1909 that

included a Mediterranean cruise, during which the lovers enjoyed an evening tryst on deck, while their mates were sleeping no more than a bulkhead away. That enticing journey had been urged by Carrie with the prospect of facilitating the lovers' proximity, their affair having by that time grown to genuine love, evidently a first for both of them. As their bonding progressed, it was supposed to bring about dual divorces that would open the way for them to remarry.

So, with their relationship having peaked, Carrie's anticipation was great. Greater yet, however, was the rage that followed Warren's reluctance to act on his part to secure their future, which resulted in retention of the agonizing status quo. His strenuous promises of action being contradicted by the failure of any follow-through added fury to Carrie's anger.

That tour of Europe had incidentally had the secondary effect of arousing Carrie's fateful infatuation with Germany, which would play a role in her deciding in a huff to pick up and leave for Berlin in 1911. Not wanting to leave Florence, as promised, any more than he wanted to lose Carrie, Warren made a feeble attempt to buy time by getting the couples to take an economy trip to Bermuda in March of that year. That did little to quell Carrie's frustration. So, not long after their return from Bermuda, Carrie, sick of Harding's temporizing, packed up and, daughter in hand, set sail.

Though she told her husband she'd be back the following summer, she told Warren she planned to stay in Germany indefinitely, perhaps permanently. She also let him know what a compatible place Berlin was for her. She wrote him of the interesting sites she had seen, as well as the interesting men she had met.

CHAPTER 33

"A Defining Issue; Carrie's Departure"

THERE WAS SOME AMBIGUITY SURROUNDING the provocation for Carrie's angry departure, the defining issue being which of the two had caused it, Warren or Carrie. A common assumption is that Warren quailed at the last moment, leaving Carrie with no choice but to depart. James Robenalt, however, has held that Warren was ready to leave Florence for Carrie, but that Carrie wasn't ready to come through with her side of the bargain. Hence, Robenalt has it that she bore the responsibility for their break-up. Hence, too, a controversy.

Since this has to do with the turning point in a revered relationship that had been going strong six years after its initiation in 1905, an inquiry into what caused the break-up brings back the context for a decisive moment in the lives of the principals. As indicated above in Chapter 7, Carrie's patience was wearing thin, and she wanted to force the decision for a terminus a quo by which they could have their adultery transformed into legitimacy. In light of the ambiguity over what (who) caused this crisis, there is a need of clarification.

This is especially needed, since there were collateral considerations, not the least of which is that it helps to define the difference between Warren's respective relationships with Carrie and Nan. The love he had for the one differed from that which he had for the other.

As previously asserted, Warren would look good if he were the one who was ready to uphold his side of the bargain, while Carrie was not ready to uphold her side. In effect, Warren would have done what was necessary to avoid the break-up, and Carrie would presumably have brought it on. With Warren looking good that way, the obverse would have made him look bad. A letter from Carrie to be cited shortly indicates rather conclusively that Warren kept promising he would be ready, only to have all of his promises "broken."

Warren had lost his run for Governor in 1910, which deflated his enthusiasm for politics; that being just what Carrie had wanted. Since he ran a half-hearted campaign (unwilling "to organize any machine to promote [his] candidacy" [Affair, 38]) chances are Carrie had something to do with his diluted effort. He was, in fact, as he had written Charles Hilles (Assistant Secretary of Treasury under Taft) completely "cured of any attack of ambition along political lines" (Shadow, 214). Warren had lost by 100,000 votes, which was obviously deflating, and coincidentally the same total by which he would beat Tim Hogan for the U.S. Senate seat in 1914, an overture to making him a potential candidate for the Presidency.

Carrie, meanwhile, had had her fill of small town gossip, which had grown to be a major irritant preying on her peace of mind. Hence, the situation should have given the lovers exactly the opportunity they wanted in order to follow their hearts' desire. Assumedly they would negotiate dual divorces and remarry. As Russell contends, based on his having seen Warren's love letters (and supported by Carrie's letter of 7 July, 1917, cited below) Carrie explicitly asked "whether he was prepared to leave the Duchess and marry her" (Shadow, 214). That he wasn't would presumably have been the last straw for Carrie.

James Robenalt sees this break-up as having been a somewhat complicated affair, and his analysis of it is itself somewhat complicated. He observes that few of the Harding love letters "tell the story of exactly what happened in 1911 that led to her decision to leave her husband in Ohio and take their daughter, Isabelle, to Berlin to be educated." (Affair, 47). However, there clearly had to have been more than that to her motive for leaving. It doesn't make much sense that her daughter's education (supposedly in the German language) would have been the reason for Carrie's departure, when that education was abundantly available, and far less expensively so, at Ohio's Universities. Carrie loved Germany; under the circumstances, an attractive refuge.

At one point, Robenalt proposes that it was Warren's 1910 run for Governor that "would open a rift that would leave her packing for Berlin" (Ibid., 29). But his dating here is confusing. To pack means to leave—or at least to prepare to, shortly. It was true that, for Carrie, Warren's involvement in politics was the bane of their relationship. If he was well out of it after losing the election, his severing an involvement in politics would have disqualified anything political as the motive for an August, 1911 departure.

To be more specific, Warren, after all, had lost the election for Governor in November, 1910, and, as this was followed by his renouncing politics, he had had it behind him for almost a year prior to Carrie's leaving. As an explanation for that situation, Robenalt offers the "possibility that Carrie lost faith that she and Warren would ever be able to be together in an open relationship together" (Ibid., 48). With politics out the window, what then would have been the reason for Carrie's losing faith, were it not that Warren wasn't ready to do anything that might bring them together? Since he talked as if he were ready to leave Florence, but took no steps to do so, that could only have been galling to Carrie—galling enough for her to start packing.

Robenalt observed that Harding had "continued to plainly state he was ready to give up his marriage for her [Carrie] and that she was the one who was not ready" (Ibid., 81). Harding had indeed emphatically pledged that he would get out of his marriage. "If you said you could and would be ready," he wrote, "I would cast the die. I have said it before and will repeat it now" (Ibid. Harding's itals.). But—to re-emphasize a point previously made—the interesting part of this pronouncement is that it was made in a letter not of 1911, but one of January, 1913.

In other words, his proposal to "cast the die" came well after, not before, she left for Germany. It came when their separation was hurting, and he'd say anything to bring Carrie back. In 1913, she was in Berlin, not around the corner in Marion, Ohio, or—considering the presence of Florence—anywhere that the matter could be discussed face to face.

There had been sufficient time prior to the summer of 1911 for Warren to have made a specific pledge. It could, for example, have been appropriately given after the couples' short holiday to Bermuda in March, 1911, which Warren had proposed as a delaying tactic. In any event, if he had talked of casting the die "before," he left no record of when. If the idea was to deter Carrie from leaving in 1911, then, come 1913, the barn door had been closed well after the Filly had been gone—for going on two years.

The die had indeed been cast—but by Carrie. Had the pledge been made in 1911, it might have had some credibility. In 1913, it was empty talk. Carrie was happily settled in Berlin, and gave the impression she wanted to stay on indefinitely. The more emphatically Warren gave the pledge, minus any follow-through, the emptier it was. By 1913, Carrie had already told him that she had been "cooling" and taunted him with the news that she had been seeing German men.

If he was fully truthful about doing what was necessary to win Carrie on "an open and honored" basis, he would, without further talk, have proceeded to divorce Florence. An empty pledge, uttered almost two years after it might have been effective, could only have been regarded by Carrie as a clumsy ploy to bring her back within range, which could only recapitulate their frustration, hers in particular. It had happened earlier, several times, according to Carrie, in a letter to be quoted shortly.

As for Robenalt's contention that Carrie was supposedly "the one who was not ready" to take the necessary step for consummation of their union, the context in which her being unready appeared had to do not with their seeking separate divorces followed by their coming together in marriage, but rather with their "dream of becoming parents together." Carrie's unreadiness was "for I's sake [i.e., daughter Isabelle's] and for the sake of the one we hope for [i.e., the child they would have]." She does offer a "doctrine" he can live with; namely, that they "must wait and hope, and trust a favoring fate," which would be the death of chronically ailing Florence—possible if only Carrie's patience did not give way (Ibid., 81).

Robenalt here had tried to make the case that this statement about parentage, by virtue of immediate succeeding proximity, was connected to Warren's statement that he was ready to "give up his marriage for [Carrie] and that she was the one who was not ready." After a sweeping generalization, one looks for supporting evidence for it in the following quote, but what is given instead in the quote is "their dream of becoming parents." Unreadiness has to do with parentage, not divorce.

On Carrie's continuing to complain of his staying in his marriage, Warren, in August, 1916, wrote her his defense that, if he left Florence, she would have a recurrence of her kidney problem, and Marion would never forgive him for abandoning her. Moreover, if well, Florence would take extraordinary revenge on Carrie (Affair, 185). Interestingly, Florence did come down with a recurrence of her kidney disease shortly after the Bermuda Trip taken by both couples (Ibid., 49) and that would have shortly preceded Carrie's departure. Which would have added an exclamation point to Carrie's "doctrine."

But Carrie the laggard in 1911? It isn't until Robenalt brings forth a passage from a letter Carrie had written Warren in July, 1917 that the real reason surfaces as to why, back in 1911, they just couldn't have come together then. The onus of unreadiness clearly fell where one would logically expect that it would have fallen: on him, not her.

Carrie was not the type of woman who would suffer disappointment in silence. She would not have waited till 1911 to complain about his failure to get the divorce that would insure the future which he had been promising her. Her July, 1917 letter indicates as much. It seems that she likely had been at him to come through well before 1911, and that he had been breaking commitments continuously, over the years.

In July, 1917, Carrie happened to have been in a foul mood. Warren's Marion Star had been printing serialized passages from a mystery novel that contained, as Robenalt described it, "insider gossiping about the 'gross scandals and wily intrigues' of the kaiser's family...leading up to the Great War." A committed Teutonophile,

Carrie was in high dudgeon, and let Warren know that a comparable exposé could be done on the scandalous secret life of the owner of the Marion Star. As for his reneging on promises to divorce Florence and marry Carrie, she spelled it out in this letter of 7 July, 1917:

"I remember your telling me many times that all I had to do was 'say the word' and you would divorce her (she isn't yours really for her husband was living when you went through the wedding ceremony), that I should 'pretend to visit friends in the West' and you would meet me and we would 'leave all behind and start anew.' We would travel until a hoped for time came, and then stop till we were able once again to journey on—beautiful dream. Yes, but that was some time ago. This was renewed once again after a defeat in 1910. … All promises were broken and I was 'imperious,' 'demanding,' 'lacking all courtesy,' and 'trying to wreck you,' when I believed in you and asked you only to keep your word to me that I might not lose my faith in you." (Affair, 258).

CHAPTER 34

"Love May Die, But Sex Lives On"

IT SEEMS INCONCEIVABLE THAT THEY would continue to yearn for one another. However, although their relationship had been volatile, it was also resilient. Carrie told him, for example, that her love had begun to change in 1911 (Affair, 58). But that didn't end it. Less than half a year after they had had exciting trysts in Boston and Montreal at year's end, Warren would be writing Carrie he had the feeling that she has "gotten away" from him and was "somewhere beyond [his] reach." Furthermore, if she should want the attention of other men, he told her she should feel free to seek it (Ibid., 62).

But the cooling noted by both of them notwithstanding, they met in London in August, 1911, nighting it at the Devonshire Hotel. And Carrie would book passages to cross the wintry seas of the Atlantic in December 1911 and 1912, for physically urgent trysts on each of those occasions. In Montreal on December 31, 1911, their love-making happened to have climaxed at the moment of a ringing of the bells that brought in the New Year, which Warren recalled in detail.

They had made December (specifically Christmas) the anniversary that celebrated their having fallen in love. As late as December 1916, not long after Carrie had sought legal advice over a public insult from Florence, the lovers were getting together in Washington for a typically intimate remembrance. Warren wrote Carrie, "You rejoiced me and I dwell in bliss, though I was fearfully disappointed in myself. You never disappoint at the alter [sic[of love (Ibid., 193f.).

As Robenalt had commented, regarding their August, 1911 night in London, "These encounters were some of the most passionate and amorous experiences of their relationship" (51). Their eagerness for one another seemed to have surpassed all else. The fear that it might be lost seemed to increase their appetite for more. The "New Year drowning in ecstasy in Montreal" had inspired "such unending worship"—at least, so long as the occasion presented itself, usually at her discretion. What these trysts signified was that whatever the bitterness over their failure to do the double divorces and marriage in 1911, their sexual pleasure went on unabated, and was great enough to suppress all else.

Strange as it seemed, their continuing relationship raises the question of whether it was really love or sex alone which sustained them in their periodic get-togethers after the break-up. Of course, by July, 1917, when Warren had discovered Nan Britton, it was probably an irrelevant question—-except that it invites comparison with the kind of relationship he had with Nan. It was not until 1920 that Warren had, de rigueur, to conclusively end his relationship with Carrie Phillips. But she did not go quietly.

CHAPTER 35

"He Got Away With A Lot"

At some point there arises the question of culpability. It is as much a matter of attitude as deed; apology as lack thereof; decency as lack thereof. Obviously most culpable was the blamelessness that became a pervasive spirit of the times. There was almost no time during his marriage that Warren Harding was not seeing other women, with the two women cited, mostly one at a time. But his desire could be insatiable.

While Warren's affair with Carrie was deteriorating, his fresh relationship with the other other-woman (Nan Britton, thirty-one years his junior) was blossoming. Responding to the rebound effect, Warren's eagerness converged with Nan's schoolgirl dream, which hastened excitement in their first private meeting. Sex was not instantaneous then and there, but it was not long in coming. Their heated affair, begun during his Senatorial term, would continue even while Warren was maintaining the respectable front expected, noblesse oblige, from a President of the United States.

The casual treatment given the matter had a double irony in that, scandalous as his adultery might have been, it was easily passed over in his lifetime, excusable perhaps for Warren's tolerance of a barren marital relationship, and posthumously screened by the smoke arising from big-money scandals exposed in his Administration. Nonetheless, the special attention given a mistress likely had something to do with the low profile he maintained as a freshman Senator, when he was busier writing secret love letters than legislation.

He might have been physically on the job, but sometimes not all that effectively when his thoughts were lost in reveries that produced those impulsive letters. Of course, it was also true that, though trying at times, his relations with both mistresses filled a need in his life. Private satisfaction gave him public confidence, as evidenced by his respected presence in the Presidential news conferences enjoyed by reporters.

In any event, despite the distraction caused by his involvement with women, it would be difficult to pinpoint any aspect of Warren's official responsibility, as President, that directly suffered as a consequence of it.

After all, among Presidents, Warren Harding's wandering was scarcely unique and was likewise never treated with other than discretion by the Press. By the same token, other Presidents were fully able to take care of Affairs of State without impediment from their unofficial affairs, as had been the case with Harding's predecessor, rather incredible for the scholarly Woodrow Wilson. Decorum ruled that the Office of President had to be accorded respect, sometimes regardless of the activities of its occupant. Morality in high office had its own standard.

Nevertheless, with Harding, ironies do multiply. For, while infidelity was one scandalous malefaction that he was truly guilty of, it was a sin which Harding was never held to account for during his lifetime. Except for questions raised about competence in office, it was there, in the very area of character, that his immoral conduct would be deemed irrelevant. This, while an overblown relevance would be attached to the scandals perpetrated by members of his Administration, which got rubbed off on him anyway, as did everything else aired by Congressional Investigators. Bad as Harding may have looked for that, it scarcely touched on suspicion of his love affairs.

Concrete exposure, with Nan Britton's revelations, did not occur until four years after his death, creating an ephemeral sensation, which at that point didn't much matter, except for the benighted reputation that lingered on, and the bite it retrospectively gave to Samuel Hopkins

Adams's satire, Revelry. Published a year earlier than The President's Daughter, Adams' book made a big splash, going through three editions in three weeks (Shadow, 631). Beyond curiosity, it produced no more than a passing laugh.

Clearly, the time and attention that were reserved for Harding's amours were more than a touch beyond what a President could afford. On top of the evenings he spent in assignations with these women, who often required assuaging, he would be carrying on an active correspondence with them, particularly with Carrie and Nan, to each of whom he would write letters of amorous longing—notably longish. During his Senatorial days, he would scribble those letters on memo paper, or Senate blue stationary, while heated political discussions were going on around him.

At Christmas time in December, 1917, five pound boxes of Martha Washington chocolates were sent to both women, with whom Warren's contacts were maintained with equal fervor. Much effort had to be expended on the secretiveness of it all, which involved time spent on the hustle of evasion and cover-up, particularly when Warren became President. But, since none of that sort of thing was much noticed, it was as if it was nobody's business anyway. Who would have had the effrontery to pry into the privacy a President was then entitled to? In other words, in his adulterous misconduct, Harding got away with a lot.

H.L. Mencken put the matter in an appropriately jaded context as part of his "review" of Nan Britton's revealing book: "That men of the highest eminence sometimes have pianissimo love affairs is surely not a secret to anyone who has been working for newspapers as long as I have. They are more apt to have them, in fact, than more obscure men, for women pursue them with greater assiduity, and they themselves stand in greater need of sentimental relaxation." [82]

CHAPTER 36

"Nobody Really Cared"

COMPOUNDING THE CASUALNESS WITH WHICH illicit affairs in high places were taken for granted—among men, by code—there was Warren's own attitude, which was an extension of the accepted one. According to the oft noted George Harvey version of what happened on a critical June night when the Nomination was about to be handed to Senator Harding, it purportedly took him no more than ten minutes to brush off questions of whether he could in good conscience say: there wasn't anything "that might be brought up against [him] that would embarrass the party, ...disqualify [him] or make [him] inexpedient, either as a candidate or as a President."

Though there is doubt as to whether Harvey had put such a question to Warren Harding, it does seem that some such situation—of concern to the Party—may very likely have taken place. The image of its having happened in a "smoke filled room" had of course been Daugherty's news-grabbing invention.[83] But that doesn't rule out the possibility of Harding's still having been queried by the powers-that-be about the vulnerability of his personal life.

The first person among those 'powers' to have been most interested in questioning the Nominee-to-be would surely have been Will Hays, the Party Chairman, who had also become his Campaign Manager. Hays happened to have been there in Marion the morning after the election conferring with Harding about what lay ahead (PD, 152). The need of questioning was important enough, since so little was known of Harding, almost nothing nationally, and, among candidates, merely that he was "the best of the second raters." (Florence, 193).

That said, it is also true that there was reason to question the need for questioning Harding about his personal life, since he had already made some significant disclosures. Somehow he had apparently told Senator John Weeks about his young mistress, in addition to which supporters of competing Candidates Leonard Wood and Hiram Johnson had spread rumors of Harding's adultery (Ibid.). Gambler that he was, Harding had reason to conclude that, since word of his womanizing was already out there, with little effect, that would pose no grave threat.

Nor was Harding especially bothered that Carrie Phillips was being attached to the rumors. What did worry him was her impending blackmail, as her disclosure of explicit love letters would be a good deal more damaging than rumors. So, in addition to his incentive for doing what he had to in order to obtain the Nomination, as Nominee he knew he'd have access to funds with which to pay Carrie off.

Strikingly, Harding had already ignored the impropriety of his having Nan Britton sitting openly in attendance at the 1920 National Convention. And she, to boot, was a lady, young enough to have been his daughter, who less than a year earlier had given birth to the daughter Harding had fathered. Though the child was kept well hidden, the Party being unbothered by thoughts of a scandalous liaison, wound up making Harding its compromise Nominee for President—no further questions asked.

As precedent, Harding had thought not much would have been made of his brazenly placing Nan in a front seat at the 1916 Nominating Convention, had he been able to do so, regardless of the conspicuous role he had of putting Charles Evans Hughes's name in nomination. Although that Convention took place a year before he and Nan got together, Harding regretted she hadn't been in touch with him then, so he could have had that front seat reserved for her (PD, 23).

Even considered as a hypothetical, his idea of having an illicit relationship publicly exposed didn't seem to have fazed him. Nor did he seem to think it would get in the way of his political future. So powerful, and so much needed in his life, was the budding relationship with this devoted young lady (PD, 23). The situation was all the more interesting, as Nan herself did not think such placement would have created a public embarrassment, as harmful to her as to her lover.

If one seeks an answer to how Warren Harding could have been oblivious to the activities of thieving grafters in his Administration, it could be said that it all started with the easy attitude fostered by the morality of the "Twenties." How could Warren Harding have been other than very much a part of the times? The fact that he could get away with a lot, made it possible, for Jess Smith, for example, to think that he could too.

CHAPTER 37

"Sex In The Limelight Anyway"

Warren's relationship with a married Carrie Phillips, well known in Marion, had created no great stir there, despite the small-town gossip, which, much as it had hurt Carrie, got stale after a while. Nan notes that there had been so much talk in town about the Warren-Carrie liaison that "gossip mongers wondered how Mrs. Harding could [have been] so blind to such a mutual infatuation" (Ibid., 10). There is indeed evidence, cited from Florence's diary, that she was too observant to have been ignorant of what was happening under her nose.

Carrie, not wanting there to be any doubt about her liaison, made overt gestures (cited in Chapter 48) precisely meant to aggravate Florence's irritation. She wanted to provoke the divorce that Warren couldn't plead for himself. Compounding the offense, and intensifying a wife's grievance, is the fact that Carrie happened to have been a statuesque beauty, attractive as well for her wit and charm, in addition to being fourteen years younger than Florence, who, five years older than Warren, was made all the more unattractive by the comparison.

A lady of dour appearance, with marcelled hair, prince-nez glasses, and looking somewhat oldish (more like a mother than a wife) Florence, being self-conscious, had been elusive about having her picture taken for campaign purposes during Harding's run for the Presidency. Political force that she was, it was only necessary for her to be his guiding light. Compensatory was Warren's dependence on her practical frame of mind.

Rumors of the Carrie-affair had indeed been so broadly spread that the Democrats used it against Harding in the 1920 election campaign, to no effect. Duly noted by Nan, she was herself undisturbed that there was a rival in town. Instead she saw it as a "source of greatest protection" for her relationship with Harding. So, she added, as people "played" with Carrie's name, "they were not looking for mine or any other."

Obviously, she had to suspect that, in addition to Carrie, Harding's experience with women had to have included "others" he had known prior to their relationship (PD, 102). Assumed by her, this suspicion could not have been lost on others, who would have taken it for granted as a natural part of this handsome politician's personal repertoire.

After all, what was known in Marion about Harding and Carrie, would not have been unknown in Washington about him and Nan, certainly not by persons who had lent them their apartments. There were times during Florence's illness when they were unafraid to dine in public restaurants, where Harding could be recognized, and at times even greeted by people known (and unknown) to him. Nan recalls that one evening when they went to dine at the Biltmore, as they passed through the aisle of tables, she heard a woman say, "There goes Harding!" His incredible explanation was that the lady was a friend with whom he "sometimes played billiards," of all places "in Washington" (PD, 74).

So, there were circumstances in which secrecy could be ignored, so long as it wasn't a touch too flagrant, and didn't get the attention of the wrong people, beginning with Florence. Her good friend, Evalyn McLean noted that Florence was habitually anxious about other women getting her husband's eye (Florence, 284). Despite that, obliging Evalyn gave Harding the liberty to take Nan to the McLean estate, interestingly named "Friendship"—and Evalyn happened to have been Florence's best friend. That hide-away was ideal for Harding. Overall, he had to be more than usually cautious during his Presidency.

However, even at that, Harding, on impulse, could also behave as if he really didn't have to be overly guarded. As suggested by Mencken, it was almost expected that men in high places would be prone to dalliance, on a scale commensurate with the person's position. According to the latest scandal sheet of any era, it was common practice, but particularly notorious in post World War I America, extending through the Twenties. It was welcomed as a release from wartime tensions, and pre-war morality.

Overlooked if an affair was extra-marital, as it usually was, justification was unnecessary, particularly if the wife happened to have been uninviting, personally and physically, and made out to be a Nag.

Or the wife might be having affairs of her own, equally well known, as was not unusual with the stylish wives of the Washington elite, and as with that same Evalyn McLean. Silently accepted, mention of such affairs (either type) was unusual, and, if voiced, ignored, or, when necessary, explained away. Since when had Harding played billiards with a lady acquaintance?

Frederick Lewis Allen, taking note of the "revolution in morals" that marked the "Post-War Decade" during which "sex was in the limelight," cited how the new morality would "proclaim that married couples should be free to find sex adventure wherever they pleased and that marriage was something independent of such casual sport" (Only Yesterday, 99). Fitting for Warren, but something that gave Florence fits. Nonetheless, she had to get used to its occurrence, and she did, unhappily.

CHAPTER 38

"Male Immunity Yields Contact With Nan"

In light of what was known of Warren Harding's womanizing, it would seem remarkable how little he was hurt by knowledge of his love affairs. A good deal of the free rein Harding was given in his adultery could be attributed to social mores that gave him male immunity. As opposed to the role levied on women, he didn't have to defend himself for the freedom he enjoyed. Then too, there was the protective mantel of the Presidency, which entitled him to a privacy it was unseemly to invade. Battered as that mantel became, graft was one thing, sex another, readily swept under the sheets.

Of course, politicians cultivate a thick skin anyway. However, a clear sign that Harding would be given a pass on his adulterous affairs is the fact that publishers uniformly shunned Nan's book, even though one editor admitted that his house was "passing up [the opportunity for] a hundred thousand dollars" (Shadow, 631) big money. As previously noted, the book also survived seizure of its plates by Anthony Comstock's successor, John S. Sumner, acting on behalf of the New York Society for the Suppression of Vice, a sensation ballyhooed in the Press.

Nan, in fact, would not have attempted private publication of her exposé had Warren's brother George (aka "Deac", short for "Deacon" due to his puritanic personality) consented to the allowance that Nan pleaded for on behalf of Warren's child and of herself, who, as mother, was left with sole responsibility for raising their daughter. Harding acquaintances, and reputable people generally, were dismissive of Nan's account, some charging, as did Harding's brother, that Nan was a "gold digger."

Of course, she actually wasn't playing the role of extortionist. It was not in hopes of getting money from the Harding family that she published a memoir which exposed Warren Harding's love life with a mere girl three decades his junior. It was Nan's dire financial need which forced her to do that. Once out, the published memoir couldn't have been used as a means of squeezing the Hardings for money.

For the financial support Nan requested, the central question was whether the account she gave of her relationship with Warren Harding could be verified. That was the insistent point brother George made with her, on which she said she could satisfy him. I have treated this matter earlier, and will bring it up again, but it is necessary to look at just one verifiable encounter here to provide context for the proof demanded of Nan. Since it had a strong bearing on Warren's culpability, its truthfulness needed to be firmly established.

Weak as Francis Russell was on documentation, he did offer evidence that gives credence to the factual truth of Nan's narrative. He personally verified signatures of Warren and Nan in the register of the New Witherill Hotel in Plattsburgh, New York, where Nan records that they had stayed on 17 August, 1918. As Nan describes that meeting, they registered separately, with her using "the usual fictitious name of [Elizabeth Ann] Christian." She arrived at 8 a.m., and went to Warren's room, not far from hers, shortly thereafter (PD, 61).

Phillip Payne's fellow Harding scholar, Dean Albertson, reported that he had likewise visited that hotel and gained grudging confirmation from a chary manager (W. H. Howell Jr.) that at least Harding had registered there on that date (Dead Last, 181). Albertson knew that Nan had registered as Elizabeth Ann Christian, based on its being her practice to use that name at other hotels where she had joined Warren on his travels.

Howell, on the assumption of scandal mongering, refused to

disclose whether anyone by that name had appeared on the hotel register on the date in question—which, in itself, suggests he had something to hide, knowing exactly what was being sought. If this was proof of the one tryst with Nan Britton, there was reason to believe there were others.

Doubters have persisted. Among relatively recent ones, lawyer/biographer John Dean, would hold that, lacking DNA evidence, the credibility of Nan's account would have to remain unsubstantiated (Dean, 162). Since substantiation means to back up, lack thereof doesn't mean the child in question therefore wasn't Warren's daughter. Nor does it mean that she couldn't have been. Since Nan's role in her prolonged affair with Warren had been completely monogamous, Elizabeth Ann couldn't have been someone else's daughter.

Evidence of his having had that affair with Nan was widely enough known in Harding's time that it satisfied seasoned critics like Frederick Lewis Allen and H.L. Mencken. Even James Robenalt, who tried to disprove Nan's account, had to concede that "since so many of [Nan's] dates and 'facts' are corroborated by the [Carrie] Phillips letters, her story could be true" (op. cit., 347).

Indeed, as no one has denied that Harding actually met Nan, one important result of his intuitively relying on male immunity was that it easily brought him into contact with her, details of which will be forthcoming.

So little did Harding fear detection during his balmy Senatorial days that, in addition to the couple's dining out, he and Nan would think nothing of walking the streets of Washington, en route to being convenienced by use of the apartment of a card playing friend (PD, 73). They had rather enjoyed such walks, "[her] arm through his." In New York, they had gone to the theater together, and someone sitting behind them seemed to have recognized Harding (Ibid., 71).

They were "so happy," over their limited freedom, Nan recalled Warren saying, "We're just a couple of small towners together, aren't we, Nan?" As close as she came to giving particulars of their intimacy was her asking if she could kiss him all night, to which he replied, "do what you want to me. I'm yours." He, in turn, treasured her physical image, telling her he "loved…[her] woman's body" (PD, 284, 332).

Interestingly, this last was contained in a heart-rending reminiscence that came to Nan on her return from her Armstrong Tour of Europe to mourn Harding's death. Much as they might have indulged their physical love, Nan rarely mentioned anything physical. She in a number of instances indicated that their relationship meant much more than that. She, in fact, etherealized their "love," calling it "a divine thing" (Ibid., 338f.).

Of all the worries that oppressed Harding during the trip to Alaska, one that never crossed his mind was fear of revelations about his sex life. He had entrusted Nan to preserve the secrecy of theirs, and she did, until she was repulsed on seeking financial aid from the Harding family to raise their niece. She was broke and in debt—more of which anon.

Many of Harding's contemporaries, who, like Daugherty, took a fellow politician's affairs for granted, knew that moral judgment would have no bearing on selection of a Presidential Nominee. Harding himself had grown so used to getting by with the Nan Britton affair that he never saw it as an impediment to his political career.

The situation, however, with Carrie Phillips was more complicated, particularly since his affair with her did get out. In fact, Carrie's husband, Jim Phillips, would eventually find out about it, disclosed to him by Carrie herself, around the time of the 1920 Convention.

It is hard to imagine how Jim, like Florence, could not have had suspicions well before that, which cuckoldry might have inhibited Jim from pursuing. The Marion gossipers who angered Carrie wouldn't have been tactful about the latest they could chew on regarding the most notorious couple in town. Interestingly, although Carrie was bothered by the gossip, Warren deftly ignored it.

Despite the risks Harding had exposed himself to with Carrie early on, he had become used to blocking out how so potentially damaging a situation might affect his future. The same sense of immunity prevailed in his relationship with Nan, which worked satisfactorily, except when official duties, especially those of the Presidency, called for his attention, and he couldn't "have her."

Though riskier than his affair with Carrie, the relationship with Nan lasted throughout his Presidency up to the year of his death in 1923. So great was Nan's appeal and so little his fear of detection that it didn't preclude love-making inside the White House itself. More than anything he could have acknowledged, the Nan Britton liaison gave Warren Harding emotional sustenance during an increasingly difficult Presidency.

In his final year, he found himself resisting any sense of fading prowess, as failing health, worries about corruption, and the Office per se began bearing down on him. It was inevitable that the lovers' relationship would reach a crisis stage on their last meeting. Nonetheless, Harding never gave up on a romance that had affected him so deeply. Desperation aside, he had still planned to reunite with Nan on his return from Alaska, though not immediately, in light of the to-do that would attend a President's return home.

In sum, just as Harding's political performance survived misplaced friendships, so too did he get away with courting political suicide if caught in bed with the wrong woman. Since he had indulged in illicit sex unscathed prior to his getting into politics, he had grown so used to getting away with it, that he maintained the same attitude while holding public office, sometimes getting away with it by dumb luck.

On the occasion of his getting caught with Nan in a New York hotel room, he was surprised to find the police were letting him go free, on the basis that a member of Congress couldn't be detained while en route to Washington in order "to serve the people" (PD, 47-50). Circumscribed as his extra-marital assignations might become during his Presidency, those limitations made his finding opportunities for them all the more rewarding. So rich was the experience Harding would have with Nan Britton that, supplanting Carrie Phillips, she became the woman who, in his late years, most touched his heart.

Warren's relationship with Carrie played out on a different level. For one thing Carrie was tough; Nan soft. Harding had had to face Carrie's anger on a number of occasions, but never so threateningly as around Convention time. For starters, she detested the idea of his running for President, and never forgot that, against her objection, he had voted for the declaration of war on Germany.

Carrie's husband was a debtor, and she had spent money more freely than she should have—for one thing on an expensive car. After all she and Warren had been through together, she felt he owed her something. Commenting on her motive, Robenalt figured she "probably needed money to maintain her lifestyle" (Affair, 341).

Much as he felt he could ignore gossip about his affairs, Warren knew his love letters contained the kind of details that might do him in. With them held over his head, Carrie demanded to be paid off. Having put the fear of ruination into his head, she pushed Warren to the point of his contemplating suicide. He made her an offer of $10,000, to be paid in two $5,000 installments, the money to be most available if he had an income from public office.

In any event, made dangerous, Carrie was a woman to be reckoned with. As noted, there had been a similar crisis, ten years earlier, when Carrie, harried by gossip, and, faced with a situation that couldn't be mutually resolved, decided to decamp for Germany (Shadow, 214).[84] In 1920, with Harding's Presidential Campaign about to get underway, there was sufficient reason for the Party to send Albert Lasker over to buy Carrie's silence, probably funded by wealthy backers, the likes of newspaper baron Ned McLean.

The price was $20,000, in cold cash, plus a monthly allowance for so long as Harding held public office. Carrie's compliance was to begin with an expense paid trip around the world accompanied by her husband. They were to be gone rather swiftly, and by summer's end they were indeed going by way of the Orient, their first stop being Japan, where Jim Phillips could study the "raw silk trade." The reasons for this, as for much else, were naturally confidential and, to all intents and purposes, down a well.

One important sidelight to Carrie's threat of blackmail was that she had earlier shown her disgust with Harding's vacillation by returning his love letters. His response was to ship them back, indicating how, by destroyed them, she would lessen the fear of disclosure (Florence,

110). This was to serve as a reminder that, if the letters were to be gone, his love was not.

Hostile to any requests from him, Carrie contrariwise held onto the letters, possibly with a thought of the potential use she could make of them. Alas, Harding's destruction of those letters would have forestalled blackmail, as well as disclosure of his love-sick ravings, some quite graphic—to say nothing of depriving historians of a future treasure trove.

PART V:

THE REIGN OF FLORENCE

CHAPTER 39

"Who Really Was In Charge?"

THERE WAS A NOTABLE DISTINCTION between the experience of Harding as politician and his experience as consort of the women closest to him. But the difference was not quite what one would expect. While in the former he was in position to assume command, and did, in the latter it was the women who took charge, based on a vulnerability which they perceived could be taken advantage of. He was weakest where, according to gender psychology, he should have been strongest.

Florence, a lady lacking in feminine appeal, took on the authoritative role reserved for men, silently conceded by Harding. Knowing his weaknesses, as no one else did, Florence felt he needed all of the administrative help he could get, both before, and after he achieved elected office. She was his Boss, and he trusted her to be a good one. Publicly, he got away with a lot; privately he conceded a lot.

With Carrie, he had been chided often enough over her recurring disappointment that she was able to use it as a club with which to induce a guilt-trip. Like Florence, Carrie also took advantage of his weaknesses. Thus, there were times when her rejection had him abjectly trying to recover their past love.

Nan, on the other hand, ruled him by virtue of her docility. Desperately in need of her love, Harding strove to cater to <u>her</u> needs, beginning with the financial ones, so he could claim her as his own. His repeated pleas that she outright <u>say</u> she loved him resembled a childlike desire for reassurance—a "crying" need that she readily fulfilled. It was as if he couldn't trust the delicate turn of events that enabled him to claim she was truly his.

On their final meeting, when it hit her that their dream might never be realized, she came down hard on him in a flash of anger. Her unhappiness was hard on him. They would have an emotional parting, both wet-eyed, as Warren, looking for some sort of consolation, pleaded with her to tell him she was happy, and, "with quivering lips and brimming eyes [she] bravely lied," that she was (PD, 241). Her enormous let-down broke him down.

While it is also true that each of these women needed him, Warren didn't exploit it. On the contrary, with each of them, Harding, at best, had a way of incurring a sense of mutual indebtedness. His, at times, made a virtual mendicant of him, especially with Carrie. This behavior was an important marker of the self-doubt that would cast an ironic light on the commanding presence he assumed as President. His subservience to these women was an extension of the attitude he had had with a political friend like Albert Fall, who caused near-terminal trouble for him. Harding's insecurity showed up in the worry over his competence for handling the responsibilities thrust upon him by the Presidency.

He worked hard because of the doubts, and did have some remarkable success at it. Unfortunately, his best showing as President in the first two years of his term in office would get erased from public memory. Having achieved far more in less time than either of his successors (among others) his downfall made him a tragic figure. Sadly, one of the few discernable recoveries afforded him, after the disclosure of scandal, came to him posthumously from readers responding to Nan Britton's portrait of his humanity in her memoir of the love he shared with her.

In his relationship with Florence, it didn't take Warren long to arrive at the realization that intimacy would, for the duration, be set aside. As instanced, one of the first things she requested when they were to set up residence in the White House was that their bedroom be furnished with separate twin beds, (Florence, 241) as had been the arrangement in their Marion abode.

Eventually dead-ended as well was any hope that he could have Nan on a permanent basis. Dead-ended prior to that had been his relationship with Carrie, several times over. With each of the two women he had been deeply attached to, he could not enjoy a lasting love life because of the third, his wife. Bad luck for a natural lover who could not assert male dominance.

One-on-one with Harding, each of these three women had the whip hand. Significantly, his lack of assertiveness with them was a trait that, in a subtler way, carried over into other phases of his life. In politics, a comparable attitude of appeasing others merged into his role as harmonizer, a tactic that paid off for him. The fact that as Lieutenant Governor he showed how he could bridge opposing factions, Conservatives vs. Progressives, got him the attention of Party Leaders. That was "typical Harding," the master of congeniality who had a gift for smoothing out differences.

In his private life, paradoxically, his agreeable nature would be seized upon by Florence, to be used for his benefit from the time that she took over running the business side of his newspaper, a chronicle of good management, her specialty. She had the upper hand in much else. But her managerial control really flourished when she used it to help mold his political future.

This began in 1899, on Florence's talking a hesitant Warren into running for the Thirteenth District seat in the Ohio Senate. However modest a beginning, he not only won as a Republican from a predominantly Democratic Marion County, but he was re-elected. As with his winning the Presidency, he gave people the feeling he was one of them. Just by being himself, and bearing a small town heritage, he easily likened himself to them, and the electorate liked it.

In the background of his entry into politics was a conflict between his influential father-in-law, Amos Kling and Florence. Warren was almost persuaded by Kling's reasoning that he should stick to his newspaper business and avoid a venture that abounded with uncertainty, only to have contrarian Florence buck up his courage and convince him to have a try at political office, regardless of its risks, and regardless of Father (Florence,72).

Having gotten Warren's feet wet, Florence had him raising his sights, which got him elected to the influential office of Lieutenant Governor and beyond. In the process, Florence seemed to enjoy the rough-and-tumble of politics more than Warren originally did, and she left her imprint on much of what he accomplished, up to and including his handling the office of President.

However, Warren's deference to Florence, was world's apart from his attitude in the incidental affairs he continued to have with women he scarcely knew. As opposed to his long-term relationships, in those other casual ones, the giving-in was all on the side of the women. Harding wanted nothing other than transient gratification, which, being mutual, was evidently accepted by the women for what it was, without complaint, though not when there were untoward consequences. With notable exceptions, Harding's casual affairs, a carry-over from his bachelor days, were generally meaningless to him; though, for Florence, they became a constant irritant.

Indeed, the area in which the two-sided phenomena in Warren's relations with women arose most painfully was precisely in that marriage. With sex being a strong component in Harding's experience with women, on those grounds, Florence seemed the totally wrong woman for him. What would unexpectedly make her the right one, was her ability to fulfill a material need in a world all business, where sex was mostly immaterial. But, as the scope of his political career took time to develop, the heights to which Florence might take him could scarcely have been foreseen.

A small town Representative in the State Legislature, he started out as a political nonentity. While Florence was helpful in getting Warren to run for the U.S. Senate, it was when he reached the Presidency that she was most in her element, which meant nothing less than taking command. She became so indispensably helpful that she assigned herself a role comparable to Chief of Staff, and she was depicted in the Press as the virtual Surrogate President.

That being the case, Harding could have simply made her his Executive Secretary, for which marriage would have been unnecessary. However, marriage, being the prerequisite Florence wanted, it became the only basis on which she could be there for him when she was most needed. What ensued was a trade-off. Since he couldn't have had the one (managerial help) without the other (marriage) he had to capitulate. In the end, that worked out for the best. It was as if she reached her ambition through him, as much as he reached his through her.

The puzzle is how two people so different in temperament could have ever wound up getting married. More puzzling was how they ever got through those difficult early years as a married couple. So there they were, perplexed as to how they could deal with the unhappiness they had brought upon themselves.

What started out as an unendurable married life for them, would radically change when, thanks to Florence, they happened into an area where a joint endeavor awaited them. Discovering that the missing factor to be arrived at in their married lives was a partnership devoted to politics, they over-night found their mutual calling. First, however, they had to get through the terrible beginning years of their union.

CHAPTER 40

"Was This What They Wished For?"

Whatever forethought—if any—Warren and Florence had had about how marriage might turn out for them, they could have hoped Florence had been more careful of what she wished for. They had every sign that this was a marriage which shouldn't have happened. Since it did, and the promise of happiness ever after was nowhere in sight, their shocking unhappiness had to have told them that what should have come afterwards was a quick surgical solution. Since that didn't happen, we learn something about what these two very different character types were made of by virtue of their ability to get through a self imposed disaster.

As for their getting married, far more important than the event itself was what they failed to anticipate of its consequences. Since they had gone through a period of courtship, they had known enough of one another's faults beforehand. Still, they had no idea of what it might be like to experience those faults at close range, when they would have to tolerate them daily, martyred by matrimony.

A glimpse at their post-marital travail highlights the dramatic irony of the adversity they didn't realize might lie ahead for them. And speaking of adversity, this glimpse discloses how poorly Warren might behave on finding himself stuck in a marriage so contrary to his nature that it pushed his wandering to its morally low point.

The marriage also went contrary to the nature of the suddenly innocent bride who had instigated it. A woman who, in all else, was anything but innocent, Florence Kling, whatever one might say about her flaws, was nobody's fool. Yet there she was having made one of herself once she set her sights on marrying, at all costs, a sex-obsessed Warren Harding. The costs were considerable, and they grew.

However, Florence was a strong woman, and knowing what she did about Warren, she obviously thought that her expertise at control would see them through. Warren might have silently thought she could get things smoothed out, but it looked like he was not going to hang around, waiting for it to happen. Given their awesome start, who could have guessed that this was the rough beginning of what was destined to become a remarkable success story—certainly not the principals.

All else being equal, normally, the reason that two people want to get married is that they have fallen in love. However, in this instance, there was the question of what love meant for Florence, as opposed to what it meant for Warren. For her, it would seem that love mostly came down to possession, the end result of her drive to get what she wanted. In Warren, she saw a special man that she had to own. On the other hand, love for Warren mainly came down to an incentive for physical pleasure, as that was what brought out the overboard professions of love declared in his dazzling relationships with Carrie Phillips and Nan Britton.

The way Warren described his feelings toward Florence in the entry he gave for the History of Marion County, was (as quoted by Carl Anthony) distant and dispassionate, as well as clichéd. He was "united in marriage with a lady of many social graces and of charming personality." Anthony goes on to summarize Warren's praise for "her loyal devotion, acumen, drive, intelligence, and wisdom and [his] acknowledged...reliance on her." There was not a word about any emotional involvement—a bond of love—and, least of all, any reference to her being at all physically attractive to him (Florence, 60).

By contrast, Warren's affair with Carrie began in 1905, and two years later they realized that what they had together was truly love, above and beyond the physical attraction. As previously noted, they designated Christmas as their anniversary day, to be recognized annually. On their third anniversary, after Warren had lost his run for Governor, which delighted Carrie, he sent her a picture, inscribed with a note on the back, telling her "I love you more than all the world, and have no hope of reward on earth or hereafter, so precious as that in your dear arms…." He went on with explicit mention of her arousing physical features; yes, lips, breasts, etc. (Ibid., 93).

Absent any component of love in the early years that Florence and Warren were living together in marriage, the dissatisfaction working on them should at least have given them pause over whether to go on with it. For Warren, the spells of indigestion that had been a chronic symptom of stress, were becoming more severe.

He found himself seeking advice so often from his homeopath father that it finally seemed best for the newly weds to simply move in with him. With them staying on for all of six months, tensions arose, which made Florence querulous and Warren more severely dyspeptic. As those attacks couldn't be quelled, Warren got himself to the brink of a nervous breakdown.

Unable to contend with their disillusionment over the mismatch they had innocently rambled into, and somehow unable to peremptorily end it, they suffered the consequences. Florence's displeasure made her irascible, and there being nowhere else to go with it in her father-in-law's house, she directed it at her husband. And Warren, demoralized over a wife's aversion to pleasures of the bedroom, apparently felt he had justification for finding them elsewhere.

That part aside, Warren had to seek refuge for his combined dyspepsia and dysphoria by packing himself off to Dr. John Harvey Kellogg's noted Battle Creek Sanitarium, looking for the curative disciplines of diet and exercise to restore his mind-body equilibrium. That visit occurred twice in 1894, the troublesome third year of the marriage, and there were additional visits thereafter, which at least got him out of the house, and out of range for Florence's displeasure.

Presumably anticipatory, he had, in fact, visited Kellogg's "San" in the year prior to his marriage, which his sister Charity claimed was due to a nervous breakdown. His visits ceased after his relationship with Carrie Phillips began in 1905, and likely before, as they had had their eyes on one another prior to that. (Florence, xiiif., 61; Shadow, 90, Affair, 16).

Clearly, much of this upheaval could have been traceable to sexual incompatibility, abruptly revealed. Since the onus of that would have fallen heavily on the partner in want, his stress created greater stress for Florence. He had found an outlet, but she didn't, except to register the annoyance that made her nag. Obviously, Kellogg's therapy had not had a lasting effect, so he went back. Unable to alleviate the source of his problem, Warren, looked toward means of escaping it.

So what had previously passed for a harmless addiction to random encounters with consenting partners would, at times, become wanton recklessness. Some of this persisted throughout his marriage, continuing even during his tenure as President. Ike Hoover, the head usher at the White House, alluded to Harding as a "sporting ladies' man" (Florence, 302). While there may have been occasions when Harding had resorted to professional women, he had to have been careful of that during his Presidency.

Warren's habitual wandering as surveyed by Carl Anthony, sometimes resulted in serious consequences, among them pregnancies and abortions. As previously alluded to, an especially troublesome episode occurred, when, three years into his marriage, Warren connected with an unhappily married Susan McWilliams Hodder. As chance would seemingly have it, Susan's family had lived right next door to Florence's family, and, in their youth, Susan and Florence had been best friends.

It was a deplorable situation all around for Susan, who, unhappily married, was separated from her husband and staying in her father's house, right next door to Florence's family residence. After going out to Nebraska to bear Warren's daughter, Susan formally broke off her marriage. The daughter had in time married and moved to New York City where she came down with tuberculosis and tragically died at the age of twenty-two. Though Warren had sent some support for the girl during her childhood, he did not come off looking any better for that.

There were other situations that were quite as bad during the early days of his marriage. Among them, was a short term liaison Warren had had with Augusta Cole, who allowed herself to be shipped off to Battle Creek for termination of a pregnancy, whereupon her husband divorced her. There had also been a brief one with a maid that resulted in the claim that Harding was responsible for her illegitimate son. The boy's adoption had supposedly been facilitated by none other than Carrie Phillips herself (Florence, xiif., 150, 302).

But the real Susan Hodder story has to do with the question of how Warren could have undertaken such a glaring outrage, and one so directly insulting to Florence. Why Susan? To have selected just that woman, he had to have had a purpose in mind. After how mutually miserable he and Florence had been made by their marriage, it can only be deduced that Warren was trying to send Florence a message. Nothing could have been a more insistent call for divorce. Since unhappiness alone hadn't done it, neither would words.

So the affair with Florence's good old friend Susan had to have been Warren's shock solution to a marriage bond that could only be severed, for cause, by direct action. Logically, it had to have been an eye-opening surprise, meant to cause a major response—certainly some manifestation of uproar—from intractable Florence. Surely this should have cinched the argument for a divorce matching the one thrust on Susan. The biggest surprise, however, was how miserably Warren's unspoken plea failed of its purpose.

But, then, while Warren had seen enough women in his time, he hadn't seen enough of Florence to know the resilience this woman was capable of. His turning around and taking himself right back to Kellogg's Sanitarium upon learning of Susan's pregnancy in April, 1894, indicated how great the shock was to him. Doubly shocking was the apparent lack of a known response from Florence to her husband's misdeeds, much as this one must have disheartened her.

In short, it hit him worse than it hit Florence, a sign both of his reaction to this failure, and his humiliation. Apparently, she was calming herself with distancing nostrums that she confided in her calendar diary, such as, "The 'misunderstood husband' is he who makes his wife's frailties his excuse for the full dialogue of sins against her—and every other woman he meets" (Florence, 62).

Incredible as this may sound, what it importantly suggests is that Florence looked upon her husband as incredibly weak, which explains why she felt she had to take on so great a part of his professional life. In time, she would believe he probably wasn't up to the job of President, and she felt she had a better feel for this than others who may have had similar thoughts.

CHAPTER 41

"Further Consequences; The Carrie Factor"

Meanwhile, one is left to wonder how this pro-active woman could react so passively to so blatant an insult as the Hodder affair, incongruously seeing her husband as simply "misunderstood." Did she fear losing him, think chastisement would be futile, or take his departure for the "San" as a sign of repentance?

Whatever—the simplest answer to all such questions is that tenacious Florence wasn't going to let go of this man, regardless—a prognostic of her being able to put up with more of the same, if need be. With Warren having been rather manic in his pursuit of women before their marriage, Florence had had sufficient warning of what she was getting into.

So great was her determination to hold on to the one man she ever wanted, that the more she learned of his adultery the harder she tightened her grip on him. She would, after all, have incredibly ambitious plans for this womanizer, believing that, under her tutelage, she could yet bring out the best in him.

In other words, she was as single-minded for what she wanted, as Warren had originally been for what he didn't want, but succumbed to. As things turned out, Florence was able to prevail in this matter as in all else, curbing Warren as she could.

Much as that restricted him, he was still able to carry on as before, since he could rely on Florence's refusal to throw him out. Revealing of how much leeway she would give him is that unexpected diary nostrum previously noted. "There is no devotion like a husband's provided he is far enough out of his wife's sight to do as he pleases." Warren obviously took considerable advantage of that. But, as he had been used to doing so, it happened not only in the case of his wife. The situation was not greatly different for the two mistresses with whom he had fallen in love.

For example, in 1918, when his relationship with Carrie was in an uncertain state—not on, but not quite off—and there were gaps between his meetings with Nan, into his office stepped Grace Cross, a stately blonde. One look and she was taken on in lieu of her husband, who had actually been the one recommended to Harding for a job. Grace was almost as swiftly bedded as hired. Since her salary exceeded his Senate allowance for staff, she had to be paid out of pocket. There were love letters for a while, then a spat over money that provoked Grace to violence, in which Harding evidently had difficulty defending himself (Florence, xiii).

Though Grace claimed she could identify scars on Harding's back, her attempt to use his letters for blackmail was foiled by a lady reporter, who, on being contacted by Jess Smith, managed to seize them. She had cleverly asked to see those letters, pretending to be dubious of their existence (Ibid., 262).

As evidence of how errant Warren could be in relations with his mistresses, while he was having an assignation with Nan in Plattsburgh, New York, he became nostalgic for Carrie and wrote her a letter then and there to say so. Beyond nostalgia, it was as if he felt he did not want to lose her for good. There is no avoiding the conclusion that, in his love life, Harding was capable of capricious behavior.

Meanwhile, with that sort of thing going on around Florence, she recorded her resignation in yet another diary entry: "The happy wife is not the woman who has married the best man on earth, but one who is philosophical enough to make the best of what she has got" (Ibid., 62). It was an attitude she was in need of to see it through with Warren. It was also something that might have sounded hollow when she learned, belatedly, that her husband was having an affair with a lady who was a close friend of hers, Carrie Phillips. That one was particularly devastating to her and was so noted in her diary when she found out about it (Florence, 41; xiii).

Worse yet were the circumstances under which the Carrie affair had been initiated. When Carrie was distressed by the loss of her two year old son, Jim Junior, in 1904, Florence sympathetically comforted her. In the following year, Florence had an acute attack of nephritis that assumedly resulted in the removal of a kidney. Her post surgical convalescence restricted her to bed rest for some five months, from February to July, 1905.

Meanwhile, Warren had been trying to console Jim Phillips. There had been so great a stress on his marriage after the loss of their son, that Jim was nearing a nervous breakdown. Recalling how, under similar circumstances, a stay at Kellogg's "San" had helped him, Warren recommended it to Jim, who was clinically depressed. Warren added the comforting thought that he would take care of Jim's wife and daughter while he was away.

With Warren and Carrie having already had a strong physically affinity for one another, it would seem that they were presented with the chance to realize their longing. While there is no direct evidence of how that situation played out, Anthony puts it together that, when Warren in a love letter recalled for Carrie how "fate timed that marvelous coincidence," his reference was to the specific instance when, absent their spouses, they enjoyed opportunistic sex. This is backed by a similar reference Warren made to what seems to have been that treasured gift of fate: "It was impossible for us to have planned [it], and I count it to be the best remembered moment of my existence" (Florence, 81).

In Warren's follow-up letter, the first of the available ones written to Carrie, he was euphoric over their "blissful affinity," as contrasted with its absence in his marriage. He wrote of the "weld[ing of] bodies…the divine embrace, the transcending union,…and... all the excruciating joy and unspeakable sweetness that [he] never did know and can only know when fastened by [Carrie]" (Ibid.). Implicit in his reciting this level of excitement is an indirect contrast to life with his wife, who had been writing in her diary that "the life of a woman is completed by her love for her husband." (Ibid., 41). It had been just a year since Florence had comforted her friend Carrie over the loss of her son.

There is a need for clarification here with respect to 1905 dating. James Robenalt contends that the Warren-Carrie relationship "began with courtship [only] and did not become intimate for three years." He bases this on a love letter of 11 February 1917, in which Warren wrote about "twelve years of love's worshiping and more than eight years of intimate revelation" (Affair., 210).

No need to quibble over "more than eight years," but more being more, one can't assume he meant no more than eight. Lacking any further substantiation of sex avoidance for three whole years, an alternative view of the 1905 encounter is worth considering. First of all, three years of celibacy with a woman he ardently loved does not comport with Warren's history. His pursuit of women tells another story.

In the special case of beautiful Carrie, past performance suggests that "love's worshiping" was synonymous with sex. Regarding a three year interval, if "the best–remembered moment of [Warren's] existence" could only mean sex was initiated, it wouldn't have ceased thereafter. There would be regular out of town trysts, and, excitation having been keen, most likely early ones.

Again, there seems to be a problem with Robenalt's dating. Twelve years prior to 1917 takes the worshiping back to 1905. But, accepting three years of celibacy from that point, and dating "intimacy" as eight years from 1908 would have it running to 1916 (when togetherness was rare) a period, which includes the years Carrie was out of the country and those when their relationship had "cooled," and, in early 1917, frigid, prior to the arrival of Nan in May.

Francis Russell outright states, "With the Duchess in Columbus and Jim at Battle Creek they became lovers" (Shadow, 167). This is followed by dashes attached to a deleted letter, presumably documenting his statement. Also fitting the strong possibility of sex in 1905 are the quotes Anthony offers about "fate" having timed "that marvelous coincidence," and the impossibility of their having planned "the best remembered moment" of Warren's life. The reference is obviously to one remarkably memorable event. Clearly, sex initiated at the level indicated would have compelled further indulgence.

There is yet another piece of significant evidence that Warren was recalling activation of a sexual event. When he comes to the Phillips home to help Jim pack for his 1912 trip to visit Carrie in Berlin, Warren has memories ("almost a riot of recollections") of his having been there with Carrie. The memories are overflowing.

As Robenalt himself describes the situation, "He [Warren] couldn't help but travel back in time to the erotic moments he and Carrie shared in her home" (op. cit., 90). Obviously, the lovers could only have had the freedom for such a visit when Jim was safely out of town—to, for example, Battle Creek, Michigan, as advised by Warren. When Warren reaches the upper hall of the house "trooping came the memory of our sacred day, and the bridal breakfast that was served there." Obviously, he is recalling <u>one</u> "sacred day." "Bridal" clearly suggests honeymoon consummation.

When he makes his way to Carrie's room, he reports that "memory deepened and blessed even more—the memory of the first time I saw you garbed for your couch...and there were memories there, in such a short time, of fuller visions of your great beauty, memories of grander realization, of ecstasies and raptures,...memories of you giving of yourself as only you can give—the surpassing experiences of my life" (Ibid.). He begins with one ecstatic experience, but, significantly, ends by pluralizing it. Jim was gone for more than a day.

The coincidental upshot of Warren's having formed a relationship with Carrie in 1905 was that he would pull himself out of Ohio politics, refusing to run again for Lieutenant-Governor, a prestigious position he enjoyed. It was a decision which would have been pleasing to Carrie. He lost the run for Governor in 1910, and though he continued to circulate in the State's political circles, he did not get major recognition, until he won election to the U.S. Senate in 1914, for which he received the personal congratulations of young Nan Britton, not Carrie. For all that could be said about the weakness engendered by Warren's need of the principal women in his life, the need that each of them had of him was a comparable weakness. In short, they wanted him as much as he wanted them, and it hurt both ways. Florence, of course, was a special case. Her diary nostrums show that, having a husband inclined to wander, she spoon fed herself to believe she could be reconciled to it.

Whether or not she guessed what may have transpired in her absence in 1905, she did come to specifically know of Warren's affair with Carrie, and put up a fight over it (covered in Chapter 46). The issue being love, they each had a claim on him. On his side, it was also a matter of love, but a moveable feast.

Warren exchanged a deteriorating relationship with his treasured Carrie for a flourishing one with a newly beloved Nan. Wanderer that he had been, it did seem that he had at least been faithful to Nan, in which case what brought about a change in Harding's mindless eroticism was, finally, a lasting love, emotional satisfaction when he needed it most.

From the time he was elected President, Nan Britton was his bed partner, the occasion permitting, for the rest of his life. As previously indicated, Warren's attitude simply reflected the conscience-free detachment which enabled persons of position—in his time, as in others—to indulge desire, pretty much as temptations might present themselves. In Warren's case, it did not prevent either him, or others like him, from becoming effective politicians, eventually Presidents.

The self-indulgence that reigned in the Jazz Age freedom adopted by flappers and their companions seemed to have been part of an amoral atmosphere in which sexual license could be treated as other basic needs routinely were. That Warren Harding could find that constancy finally suited him was remarkable. For he was a man of his times, as it has been described by social historians like Frederick Lewis Allen.

Obviously none of the amoral freedoms applied to Florence, despite her resistance to the rule of a hard-line father. Her pseudo marriage to Pete DeWolfe was an aberration, soon severed and forgotten. How, then, did Florence and Warren ever get married, and, more strangely yet how did they manage to stay married? I have indicated some of Florence's motivation, but the bigger problem lies in accounting for Warren's, when she obviously didn't have the physical appeal of women who got his attention.

Totally mystifying is what could have motivated Warren, of all men, to allow himself to be bullied into marrying this less than beautiful lady, hard featured and far from soft in personality. To take it one step further, she just wasn't the type of woman a man would fall in love with, and, the truth is, Warren never did, compared with how he felt about Carrie and Nan.

Nor, for that matter, did Florence react to Warren with the abandon of a woman who had fallen in love with him. She did love him in her own way, but it was ownership that motivated her. She knew all too well that she had competition, and fought it.

On the other hand, much as Florence may have loved Warren, the sentiments on his part were far from strong. To put it more explicitly, a man could not have been in love with his wife and have written such sexually graphic letters to another woman, of a kind that Harding wrote in telling Carrie how much he loved her. Carl Anthony offered a sample passage from one of Harding's steamy letters to Carrie that illustrates how greatly his love was based on savoring their sexual experience (Florence, 81).

With so much going against that seemingly ill-advised marriage, the outcome of their combined unhappiness was that it didn't compel the logical solution for an end to their grief. Quite the reverse, for, having strangely enough skirted divorce, they lingered on with the marriage long enough for them to discover that the longer they remained married the greater the reasons for their continuing to stay married, as they each derived something advantageous from what they found in one another.

Having learned to live with what continued to eat at them, Warren and Florence experienced the growth of a mutually beneficial bond, seemingly absurd, particularly when taken in context with the Jazz

Age background against which it took place. Difficult as it might become, Florence was confident she could derive what she wanted from the relationship, which Warren didn't object to her doing, as he appreciated what it did for him.

CHAPTER 42

"They Shouldn't Have; But Florence Proved They Should"

EVERYTHING ALREADY CITED SUGGESTS THAT two persons so vastly different as Warren and Florence were should never have so much as contemplated marriage. After experiencing what it was like, Warren had openly demonstrated as much. In a small town like Marion, people familiar with the newly weds wondered at what a rash decision it was for Florence Kling to insist on marrying a man looked upon as a philanderer. Representative of local opinion was that of George B. Christian, Sr., Warren's long time friend, who was reported to have found it strange that two persons who had long been known as wholly different in personality would get themselves paired in courtship (Florence, 37).

So, why did they get themselves married when there was so much to warn them against it? And, given the question of what happened afterwards, two people awakening from a bad dream, how could they have stayed married long enough to realize some benefit from it? If one can see why they got together, one can understand how.

The short answer as to why is that what seemed like a bad match was what would make it a good one, if they but stayed with it long enough, as, thanks to Florence, they did. His negatives were her positives. On his part, there would be obligation incurred out of dependency, on hers, incentive for control. The kind of woman whose motor was always idling, Florence was a type of person who, at some point, had to put it into gear. Since being in the driver's seat was so integral a part of who she was, Warren would find himself being the one who was to be driven.

Domination came across as something of a surprise for easy-going Warren. Since that was a large part of how Florence had made him sick, physically and psychologically, he would have needed to be persuaded there was a reason for him to stay put. 1894—three years into their marriage—was a make or break year for the couple. There had to be a sign that some sort of cure was possible.

How it might edge into sight was all about Warren's tendency to let things happen as they would, and Florence's to make things happen as she wanted them to. Put another way, as Harding's habitual inertia allowed Florence's determination, in essence, that was what rescued them. She took charge of the Star and turned it into a respectable money-maker. That would get Warren's attention.

The turning point occurred at the darkest time of their young marriage. Warren, in that dire third year, kept seeking relief at Kellogg's Sanitarium. As previously indicated, the quixotic outcome of their managing to avoid the logic of separation was that, absurd as it seemed, Florence wasn't going to let it happen. With Warren's reputation being pretty much afloat in town, she had had a good preview of what lay in store for her. Since Warren had already experienced the overbearing attitude that did in poor Pete DeWolfe, he too had had a foretaste of what awaited him.

Then, while he was away, seeking help from Kellogg, the circumstance that would give them hope took place. Warren's circulation manager at the Star quit, and Florence stepped in to take his place. She would move on to appropriate the entire business end of his newspaper, in due time delegating daily management, to free herself for more expansive assignments. As she once asserted, "I love business" (Florence, 55). Warren loved her for it.

Having full control, Florence made the paper run more efficiently, and, above all, more profitably than when Warren had it, which was loosely. Seeing Florence at work gave Warren a new perspective on a wife suddenly capable of giving him a different kind of pleasure. The paper had been moving along at a modest pace and making a modest income. On Florence's take-over, what ensued was an efficiently run management, and a dramatic increase in the bottom line. Warren, who did not excel at organization, could relax and just take care of the editorial side of the paper. This could only have opened their eyes to prospects of their having a beneficial bond.

It was not as if everyone else in town, but Florence, knew how difficult it would be for her, of all women, to hold on to a man like Warren Harding. It therefore didn't take long after she got him to the altar for Florence to look for tasks which showed a reluctant husband that, regardless of what he—and the rest of Marion—might have thought, she was exactly the helpmate he needed. In common parlance a "Bitch," she would be prepared to pave the way for aimless Warren Harding to make a mark for himself in politics, and eventually become the most incredible Presidential candidate to ever win the Republican Nomination, and get himself elected by an eye-popping margin.

That climb started from incredible origins. Having put herself in charge of the Star, Florence showed her financial skills in areas that Warren scarcely looked into. For example, she renegotiated at a lower rate loans that had been incurred for the purchase of new printing equipment. Much of that sort of thing was put in motion while Warren was taking trips to Kellogg's Sanitarium, followed by her taking care of him on his return (Florence, 49-54). Moreover, Florence's running the newspaper occurred at a time when it was deemed unusual for women to assume managerial positions in a business office.

For Florence, it was something she was naturally attracted to doing, and, collaterally, her success provided evidence that she could divert a dubious husband from the dissatisfactions that were creating unhappiness in their marriage. She wanted to signal what a great help she could be to Warren in practical endeavors.

This did not suddenly dispose of their personal problems, as, for one thing, Warren's philandering was incurable. Florence, however, did much to help them make the best of a difficult marriage, in which Florence continued to be Florence and Warren, Warren. Thus, when

Florence engrossed herself in work at the Star. Marion gossip assumed that her primary reason for being there was to keep an eye on Warren.

Florence had rather quickly justified her expanded role on the Star. Though the paper had been on a fairly decent financial footing, not great, but, typically for Warren, good enough, Florence, with her steady and parsimonious eye on finances, instantly raised profitability.

Whereas circulation had been conducted on a contract basis, supplemented by random over-the-counter sales, she decided the paper wasn't making the money it should. So she devised a delivery system, and, by her riding herd on the young boys she had assembled to get the paper delivered, the result was that in the first month of her management there was a $200 increase in circulation revenue.

She came into running a paper that had had about 700 subscribers, and, in time, she brought the total up by well over five times that number. With her efficient business sense, she had by 1898, upped the Star's circulation to almost 3,500 in a town that had a population of slightly more than 10.000, meaning she put the paper into the hands of almost every third person in town (Florence, 70).

Dynamo that she was, she also took charge of advertising, and telephone orders, in addition to resolving complaints. Often seen riding her bicycle to the office, she came, as she would put it, "intending to help out for a few days and remained fourteen years," during that time, training, disciplining, and, when needed, scolding, also occasionally spanking, her delivery boys (Adams, Incredible Era, 25).

Florence's rehabilitation of the Star was but the beginning of her rehabilitating Warren himself. She would open up new vistas that he probably wouldn't have ventured into, minus a push. This began with her insistence on marrying him and, more importantly, on her making the marriage secure when it seemed broken. Then, too, she was the one who would get him started out in politics. That, however, still leaves some questions unanswered.

CHAPTER 43

"How Come Warren Got Married, And Stayed"

On the other hand, what was it about easy-going Warren G. Harding and his negligible social status, the editor of a newly solvent small-town newspaper, that made him such a sure catch for Florence Kling? Since he would naturally remain silent about his motivation, biographers have been left with reasonable surmises. The most obvious of these would likely have had something to do with foreseeable advantages, primarily a huge step up socially, and possibly financially, by his marrying into the wealthiest family in town.

That was the opinion, for example, of Norman Thomas, future Socialist Candidate for President, who had been one of Florence's young delivery boys (Florence, 37). Francis Russell saw Harding as "flattered, if not overpowered, by the attentions of Amos Kling's daughter…[who] represented the pinnacle of that small town world; wealth, position, [and] assurance" (Shadow, 85).

On that basis, Warren would have had to assume that defiance of his prospective father-in-law's opposition to his marrying Florence would not be any more lasting than his bitter dispute with him over matters related to the Marion Trade Board. Warren had to have been going on the supposition that surely time and reason would prevail. More immediately, there was probably an element of spite on Warren's part that paralleled the reasons which occasioned Florence's spite, as both enjoyed the pleasure of defying Amos Kling's patriarchal arrogance.

As part of his effort to foil their marriage, Kling fostered a discredited rumor that would dog Warren from time to time to the effect that there was Negro blood in the family line. This so angered Warren that he threatened Kling with fisticuffs. Jack Warwick, Harding's close friend, original partner in their purchase of the Marion Star, and City Editor for a while, said Harding confided to him that he "would rather have [had] Amos Kling's enmity than his friendship," since, as a friend, Amos would "want to tell [him] how to run [his] business."[85]

That would suggest an after-the-fact rationalization on Warren's part, from which he could derive the practical satisfaction of feeling that Kling's ill will was self-defeating, since it gave Warren precisely the relationship he wanted to have with an intimidating father-in-law.

Additionally, his having made off with the daughter of a millionaire not used to being crossed, would give him an element of revenge. In effect, the outcome was that Warren got things his way on both counts, enabling him to make a virtue of expediency—a strategy which he would cultivate when politically challenged, as with Texas patronage.

Of course, it was not easy to outsmart a man with the financial power that Amos Kling possessed. For, whatever ad hoc revenge Warren may have exacted, that was greatly outweighed by Kling's buying up Warren's $20,000 debts with the demand for immediate payment, which forced Warren to seek desperate help from local friends.

Warren did finally succeed in winning over his father-in-law. But that didn't occur until 1903, after the twelve years that Amos Kling had kept his distance, whereupon he decided it was time to reconcile with a son-in-law who was making a name for himself in Ohio politics as newly elected Lieutenant Governor. Kling went so far as to write Warren an apology in 1907, plus an invitation for him and Florence to join Kling and his new wife on an expense paid trip to Europe—accepted with pleasure.

Florence, on the other hand, had made no overtures to heal the breach, just as Kling's early hostility had not interfered with her equally strong-willed effort to capture the man she wanted. Her father had to come to her, not the other way around. Obviously, she had a way of managing not just business, but men.

In accounting for why Warren complied with Florence's insistence on their getting married, beyond the reasons adduced above, it is useful to recall Warren's father's oft-quoted remark that he was glad Warren had not been born "a gal," because he couldn't say "No" (Adams, Incredible Era, 7f.).

Florence had been warned by Warren's mother that if she wanted a happy marriage, she had best "keep the ice box full and both eyes on Warren" (Margaret Truman, First Ladies, 234). Depressed as Warren had been in those early years, on Florence's taking over the Star with the same enthusiasm that she took him over, he saw the advantage of having this shrewd minded woman for a wife. He had no greater public ally, no truer helpmate. Thus, based on Warren Harding's good political instincts, and his being more perceptive than he is given credit for having been, one could understand how he would foresee the growth of a symbiotic relationship in his marrying Florence.

CHAPTER 44

"Compensation For A Celibate Marriage"

Once they married, the question lingered over how his desire to connect with other women would eventuate. He had an eye for them, and they had one for him. Back in college, a room-mate said he was attracted to and "frolicked with" every pretty girl on campus (Dean, 8f.). Those girls were equally attracted to him—and for good reason, as, in addition to being rather tall, his appearance in a picture from that time also showed him to have had the prototypically dark and handsome look of a matinee idol, complete with accenting mustache.[86] Predictably, he had lived in the only mixed-sex dormitory on campus.

The mutual attraction between him and the women was strong enough to last a lifetime. Seen as a factor in the distressful beginning years of his marriage, it continued unabated thereafter, as did the stress. On his return from a Honolulu vacation, Harding apologized to Scobey for not having written him a letter from San Francisco because, as he wrote, "the stenographer was so blooming handsome that I quite lost my head and overlooked some of the things I had in mind."[87]

That was Warren Harding at age forty-nine. Nine years later, at a stop in Yellowstone on the journey destined for Alaska, despite the fact that he was ailing much of the way, and feeling his age, when a bevy of young waitresses forced their way past Secret Service to serenade him, he perked up and had them stay on. He wanted them to return on his way back. As on previous occasions, Florence let him know she was not amused (Shadow, 580).

While Florence had succeeded in landing the most attractive man in town, Warren, on noticing the availability of Carrie Phillips, became interested in the most attractive woman in town. He was much more desirable to Carrie than her own weak mannered husband, in stature a foot shorter than she was, a woman with Gibson Girl beauty. As instanced, this played havoc with Warren's marriage, plagued from the beginning over other women. Carrie's marriage was no happier, to which the adjustment of their respective mates left much to be desired.

Though Florence felt fulfilled by taking charge of her husband's public life, she was expecting the impossible in believing this man could enjoy his private life with a sex-averse wife. He, on the other hand, made the mistake of thinking he could enjoy the personal management she provided, while he remained free to seek gratification as the spirit moved him. She continued to find consolation in diary nostrums, like those already cited, e.g.: "Look for the bright side, and if there is no bright side, burnish up the dark side." (Florence, 41).

Florence's greatest challenge was Warren's blatant affair with Carrie Phillips, which, at one point, sent up divorce signals. Warren had gone so completely overboard with Carrie, that his first love letter oozed with sexual delirium. As previously noted, he wanted them to "weld bodies" in the "divine embrace" and "excruciating joy" that could only be known when he was "fastened" to her (Florence, 81).

During the span of Warren's fifteen year relationship with Carrie Phillips, he from time to time found himself on the horns of a dilemma as "excruciating" as his sexual obsession. Since Carrie pressed him for the natural solution to their problem, Warren was left weighing the merit of staying bound to a marriage that provided practical advantages, or of pulling out to marry a woman he had fallen madly in love with. But to the extent that Florence provided no incentive for sex, Carrie provided none for politics. What she hated, Florence loved.

Since the feelings with Carrie were mutual, and mutually keen, she had had to bitterly remind Warren in that 7 July, 1917 letter of how he had dangled before her the prospect of marriage, which he was unable to make good on. With those love letters dangling over his head, Carrie's ill-timed demand in 1920 was focused on his paying her off. But, considering the animosity between the two women, Carrie had incentive to vengefully hint that he, at long last, envision divorcing Florence.

While Carrie's threat may have been cushioned for Warren by his other love affair, it had to be looked at narrowly. Obviously, it was as much in the Party's interest as his own that a last minute "woman problem" had to be taken care of on behalf of the newly minted Candidate for President, just prior to the election campaign that was to kick off from the front porch of his home with Florence.

One can understand why Warren would tell Nan Britton that Florence "makes life hell" for him and why he would "always speak disparagingly to [Nan] of Mrs. Harding" (PD, 72, 80)—while he was incapable of doing anything about it. In itself, the fact that his fear of losing Nan—yet another chance at liberation—did not prompt him to remedy his marital situation tells us how formidable Florence's hold on him was.

It was no secret that she was his boss, the essential person in his political life, and—going back ten years—this was something he openly confessed. Indeed, he did so proudly, as, in a typical applause line, he told a hometown crowd that he got himself nominated for the 1910 Governorship, in spite of the bosses, as Florence was the only boss he really needed, and was a very good one at that (Florence, 92).

Although his life with Florence might leave him with a sense of deprivation, he couldn't bring himself to accept a tempting a way out. The simplest explanation had to have been his realization that eluding Florence's grasp would greatly weaken him in matters that were important to him. Then, too, he'd have to face thoughts of an unwinable fight with her, which would indicate the near impossibility of his getting a separation cleanly done.

Florence herself had abundant grounds for getting rid of him, but likewise did nothing about it. Nan relates that she was told about the Hardings' stressful situation at home by Jim Sloan, the Secret Service Agent who had been Warren's go-between for his contacts with Nan.

Had Florence made herself fully cognizant of their relationship, as Sloan knowingly put it, Florence's "temperament" being what it was, she "would not have released him …[and she] might possibly have sought some form of retaliation."

Warren's own rejoinder was a succinct understatement: "she'd raise hell, Nan!" (PD, 216). Nan selflessly took this as her "cue for guarding well a situation which Mr. Harding had termed his 'greatest joy'" (Ibid.).

With Nan knowing this much, it was a tribute to her perseverance that she could hold onto the relationship, even, as its uncertain status persisted, until she had to painfully resign herself to a dreary reality. It was also a sign that Warren had long since adjusted to what Florence did not offer him in exchange for what she did.

As it turned out, they were good companions with mutual interests, and he enjoyed a certain contentment with Florence, his reliable support system. Florence, from her point of view, found Warren an interesting conversationalist, and liked their sharing ideas about the world of politics that surrounded them. So, they had a comfortable day-to-day relationship, making it easy for them to enjoy one another through common interests.

Actually, despite areas of mutual unhappiness, over its course, the Hardings' marriage worked, if not always harmoniously, which was slightly ironic for a politician whose career would be enhanced by his role as Party Harmonizer. Also overcome was an essential difference in their respective natures. Warren tended to be generous, soft-hearted and forgiving, as with his pardoning Eugene Debs, and Florence was not.

Indeed, she could be petty and mean-spirited, particularly if it was a question of money, as with her objecting to the Government's proposed purchase of the upscale mansion of Senate widow, Mary Henderson to make it the first official residence of the country's Vice President. With the Coolidges being quartered on the top floor of the Willard Hotel, Florence declared, "A hotel apartment is plenty good for them!" (Anthony, First Ladies, 394).

A key indication of how Florence was able to take Harding over, and a reflection as well of the kind of dominating attitude that made him captive appears in an unsent letter she wrote as First Lady: "If the career is the husband's, the wife can merge her own with it, [and] if it is the wife's, as it undoubtedly will be in an increasing proportion of cases, then the husband may...permit himself to be the less prominent and distinguished member of the combination" (Ibid.).

With her hard nature coming together with his soft nature, frictions were inevitable. But with him knowing her as well as she knew him, Warren and Florence got along, as both acquired something they wanted; she, control, and he, good management on and off the job. Besides they were good company for one another. They had shared interests, much to talk about, in the rich political life they had together. After all, they were colleagues.

CHAPTER 45

"Florence A Force To Be Reckoned With"

It was no accident that Warren, early on, would call his wife the 'Duchess.' She wasted no time in earning the name. As king-maker, she was dedicated to building Warren's future, climaxed by his unlikely becoming the Republican's Presidential Nominee in 1920. A tireless campaigner, Florence was admired by Mac Jennings, for her take-charge gift: "She thinks she knows the game better than anybody and will pull it off alone unless some of us fool men ball things up of course. But she is a good gal and a loyal scout."[88] Warren appreciated her meeting women in various parts of Ohio, whom she would advise to talk "'State Pride' Stuff and urge the men to go vote whether they [could] or not."[89]

More basic yet, although Carrie made him ecstatic, Florence made him comfortable. Among other things, it came down to a question of which could be seen as the more trustworthy relationship, that being the one that would wear better, and longer. Without their realizing it, the critical decision for this had been formulated way back in their courtship days, when Florence had pushed for marriage, regardless of all that weighed against it.

Used to being defiant, Florence had it in her nature to take such a step. She had to have known what others in town knew about a man who had a notorious fondness for the ladies, the same man who, as rumor had it, supposedly had left a tell-tale toothbrush in the abode of a Marion widow.[90] .But none of that would slow down the woman he would at first call Boss, and to whom he was her Sonny (Dean, 21).

Having established a pre-marital claim on him, Florence felt that, even before they tied the knot, her hold was strong enough to handle the approaches of other women. During courtship, she would, in fact, track him down on suspicious occasions, such as a jaunt out of town to see a former girlfriend. On his return, he was met at the train station by Florence's vociferous reminder that he was not going to get away with pursuing other company (Shadow, 84f.).

I have cited the advantages which they came to realize would be derived from their union, as when Florence got Warren into politics in 1899, but their sense of mutual benefits thrived well beyond that critical event. As First Lady, she almost immediately settled into a role she was naturally adapted to. On her own, she developed an amicable relationship with reporters, unafraid to give straightforward answers to political questions. In effect, Florence Harding was a force to be reckoned with.

Going well beyond what prior First Ladies did, she made public speeches, and, good at public relations, she opened the White House to tourists and escorted them through rooms, in addition to her reviving such events as the Easter Egg Roll. She would also undertake independent responsibilities, as with her special interest in looking after the well-being of wounded veterans.

However, there was a down side to her aggressiveness. For one thing, it got her a bad reputation. In Margaret Truman's book on First Ladies, she compared Warren Harding's blighted reputation with a similar one that could be reserved for his wife. Truman entitled her Florence Harding Chapter as, "The (Probably) Worst First Lady."[91] At least part of the low opinion of Florence would rest on her having shamelessly taken charge of Warren. She would do so more extensively after his election than before, which had already been much.

As a neighbor purportedly observed, she "runs her house; [she]

runs the paper...runs Warren, runs everything but the car" (Truman, 234). Florence made no effort to disguise her overbearing attitude. Nan Britton recalls that in familiar conversation, Florence would frequently correct Warren with remarks like, "Now, Warren, you don't know anything about it," or, "Well, Warren, I know better" (PD, 15).

Setting aside her doubts—and indeed fears—about his running for President, Florence's dominance not only expanded during his time in office, but she proudly brandished the fact. "I know what's best for the President. I put him in the White House," she said, convinced, she added, that "he does well when he listens to me and poorly when he does not" (First Ladies, 234, 233).

There was her initial fear, oft noted, that, should he become President, that role might be his death warrant, based on the prediction of her Psychic, Madame Marcia (Shadow, 353f.). On that worry, Florence had, at first, tried to protect him from seeking the Nomination. Not easily dismissed as a mere crackpot, Marcia was taken seriously by as rational a Presidential wife as Edith Wilson. Marcia's reputation had, for example, included a prediction of Garfield's assassination.

It would be difficult to gainsay the self-aggrandizement in Florence's protective attitude, as Warren's rising political star greatly advanced her own interests, giving her a position she savored. She made no attempt to hide her delight in finding herself at the center of power on Warren's winning the Presidency.

Her attitude was to have him simply make the most of his unrealized potential. This he recognized more appreciatively than apprehensively, noting how busy she was at "directing the affairs of government...[being] full fledged in expressing her opinion as to how the Executive should perform his duties." She could go so far as to make changes in Warren's State of the Union Address, one change being a removal of the idea that he might accept some form of the League of Nations.[92]

Harry Daugherty observed that Warren, being lucky to have good counsel close at hand, "held the profoundest respect for her judgment" (Florence, 162). As previously cited, when Warren began to lose heart over his poor showing in his early run for the Nomination, Florence saw to it that he stayed put and remained in the race.

This was but one instance of her validating the assumption that she made a President of the man, a position that many saw him as unsuited for, including importantly placed friends like Nicholas Murray Butler. In making a President of her husband, star-gazing Florence made one of herself, convinced she was the real thing.

True enough, once Florence set foot in the Oval Office, tailor made for her instinct to take command, she came into her natural element. But there was also another dimension to this situation. Going back to how they responded to a predictably difficult marriage, one finds that Florence, was clearly the more dynamic of the two, and often the more interesting one. Carl Anthony, in writing a voluminous book on the Hardings, made it primarily about Florence, named first in his title, the last part of which does not mention Warren by name, proposing only to treat the Death of America's Most Scandalous President. There was ample justification for Anthony's concentrating on Florence, she being the one who had originally made a political animal out of Warren.

At first, unsure of himself, Warren, when given a push by Florence, realized she was a reliable advisor. Without her backing, he might not have decided to try a move up from the local to a state-level office, and on to the national one. His career, in a nutshell, evolved under the guidance of his wife.

As previously noted, Florence's political involvement was greatest during Warren's tenure as President, when her management skills were at their height, and she took advantage of having a free use of them. She would practically create a dual Presidency by expanding her First Lady's role to the point of assuming an unprecedented level of power. For Warren, Florence was the ideal on-the-job helpmate, in lieu of one in the bedroom, a compromise that he was perfectly willing to accept.

He relied on her judgment in a variety of key matters, and, given that authority, she involved herself in such concerns as revising—at times, censoring—his speeches. For example, as he was drafting a Congressional address, she excised a proposal that Presidents be granted a six year term, an idea of little pertinence that would go nowhere in Congress.

As observed by Kathleen Lawler, an aide to Albert Fall, Warren had become so accustomed to consulting Florence that he rarely made an important decision without getting her opinion on it. With Warren having an easy-going style, and Florence a driving one, it seemed that the Presidency meant more to her than it did to him, which became so widely known that the Press made hay of it (Florence, 339f.).

It was Florence's nature to assume dominion where she saw an open field for it, a trait usually resented by men. The extent to which she tried to take over Warren's Presidency is reminiscent, mutatis mutandis, of Edith Wilson's assumption of the Presidential role in making critical decisions for her husband, even before his disabling stroke.

The reason behind Florence's taking part in the Presidency was simple. More than anything, what gave Florence the opening to do so was the fact that Warren came to dislike being President. For example, wearied by the railroad strike in the summer of 1922, to be shortly followed by the coal miners' strike, both nationally disabling events, Warren found himself a disabled President. He wrote Dick Child ambassador to Italy that the Presidency was "an unattractive business," adding, significantly, "unless one relishes the exercise of power" (Florence, 360).

Worse yet was the predicament of the most powerful man in the country finding himself powerless. He had to nudge his Attorney General to get an injunction that would bail him out of the railroad strike. However, it was an injunction which bordered on being unconstitutional in its severity. Frustrated, Warren felt like he couldn't win. Reason enough for his wanting to turn the job over to someone else.

But if one looks at how Florence took charge, that doesn't mean he outright turned his job over to this aggressive wife. All that can be said of his weaknesses—accented by Florence's strengths—doesn't, however, diminish his own strengths. When he took on the pressure to make a worthy record for himself during his first year in Office, he functioned very well on his own, and got stellar backing from the Press.

Florence had a lust for power. Not so Warren, who would shine in his capacity to get things done by effective persuasion, leaning on Congress to follow his leadership on, for example, taxes and tariffs. He knew how to make politics work. He was smooth, she abrasive. Florence got ahead of herself. She went so far as to consider herself more the politician than he was, ignoring how smoothly he operated in that capacity, and how effectively.

There were those complementary political skills which came naturally to Warren, such as his ability to bring opposing politicians together in the interests of Party. He had done it masterfully as Lieutenant Governor in the Ohio Legislature, which got him known in the Party. It was as if her work involved substance, and his personality. But he had a better grasp of the difficulties of running the Presidency. If, as Daugherty observed, Florence enjoyed the Office more than he did, that was because he felt its responsibilities more acutely.

Warren made no bones about giving Florence credit for being his boss, which went over big as a campaign ploy. This became so widely known that a Life Magazine illustration was captioned "The Chief Executive and Mr. Harding." She took such pride in how the Press treated her Executive role that she clipped a picture of the two of them captioned "Our Boss and His Boss." An admiring editorial wrote of "Mrs. Harding's First Year in Office" (Florence, 344, 352). The jokes proliferated, and Harding shared in the laugh.

In his Inside Story, Harry Daugherty tailored events to suit his self-serving purposes, but there was no need for him to be other than straightforward in his observation that Florence "was intensely interested in his work and watched carefully to see that he made no mistakes. If he did she was keen 'to pick him up'" (Inside Story, 170f.).

This is not to say her decisions were always for the good, as noted with her misjudgment of Albert Fall. But, as has been the case with every President, it was essential for each of them to have a trusted advisor and all purpose assistant at hand, as with Franklin Roosevelt's Harry Hopkins, to name but one. Among First Lady's few were as influential as Florence. Eleanor Roosevelt, for example, mostly carved out a separate role for herself involved with social issues, while Florence placed herself right in the Oval Office itself.

Earlier, there were two notable decisions in which she had been significantly involved. The first was her support for Harry Daugherty's persuading Warren to run for the Senate seat being vacated by Theodore Burton. Harding had let it be known that, while he wouldn't directly seek the nomination, he wouldn't decline "any draft made upon [him] by [his] party." It was in relation to this feigned reluctance that Harry made his oft quoted remark about dealing with Warren's sleepy indifference to political aspiration: the one about "a turtle sunning himself on a log," whom he "pushed into the water."

Harding had indeed been sunning himself in Daytona, Florida, when Harry approached him about entering that 1914 Senatorial race. While Harry claimed responsibility for activating Warren, Florence's close-up push was more likely to have been the decisive one.

There was another reason for Harding to hold back on what would have been his desire to jump right into the political waters. The situation with the Senate was complicated by Florence's having fallen so gravely ill in October, 1913, that she had to be confined to bed for six weeks. As she was suffering from a heart problem, exacerbated by a nervous breakdown, the doubt over her ability to survive was greater than it had been on other occasions, such as that on the kidney operation in 1905.

That warm feeling Warren had for Florence went beyond practical considerations. Her loyalty meant everything to him. She had stood by him at every turn in his political fortunes, as, for example, with her having been right there beside him when he made the inflammatory speech in Birmingham, Alabama advocating the enfranchisement of blacks. For a man whose sex drive could demolish decency, it spoke volumes that he would prefer an unattractive woman with piano legs and a practical mind over Carrie Phillips, a Gibson Girl beauty, images of whose naked figure bedeviled his reminiscences.

Warren liked Florence's boldness, based on which there were occasions when Florence took it upon herself to reverse a decision of his that she disagreed with. One important instance of this occurred when Warren, seeing his low vote count in the early going at the 1920 Nominating Convention, decided that he wanted to tell Harry Daugherty he was pulling out of contention. Florence, on the spur of the moment, seized the phone to cry, "we're in this fight 'til hell freezes over!" (Florence, 178). They were in it together through every turn in his political life from that point forward.

CHAPTER 46

"The War Of The Women"

WARREN HARDING HAD A KNACK for putting himself in maximal jeopardy only to come out with minimal pain. On the job, this applied to unsupervised staff and ill-advised friendships. In his personal life it was women. His need of them could at times become manic. There was an instance, during his term as Senator, when it apparently got out of hand. As Russell reports, Harding had written "several sportive letters…to a Washington woman of clouded reputation." So great a risk did Harding hazard, that, when the letters were put up for sale, Daugherty had to quickly pay for their retrieval (Shadow, 432).

Although Warren was forced to make some critical decisions regarding his marriage, there was one Florence made that would seem to have put his reputation in jeopardy. And she put it out in the open. It had to do with her rivalry with Carrie for possession of him. This got to be so intense that it broke out into nothing less than public warfare.

Warren's soft-natured temperament brought out the aggressiveness with which each of these women asserted her claim to him. Both had a case that was backed by his stated allegiance to each of them. His contradictory desire for attachment to the two of them was a fragile fantasy, which he took as far as he could go with it, banking on one for sex, and the other for advice and management.

This collapsed when Carrie, in 1911, just prior to her leaving for Germany, made a last minute effort either to snag him, or at least break up his marriage to the woman she hated. Carrie deliberately wrote Warren a letter which she posted to his home address, knowing Florence would intercept it. Carrie evidently was as frustrated with Warren, as he was with himself for having to live a double life. She wanted to end it, as he couldn't bring himself to do so on his own.

Carrie's use of a vindictive device to pry indecisive Warren loose from Florence had the additional objective of embarrassing Florence, and provoking her to act, if Warren wouldn't. As another effect of Carrie's frustration, she tried to awaken Warren's jealousy by sending him letters she had received from a local admirer, assumedly a Mr. Robinson, just as during her stay in Germany she had let him know she was seeing men of interest to her there.

While the 1911 letter intended to be opened by Florence did get her sufficiently enraged to consider divorce, she was evidently assuaged during a session with Warren's lawyer, Hoke Donithen (Florence, 95f.). The net effect of Carrie's ruse was that it backfired. With Warren having to face a divorce he wasn't prepared for, Carrie only reinforced his fear of losing Florence.

Since Florence's thoughts of divorce were dissipated, Warren's sigh of relief would accompany gratitude for Florence's willingness to keep him. Based on elected offices to come, the incident also cemented their political partnership. Meanwhile, since there was no discernible difference in their relationship in the aftermath, Florence could relish her victory as spite vanquished.

In another instance of the warfare between these women, Florence enjoyed the pay-back of giving Carrie a public scolding for making remarks about the inanity of America's joining the fight against Germany. This happened in the summer of 1918 at the train station on the occasion of Marion's young men entraining to go off to war (Ibid., 152). Florence not only had the satisfaction of having been able to fend off her competitor, but there she was inflicting public embarrassment on her rival.

Nor did that end the dueling. It took two more gratuitous turns. On Notification Day, July 22, 1920, when Harding received official notice of his having won the Republican Nomination for President, he made a speech before a large gathering of proud Marionites. Florence, who had helped Warren put the speech together, was seated on the platform beside him, moving her lips in silent recitation of his words, many of which were hers. On surveying the crowd, she spotted Carrie and getting up, very pointedly shook a fist at her, assuming people would know whom she was singling out, and could guess why (Ibid., 204).

Carrie had to have her pay-back. Violating the agreement she had made to hold her tongue, on being paid off by Albert Lasker to get out of town, she hosted a lawn party to which she invited reporters covering the newly designated Nominee, and as much as confirmed the rumors of her affair with Warren.

Not content with that, knowing what would really provoke Florence, she deliberately approached Warren while he was idly sitting on his front porch. Enraged, out came Florence to pitch a feather duster, followed by a wastebasket, and finally a piano stool sequentially aimed at Carrie. At her departure, Carrie countered by throwing Warren a sweet goodbye kiss. (Shadow, 401f.).

Beginning with the train station episode, these incidents were publicly observed, the last by a history professor, who had no reason to keep his observation confidential. The warfare was out in the open for all of Marion to witness. However much this may have reflected on the two women, it really had no adverse effect on the man over whom they were fighting. Purportedly, it should have, but instead became an extension of Harding's ability to dodge the adverse effects of his liabilities. A likeable person, he liked being liked and somehow cultivated a certain immunity that did much to enable him to advance his career.

However, he was not free of complications. Warren's having had a ravenous entanglement with the most beautiful woman in Marion, who was someone else's wife, while he could not give up his own incompatible wife, made life difficult for all three. Unable to overcome his addiction, he went ahead and got himself heatedly involved with yet another mistress, whom he would genuinely love and want to marry, suppressing the difficulty—indeed impossibity—of getting it done. Remarkably, he survived all of that, and could have gone out a successful and revered President, his personal chaos confined to dismissible rumors, had the grafters in his Administration not brought corruption down on his head.

Carrie had wanted it to be known that she had had an affair Warren just prior to his Presidential campaign. Though embarrassing, not much was made of its occurrence, that being, in a way, understandable, even permissible for a President-to-be frustrated by a marriage that lacked intimacy. Carrie had an ax to grind against Warren, but gave no particulars, beyond what could be observed. Nan had no ax, and had no intention of using something comparable, until forced to publish post-mortem particulars, not commonly done by Presidents' mistresses.

Nan's publication of her poignant love affair with the President was so effectively told that readers ate it up. Obviously, it did not help the image of a President already disgraced. While Warren didn't deserve cries of scandal regarding what went wrong during his Presidency, a sample of his scandalous conduct with a young woman, once in print, was not easy to deflect. When Nan, in frustration—and need—published her memoir, it turned out that the President really had no clothes.

CHAPTER 47

"Warren Deals With Tensions At Home"

From Florence's self-promotional style, one might conclude that she had complete dominance over Warren, whereas, based on numerous incidents, some already cited, it would be closer to the truth to say that she actually had to give him more latitude than he gave her. Unfortunately, that didn't pave the way for a smooth union. Difficulties they continued to have. On the one hand, how they lived with them made for additional problems, and, on the other, it produced some interesting compromises. They couldn't have lived inharmoniously on a day to day basis without driving one another crazy.

Warren Harding was not a complicated man. Unpresidentially, he had all of the "regular guy" attributes. He drank, chewed tobacco, enjoyed poker, golf, fishing, off-color jokes, and a prurient interest in women. Much of this was innocuous enough, as with his enjoyment of the "Hulu" dancers on a trip to Hawaii. As for where Florence stood in that world, since she served cocktails with illegal booze in the residence quarters of the White House at the regular poker parties, she could apparently tolerate their heavily male atmosphere—jokes and all.

Though none of that caused any trouble for Warren and Florence, there were instances, added to those already sampled, which disclose the irreconcilable difficulties they went through with one another, despite their ability to make the most of a bad marriage.

With their common interest in politics, they could be companionable, without especially being good companions. For all the help Florence gave him, when Warren was in his element, he was fully capable of thriving on his own. He became a gifted politician known to major figures in the conservative wing of the Republican Party, like William Howard Taft, on behalf of whose successful Presidential campaign he became a spokesman in 1908 (Affair, 27).

At home, it was his wife who had to exercise diplomacy. There were low-level irritants and high-level ones that normally would break a marriage, some of which almost did. Warren's wandering eye being what it was, one has to assume that, for that alone, Florence was finally content to chide him when necessary and otherwise put up with it. Chances are, for example, that, since Warren had a private box curtained off at Washington's Gayety Burlesque, Florence couldn't have been ignorant of it. But if displeased, since she didn't stop it, she could apparently forget about it, strip-tease being an impersonal thing.

Warren was at least shielded from public view and enjoying a harmless pleasure. Had Florence known that two years after their marriage he was taking in a performance of the belly swiveling "Little Egypt" in 1893 at the Chicago World's Columbian Exposition, it is possible that there might have been an objection, but, based on her blind-eye to burlesque, she would likewise have let it pass.

Voyeurism was a trivial thing, certainly an irritant, but it did not weigh greatly on the dissatisfaction at home. What did weigh was the fact that Florence knew she had to keep an eye on his having more than a look around. Mistrust made her edgy, which often resulted in the nagging that was a habitual part of her make-up anyway, taken for granted by those who knew her, though not always by Warren..

With his home life being what it was, Harding frequently became restless in office, and eager to find an escape. In a summary check of correspondence with his long time friend, Frank Edgar Scobey ("Edwardo") over a span of five years alone (1914 to 1919) one could find over twenty instances in which he mentioned looking for, and usually finding, an opportunity to get away somewhere. This does not count his speech-making trips to local Chautauquas, or those on the campaign trail. Nor would it account for unreportable adventures like, for example, his week-end trysts with Carrie in out of town hotels.

An indication that it was practically a necessity for him to get away is his having planned a Chautauqua tour on 7 May, 1918 that would take him on a six week trip through the Northeast and demandingly commit him to one a day speeches, six days a week (WGH to FES, 7 May, 1918). Florence suspiciously went with him on a number of those trips, and doubtless, out of a distrust she couldn't explicitly come out with, she would, en route, get on him for unspecified cause.

After Warren's affair with Susie Hodder, Florence followed a lesson she had learned from that type of experience and spelled it out in her calendar book: "never to let [a husband] travel alone." During his Lieutenant-Governorship, Warren Harding made a hit for himself with a rousing speech he gave at the State Republican Convention, whereby he got himself known as a crowd pleaser.

Shortly reputed to be a natural orator, he was picked up by the Redpath Lyceum Bureau in 1904 and assigned to the Chautauqua tours that were routed through Ohio and much of the mid-west. As his going alone piqued Florence's suspicion, she commonly went with him, which on occasion became an irritant for Warren.

Francis Russell offered a dramatization of how such a travel episode supposedly played out. He had Florence "rasping at [Warren] all the way, querulous, persistent, while he sulked in his plush [railway car] seat,...his frown growing deeper under her nagging until finally he would turn on her with 'Goddammit, shut up!' and she would lapse into brief, offended silence" (Shadow, 161). Anthony, in covering the same incident, also undocumented, added that Florence's irritation had something to do with the heat and its being one of their many "bumpy, dusty rides," during which Anthony pictured Warren as "enduring her squawks about his cigar, posture, and suit" (Florence, 78).

Assuming this wouldn't have been concocted out of thin air, it sounds like an intimate look at a credible possibility, not ordinarily knowable.[93] Significantly, what it discloses is that Warren did not suffer his dissatisfaction in silence and wouldn't allow himself to be cowed by Florence. It also indicates that she, usually featured as the dominant partner in their marriage, could herself be cowed and could equivalently suffer in silence his chastisement for her cranky moods.

In any event, for all the good they each derived from their marriage, there were sufficient grounds for mutual dissatisfaction, beyond uncomfortable trips that got on Florence's nerves. When Warren shared his dissatisfactions with Nan, it wasn't just to offer an excuse for his needing her company.

As Warren laid it out for Nan, there may have been situations that called for the husband's obligatory kiss, but, he emphasized, "My kiss for her is most perfunctory, I can assure you!" He could quite honestly tell Nan that "it had been many years since his home situation had been satisfying." More than justification for his intimacy with Nan, his dissatisfaction had been a chronic torment, for which Nan gave him passionate relief (PD, 209, 44).

Considering the three decade difference in their ages, it was seemingly an affair at once disreputable and desperate, which Warren would take as far as it could go. But, as reported by Nan, there was a lot more to it. For the love-mates, it was a genuine meeting of hearts. Whereas sex was what had kept bringing Carrie back to Warren after their 1911 break-up, from all that one can tell, with Nan, psychological relief was a necessity and love primary.

In any event, if Warren had his complaints, looked at from his wife's point of view, Florence could claim the adultery made hers greater. With Florence being plagued by suspicions of his disloyalty, the two of them occasionally let their discontent get the better of them. There were, in fact, definite occasions on which Florence's rage would reach a flash point, at least two of which are worth noting.

In one, Florence had a healthy suspicion that something was going on between her husband and another woman, of all times, during his Presidency, and, of all places, in the White House. Florence had had a Secret Service Agent (Harry Barker, the first to be assigned to a First Lady) to keep watch on Warren for her, which was more than an effort to let her husband know his Presidency might be at stake. So, there arose this climactic instance in the White House, when she was alerted that something was indeed taking place in the Oval Office. On the spur of the moment, she was all for bursting in on the lovers.

Luckily for Nan, Florence was unable to think a woman she regarded as a mere child could have been her husband's consort. Luckier yet, Nan had a Secret Service Agent of her own to be on the look out for her. At first, it had been Jim Sloan, and, when Florence had him fired, he was replaced by Walter Ferguson, "Fergy," who was equally vigilant. Nan's love letters, on the other hand, were addressed to Warren's valet, Arthur Brooks.

So, since Warren had protectors, Nan's surreptitious visits evidently were not uncommon. Florence, on the other hand, may very well have had had her suspicions, though, until the dust-up, she had apparently let things ride.

However, on the occasion of Harry Barker's alarm, Florence had to respond. She rushed to the door of the White House cloak room, Nan and Warren's favorite nook, but, unexpectedly, she was brought up short by Fergie, who told her that the Oval Office was secured by Secret Service regulations. Thus Fergie detained a fuming Florence long enough for Nan to be escorted out the side door (Florence, 374).

A confrontation there may have been afterwards, but there is no evidence that Florence and Warren were seen openly quarreling. Quarrels they surely had had, probably over situations not unlike the White House episode, and on at least one instance the aftermath was observed, and an explanation given. This occurred at Christmas time in 1921, after Harding had experienced first-year successes for his Administration, which, in addition to the season, should have put him in a pretty good mood.

However, after Florence's personal physician, Charles Sawyer, had given Charles Forbes a report of Warren's gloomy mood, Warren's sister Carolyn urged the ever-cheerful Forbes to bring Warren out of it. What Sawyer had told Forbes was, "My God! They had a hell of a row this morning" (Shadow, 487). With Harding lamenting the unhappiness of his marriage, Forbes later divulged that Warren told him the reason for his depression was the feeling of how empty his life was.

There was no reason to explain what the emptiness stemmed from, since the row had explicitly been with Florence, whose own discontent had apparently flared up, on what probably was not an isolated occasion. Warren's unhappiness at Christmas time had to have been taken as a comment on Florence, which could only have aggravated her own discontent.

Feeling boxed in with his marriage during his Presidency, Warren, being stressed at home and on the job, found relief in the relationship that Nan Britton describes. His seeing her seems to have become so great a need that, as Nan depicts his love, it was a joy that grew into another of Warren's dependencies. At the same time, his despair over the situation with Florence seems to have been an on and off thing. Prior to his finding Nan, Time, plus his leaning on Florence for official assistance, apparently worked as healers. Then, of course, pre-Nan, there had been Carrie.

Since the question of how they could continue to live with their difficulties came up on more then one occasion, as they lived through them, Florence apparently couldn't stay mad, and Warren couldn't stay hurt. They had to get on with their lives.

Luckily, they had a sense of humor. That the two of them could in fact share a laugh over her domineering, indicates there were times when their relationship seemed to have mellowed.

This included open kidding about Florence's nagging, an instance of which had occurred as early as 1907. In a Christmas greeting the Hardings were sending to their good friends, George and Coonie Christian, Florence dictated the message and Warren signed himself, "Secretary to Mrs. Harding." He added, "The Duchess has been bossing Santa Claus, because he stands for it and she likes to boss" (<u>Florence</u>, 86). Part of Warren Harding's charm was his ability to laugh at himself. Evidently, he had been able to stimulate a like ability in Florence; no easy matter.

Significantly, that Christmas, was the very one when Warren and Carrie recognized that they had fallen in love, and had agreed on using future Christmases to mark their anniversary. Conceivably, that would have been a reason for Warren's sudden joviality. Thoughts of his having Carrie could make him forgiving at home. Ten years later, in June, 1917, Warren was writing that he felt his bumpy relationship with Carrie was really over (Affair, 252). And, with Carrie's erstwhile lover ready to move on, in mid-1917 he happened to have had young Nan Britton waiting in the wings.

However euphoric at first, Warren's relationship with Nan would eventuate in heart-ache. Lady's man that he was, Warren Harding never reached a lasting homeostasis with at least one of his women. In Nan's case, as in Carrie's, Florence stood in the way. It was his dependency on her that inhibited Warren from finding closure with his first-rate manager.

CHAPTER 48

"His Heart-Ache"

THE EXTENSIVE INVOLVEMENT THAT FLORENCE had in Warren's political life occurred in an era when it was taken for granted that the highest echelons of power were, as in business, exclusively a male preserve. That Warren could accept Florence's take-over against the background of a male chauvinist environment suggests both his confidence in her and the alleviation she gave him at work, which, in year two of his Presidency, was beginning to wear on him. As Florence relished the chance to wield power, his granting it constituted a sublimating pleasure for her. Yet, as she knew he had a need she couldn't meet, her diary nostrums show a resignation that he would find his own sublimation.

Taken as a whole, Warren G. Harding's Presidential life was not a happy one. He had one fruitful year as President, the first, but, the irresolvable strikes in his second year gave him a taste of the down-side to the Office. His marriage, being incomplete, left much to be desired there. Moreover, the very fact of his having had to retain and pacify this helpful but overbearing wife, didn't make it any easier for him to live with her. A serious concern when chronically ill, she also induced a good deal of worry.

Though Warren had a satisfying relationship with Nan Britton, he repressed the idea that it couldn't be legitimized. So, all around, while there were grounds for emotional frustration, it wasn't expressly mentioned where it was most likely to have been, in Warren's correspondence with his good friend Frank Edgar Scobey. Unhappiness, as such, didn't come up.

Among the personal matters Warren would share, not once did he suggest that he had been plagued by frustration, certainly not the sexual kind, though they talked and wrote enough about sex. Suppressed, frustration would get disguised by humor, a typically male response that took some interesting turns—one being dirty jokes, low-brow sublimation. As will be seen, women, the source of both his joy and unhappiness, interestingly, were often the butt of those jokes.

So rather than claim frustration, Warren, for Scobey's benefit, would, on the contrary, register a need to observe propriety, a joke unto itself. Though it might pass as sincere (even if offered in mock sincerity) the call for propriety was declared more out of a need for cover than from a sense of guilt. Nor, for that matter, would Warren have been able to come out and voice the uncomfortable truth that for much of his life, he had not enjoyed a lasting experience of love, per se, above and beyond sex.

He thought he had had it with Carrie, but that would get dissipated. He clearly seemed to have recovered it with Nan, but the more emphatically he expressed his love, the more suspicious the expression was. For one thing, he had to keep Nan secret from Scobey, as much as from anyone else, trusted friend or not. Word of adultery was normally not shared. Since Nan did Warren so much good, any talk about it was meant for her ears alone.

There had been the incident cited above, after which he alluded to a feeling of "emptiness" in his life caused by exasperation with Florence. Frustrated that there was no way around the emptiness, he had to move on from it. As that had been disclosed indirectly, and second hand, no particulars came out.

More explicit was a very telling instance of his opening up another time about a sense of emptiness. It came to mind for Warren in the way he sympathized with Mrs. Scobey (Evaland) over her being "ill with an attack of heart trouble."

Wanting Scobey to give her the reassurance that people with heart trouble "reach a ripe old age," Warren went on to confess that he had

had "a serious spell of it" himself, adding: "as a matter of fact I have never gotten entirely free of it. More than that, I am not thinking of the kind of heart trouble that you are."[94]

This letter happens to have been written less than a year after Warren and Nan had become intimate, and they continued to share an enriching relationship, which had begun with heated kissing in the bridal suit of New York's Manhattan Hotel.[95] If heart ache was related to Nan, it would probably have been based on the unfortunate status of their love; so great and regarding its longevity so uncertain. Moreover, as Warren was "never…entirely free" of heart ache, he had to have been including Carrie, and, overall, the lack of a relationship that gave him lasting satisfaction. Under the circumstances, Warren meant to be ambiguous, and let it go at that.

On the other hand, if the heart ache had to do with Nan alone, was it based on his knowing their relationship had no future so long as Florence lived? If so, the ache was that he couldn't have his love and couldn't let her go. Obviously, that was heart ache enough—twice over, as the incomplete situation with Nan replicated his Carrie Phillips dilemma. After their apparent break-up, by 1918, his connection with Carrie had not been completely severed. In a sense, it hurt that he couldn't give up on it.

Since Scobey, to whom Warren had written of the heart ache, knew nothing about Nan (he in fact said so when her book came out) he would only know that his friend's reference to a figurative trouble of the heart might have had reference to the absence of a fitting relationship in his married life.[96] It might not have occurred to Scobey how his own wife could underscore Warren's heart-ache, but, if that were so, this friend would surely have been gentleman enough to block it out. The attention Warren gave Evaland would come up again.

Whatever the provocation for Warren Harding's thoughts of disappointment in love, in 1918, at age 53, he was doing rather well for himself, heart ache notwithstanding. Nan had come into his life in the previous year, and, with her, he had found a tender young woman who by her devotion provided a reprieve from the trail of fruitless relationships.

Sex renewed at middle age was no small element in Warren's treasuring his relationship with Nan. In fact, because of his prior deprivation, sexual allusions never having been far from Warren's mind, it took very little for them to re-surface. Several come up in the same letter (of 9 March, 1918) in which he mentioned heart-ache.

As a casual aside, he had to treat Scobey with word of how friend Mac Jennings had become "so fascinated with the short skirts and low-necks" of ladies in New York that he had little enthusiasm for returning to Washington. That same letter was begun with Warren saying he had a store of new jokes and parlor stories that, in time, he'd be providing for Scobey's "repetory" [sic]—some to be sampled shortly. Since there could be nothing specific about sexual frustration in letters to his friend, could the jokes have been a way of sublimating it?

CHAPTER 49

"Has A Heart For Florence Too"

HAVING HAD HIS REVERIE ON heart ache, Warren later in the same year would be confronted with another type of emotional incident: the recurrence of Florence's kidney ailment. Suddenly, his attitude towards a wife constitutionally given to nagging would be transformed, though she, on the contrary, was not. Imprisoned by bed rest, she could, in fact, be more of a nag, and a good deal more irritating than when well.

On the incident in question, far from wanting to strike back, Warren responded indulgently, indeed tenderly, when she would boss him around during her illnesses. He could be a prince of a husband.

There was no minimizing the painfulness of hydro-nephritis, and Harding certainly didn't. He, on the contrary, was distressed over the toll it took on Florence, having often enough seen her in the throes of pain. This was evidently a congenital problem, as Florence's father would die of the same kidney disease, suggesting a dim prognosis for his daughter. Following Florence's kidney operation in 1905, the problem recurring in 1913 was complicated by a heart condition, which inclined the Hardings' doctor friend, Charles Sawyer, to believe she was in a crisis stage from which she might not survive.

The ailment returned in 1918, and was grave enough for Florence to be once more confined to bed for six weeks. In the letter Warren had written from her beside on 30 December, 1918, in which he was sending the Scobeys a Happy New Year's greeting, he expressed his concern for Florence's well-being with just the right touch. He used a lightness of mood as part of an effort to lift her spirits.

The Duchess, he wrote, "delights to issue orders no matter what is the state of her health, and it is the writer's business to receive them," regardless of her wrongly identifying the placement of an Indian floor covering that he was ordered to mention in a thank-you letter. Should it happen that she "can't issue twelve separate and distinct orders in short minutes," Warren continued, it's time to "send for the undertaker."[97] In effect, Warren was saying he cheerfully acquiesced in her bossing and would try what he could to dispel the gloom aroused by her condition. After all, "the patient, [poor wife] was in the dumps" (Ibid.).

Divorce being out of the question at such a time, there is reason to wonder whether the undertaker reference might have been a Freudian slip. Considering the moral side of Harding's carrying on under those circumstances, probably the best that can be made of a bad state of affairs is that, since he was living a contradictory life (formally married, but physically not) he could correspondingly feel compassion for his sick wife, while enjoying the company of a woman who revived his sense of manhood.

That would give Harding an available rationalization to salve a confused conscience. Extra-murally happy, he could afford to be intra-murally charitable, which, though it earns him no great credit, indicates how he had to navigate a double life.

Out of all of the discordant emotions that complicated Harding's double life, a fairly good sampling of what that situation looked like emerges from that letter which he wrote to Scobey on 30 December, 1918, particularly when it is taken in context with collateral events which preceded and followed that date.

There are times when one comes across a letter that has several levels of meaning, all subject to relevant implications. This "Happy New Year's" letter was one of them. It was capped off by a salacious type limerick, of a sort that could be passed around in light hearted conversation, but rarely offered in correspondence, even among close friends. In the Harding-Scobey social circle, there were occasions for fun when dirty jokes would get out. These unexpectedly came from Warren, who put up a façade of restraint, as opposed to the persona Scobey offered of a dirty old man, for whom these jokes were appropriate.

PART VI:

A TIME FOR JOKES

CHAPTER 50

"A Revealing Letter"

THE 30 DECEMBER, 1918 LETTER was a rambling long-hand piece of some length, which, among other things, incongruously included a limerick containing the most explicit sexual reference that Harding would gratuitously commit to paper in any of the letters he wrote to Scobey. It was a bit of male conviviality out of keeping with the occasion, and, though an item of passing amusement, it touched on a sore point. However, it will be best to delay treating the limerick, since there was much else of significance that relates to the context of this letter.

For one thing, placed in relation to the time when it was written, the letter contains some informative ironies, in fact, dramatic ones. On the matter of chronology, it was written eight days before the death of Teddy Roosevelt, which was to reawaken Harding's prospect of running for the Presidential Nomination, a possibility that would shortly tighten the need for discretion. Prior to that sobering event, Harding had been enjoying the carefree mood of his Senatorial days.

The letter was also written shortly before another significant event that occurred on an evening in early January, 1919 (possibly not far from the date of Roosevelt's death) when Warren's relationship with Nan intensified to the point that they stayed longer than usual in his Senate Office. So carried away were they that they ignored how late it got, as well as the rules governing the presence of guests on those premises.

Furthermore, in the heat of passion, what they likewise ignored was the absence of "the usual paraphernalia which [they] always took to hotels" (*PD*, 76). In retrospect, they decided that that was the night when their child was conceived. There is further dramatic irony in Nan's recalling, just prior to this event, how she and Warren had often talked about "how wonderful it would be to have a child," which wasn't very seriously entertained, as Warren thought he could be "careless of consequences, feeling sure he was not now [at his age] going to become a father" (Ibid. 74f.).

His actually becoming one turned out to be much less of a blessing than Warren had innocently believed it would be. Suddenly made a reality, the child became an unneeded burden for him, and a burden as well for Nan, but one she would cherish all the more, considering that this 'poor girl' would be faced with an anomalous status.

Since Florence's illness hung on, at the same time that Warren's relationship with Nan was rising in intensity, he had to deal with some contesting emotions. Upset over Florence's suffering, while concealing his excitement with Nan, he also had to conceal from Nan the feeling that he was not really as happy as he said he was over her pregnancy.

Surrounding that reckless event in the Senate Office (and following others when the lovers were equally heedless of contraception) there were a number of instances in which Nan records that Warren, believing Florence might die of her disease, irrationally fantasized the opportunity he and Nan would have for a heaven-sent future (e.g., *PD*, 74). Out of mind was the question of how a child would play into that future should Florence survive. Nan mentioned times when she felt that Warren, in a flash of inflated hopefulness, would feel good about the prospect of fatherhood.

But he also wavered and would contradict himself, suggesting that the situation should best be "handled." Nan was quick to let him know that "his apparent indifference to [what] an operation" meant, did not sit well with her. It indeed made her "all the more determined to *have* the child" (My ital.). Unsettled, Warren could at one and the same time give Nan the heady feeling that he liked having a child, while, on second thought, wanting her nonetheless to consider the remedy of pills.

There was much vacillation, Harding's non-resolution of which was circumvented by his telling Nan he wanted her to be free from worry, though her attitude inconvenienced the dissimilar freedom he would want for himself (PD, 79, 80, et passim). On top of that came Florence. As her confinement hung on, the uncertainty over her fate ratcheted up the turmoil for Warren, concurrently sympathetic with a wife in her near-death condition, while looking for the resolution of it.

At the same time, there he was writing Scobey a frivolous Happy New Year's greeting, accompanied by an inappropriate limerick, and concern for his wife, at the same time that he had all-consuming thoughts of Nan, both buoyant and worrisome. Along with the joy she brought Warren, Nan at the same time added complication to his already complicated situation. In a matter of weeks, he would have to deal with the danger of possible disclosure that, as Presidential Candidate, he was going to be the father of an illegitimate child who could not be acknowledged.

There were lasting ramifications stemming from the anxious turn of events following Warren's light-hearted mood of 30 December, 1918. With the advance of Nan's pregnancy, Warren, being hard pressed for a way out, would change the subject. Again bringing up the probability of Florence's demise, he told Nan he was certain that, in any event, it would occur "far in advance of his own." This came out in connection with his telling Nan, with "undisguised enthusiasm," that he would like to "take the baby [himself] and make her a real Harding!" (PD, 130). Wanting to dispel Nan's confusion he accelerated his own.

Decisive events that needed clear-headed attention were bearing down on him. So, in the heat of his campaign for the Presidential Nomination, Warren would feel he needed to keep a respectable distance from Nan (though sending her, "$100 or $150 at a time," PD, 128).

Depressed by thoughts of the illegitimate child hanging over his head, he would unaccountably seek consolation, from whom? Carrie Phillips, of course! Hoping for a sympathetic shoulder to lean on, he would instead find Carrie's to be stone cold, in addition to which he would be treated to a tirade of mockery, including the accusation of his having other adulterous adventures topping the one secretly in progress (Shadow, 344).

Prior to the complication introduced by Nan's pregnancy, Warren's outlook had been fixed on the other complication. With Florence so near death during the time of her long confinement, it was not unlikely that, at the time of his 30 December, 1918 letter, Harding could envision her demise occurring at any time. In his perturbed state of mind, the loss of a loyal wife and valued consultant had not yet sunk in, but its likelihood was there, and compounded his awkward ambivalence toward Florence.

He was greatly worried about Florence's illness, more about her possible death, and still more about her possible survival. But he had become inured to complications. It was very likely that, not long after this same December, when his relationship with Nan would be at its best and just after Florence's condition had been at its worst, Warren would be telling Nan their situation might be resolved by fate, as the doctors were "sure [Florence] would die" (PD, 234).[98] Since there was no other way out, Time might resolve the mixed loyalties that burdened his conscience.

Florence's condition was indeed dire. As Warren had written Scobey, over a month earlier, hydro-nephritis had swelled her kidney to eight to ten times its normal size, and, at that point, it seemed as if her bed-ridden condition might continue indefinitely.[99] But, when he shortly afterwards heard that her death seemed to be impending, Warren had for a while made less of an effort to conceal his relationship with Nan, as he wouldn't mind being seen in public with her (e.g., at restaurants) presumably on the hope it might pave the way for their gaining approval as a socially acceptable couple. That was his state of mind at the end of December, 1918.

Warren was assuming that a seemingly inconclusive future would instead have a favorable outcome for him and Nan. That was what followed from the emotional high of his time with Nan that, in turn, led to her pregnancy. Surely, Nan had high hopes as well, by this time, since their relationship had apparently become regularized. Warren had been slipping out of Washington unnoticed in order to get together with her on almost a weekly basis, a pattern duplicating the one he'd had with Carrie.

His ardor, as reported by Nan, had become so strong that Francis Russell had a striking perception of it: "his pangs seemed virginal in their intensity and surpassed any longing he had ever experienced in his life" (Shadow, 295). Strong stuff.

Under the circumstances, Warren Harding was looking toward a new beginning, a promising future with the woman who had really captured his heart. He also knew it would be a struggle to get there. In the process, caught between competing loyalties, Warren's character did not come off looking very well. Amidst his several-sided tensions, being torn this way and that, it would have been amazing if that didn't test his sanity.

CHAPTER 51

"What He Wanted His Friend Had"

COMPOUNDING THE VAGARY OF A future with Nan was Warren's envy of Scobey's marriage to Evaland, a lady very appealing to men. With his own desire for fulfillment seemingly near realization, though precariously so, Warren looked appreciatively upon the relationship that his friend Scobey had found on a permanent basis. .

In comparison with the elevated feelings that Warren was enjoying, there would be an inclination for him to think Scobey didn't sufficiently prize the good woman he had. Evaland apparently had not been his initial love, as he had married her after the loss of his first wife, implying the second might have been subject to comparison. Instructively, Warren had been surprised at learning that Scobey, while married to Evaland, had been in quest of a woman from Nebraska during their 1911 journey to Europe (Affair, 52).

There were other background elements behind the drift of Warren's Happy New Year's greeting to the Scobeys. For all of the kidding that was done about Scobey's presumed extra-marital roaming, which he had his wife unsuccessfully checking up on (mentioned in various letters) there was one letter Scobey interestingly had written to Florence Harding as early as 20 October, 1914, which indicated that his relationship at home seemed quite good, and happy for both partners.

When Scobey took advantage of one of his wife's absences to

indulge in some dancing, he made the pretense of being the mouse at play while the cat was away. Warren would, in keeping with the idiom, play along with the game, noting in the 30 December letter that, whereas in her illness, "the Duchess sins so little and is punished so much," Scobey by contrast, "is punished little, and inferentially he sins awfully." Meanwhile, the presumably virtuous Harding, tongue in cheek, could claim, "it is well to be really good and have no sins to atone [for]" (op. cit., WGH to FES, 30 December, 1918). As with the limerick itself, not the least thing that is wrong with this hypocritical levity is its timing. From what the doctors were saying, Florence seemed to be on her death bed.

Nonetheless, out of this banter, came occasional truths spoken in their ongoing jests, as with an envious attitude in Warren's fondness for Scobey's appealing wife. She was a lady who, among other things, attracted Warren's interest as a great golfer (potentially, a Texas champion in the women's game) and who, far from being prudish, was also an appreciator of his "parlor stories," many risqué.

On a number of occasions, Warren would go out of his way to ask that Scobey inform his wife of a supply of stories he had in store explicitly for her, which, being luridly ripe, were of a type for male enjoyment.[100] In describing the gyrations of "Hulu" dancers (regrettably wearing grass skirts) Warren had specified a certain sensual motion for Evaland's benefit, supposedly wetting her curiosity in a manner not shared with Florence, who habitually objected to his looking at women with a prurient eye.[101]

Aware of how comfortable Harding was with Evaland, Scobey would knowingly mention his wife as one of the "Texas chickens" who could entice him to pay them a visit in San Antonio. (Scobey had certainly noticed something. And didn't mind.) As part of the freedom with which sexual innuendoes were shared with Evaland, it was in a letter addressed specifically to her that Warren noted how Scobey, as Director of the Mint, would be called upon to "choose," at leisure, the "models for the feminine figures" used "to decorate our various coins," an enterprise in which the President would shamelessly participate.[102]

Although Warren Harding and Frank Scobey were staunchly

conservative Republicans, that had nothing to do with their personal morality. Warren outright liked it that Evaland enjoyed anything with a sexual innuendo fully as much as he did. Enhancing her attractiveness to Harding, she evidently regaled their social group by bringing forth parlor stories of her own which suggested an appreciation of sex itself.

On more sober issues, Harding, as noted, had empathized with Evaland on learning of her heart condition, and he had also offered the compliment that her strength of character would help her cope with worry over her mother's illness.[103] This was a woman after his own heart, which Warren made no effort to disguise. He liked her enough to want her to know that his heart ache was figurative.

There were times when he wanted Scobey to remind Evaland that she owed him a letter, and he believed that, despite all of the supposed philandering Scobey indulged in during her absences, Warren—projecting—felt her husband would surely have reason to genuinely rejoice on her return.

As for the "chickens," whom Scobey courted in his escapades, since most were likely women in their social circle, his playing around wouldn't have been unknown to his wife. Observed by Warren, this could very well have raised the question in his mind of whether Evaland was permissive, something difficult to ignore. In contrast to Florence, Evaland's tolerance obviously would become as much enjoyed by Warren as it was by Scobey. Their jokes in themselves suggested a permissive atmosphere, which Scobey repeatedly used to bring the Hardings to his San Antonio home.

Evaland Scobey's personality had a certain appeal to men, which did not go unnoticed by others whose attitude duplicated Warren Harding's. For example, a friend, William Fordyce, likewise envious of the fine wife Scobey enjoyed, told him, in terms that might very well have come from Warren himself, that his wife was "the most attractive and interesting woman," to whom Scobey should get down on his knees and "pray every night that [he had] been fortunate enough to secure her as a life partner." [104]

Evaland's special appeal had not been disguised by Warren, who, three years earlier, had expressed corresponding sentiments. It was in the summer of 1915, that, with Evaland being ill, as was Florence again, Warren wrote Scobey: "The last time I saw [Evaland] she looked so good that I didn't suppose she would go anywhere, unless it was to a divorce court seeking the deserved freedom from a gay and festive husband like you have proven yourself to be" (Affair, 155f.)

Coincidentally, the letter from Fordyce was sent less than two weeks prior to Warren's Happy New Year's letter, which became a dual reminder for Scobey of how lucky he was—for Warren, a reminder of how unlucky he was. The effect of those letters would, by implication, also have offered a clear indication to Scobey of the contrastingly difficult time Warren was having in his marriage, never directly mentioned. Since so many knew of his relationship with Carrie Phillips, Warren's best friend could not have been unaware of it. It was certainly obvious what a lady's man his friend was.

Hence the frequent mention of enticing San Antonio "chickens," as just the way to regale this Ohio friend. And, Warren, via limerick, was returning the favor. More importantly, he was providing an item for Evaland's off-color enjoyment. She being his type of woman, could it be that he had been assuming she enjoyed the actual pleasure (denied him at home) as much as he did, in secret? Warren and Evaland seemed to have had quite an affinity for one another; certainly an understanding.

—All of this in a letter that began with mock indulgent levity intended to lift the spirit of Warren's bed-ridden wife, and a letter, as well, that would wander into a practically flirtatious interest in the wife of his philandering best friend.

CHAPTER 52

"The Limerick"

As for the limerick itself, I have called it gratuitous, and it was, in more ways than one. For, since Warren indicated he thought Scobey might already have heard it (indeed, he noted, "maybe you have <u>had</u> it"—my ital) there was no reason for the limerick to be sent, which meant Warren's doing so was primarily for his own benefit, and for Evaland's. The explicit nature of the limerick gives it a celebratory tone related to Warren's felicitous relations with Nan, for example, which had liberated him from a long void. The frivolity also helped to relieve Warren of the nervous uncertainty over Florence's future and his own.

This becomes apparent in a caveat Harding registered immediately prior to his writing the limerick: "It is useless to expect all one wishes," he sighed (op. cit., WGH to FES, 30 December, 1918). While this had to do with his regret over not being able to have a dog of his own in Washington, the caveat plainly makes a statement of broader disappointment, never far from Warren's mind, consumed as he was with a too-good-to-be true situation not yet made secure.

Security, of course, was contingent on what happened with Florence, who had had a history of making miraculous comebacks from previous sieges of nephritis. But, according to the doctors, this time it seemed different. The context of its timing makes the limerick more than the simple little thing it was. It reads:

"There was a young man named Skinner
Who took a young woman to dinner.

At a quarter to nine,
They started to dine
At a quarter to ten it was in her.
The dinner, not Skinner."

As indicated, this was embedded in that rambling seven page letter written in long hand, to avoid its getting into the hands of a censorious secretary. With sex inappropriately surfacing in a letter that begins with sympathetic tolerance for a sick wife's ordering him around, Warren's mood becomes a sign of his underlying frustration over what had been lacking in a bedroom where the orders were given.

As a sign of how flippant the use of this limerick was, Warren would add as an after thought, "This may seem like slow dining to Scobey, according to Mack Jennings." In other words, this thing had apparently been passed around among Warren and Scobey's friends. It regaled them in the retelling, and, in this instance, Warren could expect that it would do the same for Evaland.

On the one hand, ridiculous as it was, there were serious ramifications implied by this little joke. Warren's imagination, heightened by Nan, would sublimate what was absent in his marriage, while, his sigh, on the other hand, suggests that Florence's proven resilience raised the question of whether his euphoria was being enjoyed on borrowed time. Finally, though written at Florence's bedside, there was no evidence that Warren had shown her the letter, since, if so, there would have been an indication that he had. Under the circumstances, the gauche limerick would have risked Florence's outrage.

Also filling out the picture of Harding's acceptance of his wife's bossing in the midst of an extraneous preoccupation, there is the likelihood that his indulgence stemmed from a variety of conflicting emotions. Gratification might appease a physical need, but his tolerance of Florence's orders clearly involved the human side of his nature, which, since it had been there for others, would not allow him to ignore a sense of guilt that had had a long history. It was aroused, ipso facto, by the daily sight of his wronged wife in the grip of an illness that inflicted major physical pain.

Further complicating the issue, this stressful situation paralleled that identical one which had occurred years back, when in 1905, Harding had begun his fifteen year relationship with Carrie Phillips. As noted, while bedridden Florence had been recovering from her kidney operation, and Carrie's husband Jim had been shuffled off to Kellogg's "San," Warren and Carrie had the opening to initiate their longed-for love affair. The adulterers had unhampered liberty at a stage when the allure was strongest—deprivation having intensified desire. That same romantic intensity was being enjoyed once again under a similar set of circumstances, and as lovingly, with another woman, by contrast one who accepted subservience.

Since the doctors had given Warren and Nan every reason to expect that Florence would not again survive a painful siege of nephritis, it seemed that they might be freed to realize their dream-world. All they needed was patience. But all hopes would be dashed when, two weeks later, on 14 January, 1919, Warren would be writing Scobey that not only had Florence's condition improved, but "we're constantly assured she'll be restored to her normal health" (WGH to FES, 14 January, 1919).

Constantly ribbing Scobey about his prurient adventures (a cover for his own) Harding found this friend to be a more than obliging clown who, for their mutual amusement, persisted in weaving tales of dalliance. Offered as fun, those tales were but an extension of their parlor stories—probably a part of them. When Warren's own adventuresomeness finally brought him into a relationship that was genuine, above and beyond sex, the jokes receded.

The jokes were part of a superficial mentality that became expendable once he moved on to dedication, both in love and in his working at the Presidency. As such, the jokes were more like an interlude in his life as "one of the boys," prior to his adapting to situations that involved seriousness of purpose.

CHAPTER 53

"Old Men At Play"

ALMOST NO ONE WHO HAS dealt with the Harding biography has failed to make something of the baffling role that sex played in his life. Jokes were a low-level extension of that role.

The risqué material that Harding would share with the Scobeys was trifling stuff. Typical of male conviviality, it was comprised of the kind of sentiments which crossed an idle mind, and were easily shrugged off. But, as an offshoot of the larger interest which befuddled his relationships with women, the jokes have suggestive implications. Did they, for example, contain a certain male chauvinism that got superseded by a shift in attitude?

Outside of Nan Britton's account and the summary information Francis Russell and Carl Anthony have provided from Harding's Carrie Phillips letters, the Scobey letters open the possibility of our getting a more complete picture of the sex related phase of Harding's life, regarding which details are not abundant. One aspect of the sexual allusions and off-color stories in the Scobey letters is that they actually contain more talk about sex than jokes that are based on it.

The reason for this is that, from various intimations of caution over what they'd put into letters, it seemed like most of the sex jokes were preferably being exchanged orally. There was at least that much decorum observed in their sharing indecent material, normally kept private, and rare in their correspondence.

The time frame was a factor. A good portion of the tawdry stuff that did get into their letters took place during the easy-going life Harding enjoyed as a freshman Senator. Thus, it came up mainly after 1914, by which time his break-up with Carrie was mostly complete, and prior to the time when his relationship with Nan entered a delicate phase (post 1919). In other words, there was an open period when, potentially frustrated by a hiatus in his time with a mistress, Warren Harding would have been missing the company of one. Though he began seeing Nan in mid 1917, they did not instantly become absorbed with the question of their having a future in the midst of their enjoying an all-absorbing present. Thereafter, the Presidency itself dictated propriety, observed in letters, ignored in life.

Even as Senator, when he came up with "corkers" for Scobey, Harding would often write that he had to be careful about sending them, as much out of the need to observe official propriety as out of Harding's fear of offending his secretaries, like young Miss Pickens, for example, who took it upon herself to censor his letters, which made other means of delivery preferable.[105]

His fear of censorious secretaries comes out on a number of occasions. Not long after his complaint about Miss Pickens, Harding would write Scobey that he didn't have the time to write him a long-hand letter about the kind of "gossip" they enjoyed, since he had inherited from his Ohio predecessor, Senator Theodore Burton, an unnamed secretary who had "absorbed [Burton's] ideas of propriety." 106

Though Harding might still put some stories for the Scobeys into letters, his desire to share the racy ones would surely have had him reserving them for visits, making it unnecessary that he include in letters stories that would be more enjoyable if given orally, as parlor entertainment. It is not known to what extent his secretaries might have been opening incoming mail.

But, since Harding had a little earlier been complaining that the stories he was getting were too mild, either Scobey was being decorous about putting such items down on paper, or, he was being mindful of secretarial intervention. But the important point is that, as a matter of choice, sexually deprived Harding simply had an appetite for the stronger variety and said so. Interestingly, in not one of the available letters from Scobey to Harding did he give Harding so much as one dirty joke. That stuff was provided exclusively by Harding.

Whatever the bias of inhibiting secretaries, they did not greatly impede the exchange between old friends of references to off-color jokes, mainly on Harding's part, amidst his chiding Scobey for chasing after the alluring "chickens." Pretending shock, Harding wrote Scobey, "I do not think it is becoming for a Texas steer to be writing a dignified Senator-elect about the attractiveness of Texas chickens. You really offend me. If you don't cut out this affinity business and your interest in Texas chickens, you will come to a disgraceful end. I regret that you have been deteriorating very rapidly since you got beyond the sphere of my helpful influence" (There was evidently no need for him to inquire about what business a "Texas steer," would have to be going after those "chickens.")

Harding went on to suggest that the Scobeys join him and Florence in California on their way to Hawaii, a trip that, once "Edwardo" had had his "inevitable pursuit of the poultry exhibit" in Austin, would put him under Harding's "sheltering wing."[107] None of the joshing could be taken seriously, but there is an indication that Scobey was enjoying a freer life-style than was his friend, who exaggerated his pretense of decorum.

Having, at the time, just won his seat in the U.S. Senate, Harding was in a congenial mood. He played variations on the adulterous pursuit motif. For example, the humor of Harding's protecting Scobey from his "chicken" obsession rested on the irony of his having a moral arbiter who could not curb his own obsession, which Scobey was able to glean from the off-color stories Harding sent him. It additionally suggested a greater appetite for stories with a personal innuendo, which enhanced their tomfoolery.

In keeping with that, Harding comes out with the fear he'll put his liberty at risk by sending "corkers" through the mail, backed by an insistence that he "will maintain [his] virtue at all hazards"[108] As part of their game, Harding's fear of offending secretaries becomes paramount when he gets a "prim and proper Boston spinster" type who "would die of shock," if he dictated letters like those Scobey required for his repertoire.[109] On yet another occasion, while he is tempted to offer new stories, he can't commit them to the mail, as he says that his secretary freezes up whenever he starts a letter to Scobey. Joining in the levity, Mac Jennings thinks the spinster must have been recruited by the Duchess.

An interesting aspect of this correspondence is that references to the allure of women and pursuit of their company had almost entirely to do with Scobey's escapades, offered as the wish-fulfillment of a lecherous old goat and supposed adulterer. Harding, by contrast, mainly proffered chiding, or restraint on behalf of propriety. That being used as a pretext for concealment made his hypocrisy come off as part of their amusement.

Having been the butt of Harding's mock protestations of propriety, Scobey turned the tables on Harding. Well aware of his friend's weakness, Scobey would see to it that Harding was presented with a covey of adulating ladies eager to meet the good looking newly elected Senator. In an undated letter sent to Harding some time after 9 November, 1914 (but earlier than the above mentioned 2 December, 1914 letter about the trip to Hawaii) Scobey in reminding Harding of appealing Texas "chickens" he had met on a previous visit to San Antonio, wanted to tease him into paying a return visit instead of going on to Hawaii with Florence.

As bait, Scobey writes that he has "run across several chickens that would even make a United States Senator take notice." Playing on Harding's vanity, Scobey stressed that there were even additional ones, beyond those he had already met who "will make life pleasant for [him]."[110]

As a sign of the sensitivity Harding had for the Texas women who reciprocated the attention he had given them, and whose interest he wanted to retain, he writes that he wants to thank Scobey's friend, Roy Campbell, for a fine box of Texas onions sent to him, which he had, at first, thought came from a "lady friend" whom he had wanted to thank for the "fragrant offering." So great was his gratitude for the supposed courtesy that he had almost risked the "great embarrassment" of hastily writing the anonymous lady to acknowledge her gift.[111] By his eagerness not to neglect what he thought was a woman's interest in him, his almost making a fool of himself does just that.

Between the two of them, their joshing had them laughing at themselves as old men at play. A joke or two introduced on that motif vented the frustrations of age, which had something to do with their making women the butt of their jokes. However, since those were part of their social entertainment, most treated as 'parlor stories,' the women saw no harm in getting into the game when the mirth was shared mutually.

CHAPTER 54

"Stories Directed At Women Are Shared With Them"

AFTER AT ONE POINT WRITING it was best that the stories didn't go too far (27 January, 1915) Harding decided to send one that did. It involved public figures by name, and provided an example of the source for their male pleasantry: i.e., best when covert, salty in content, and targeting a woman.

This was ushered in via anticipation of the April Fiesta in San Antonio. Harding was telling Scobey it might be precarious for him to become King of the Fiesta, as he would not want Scobey subjecting himself to "the many royal temptations," that went with the crown. "I think it is best that you stay within the influence of home ties and domestic considerations." He kids Scobey about his having once wanted the authority of a Pope, so he could do whatever might arise in his imagination.

At the same time, given Scobey's lack of self-discipline, neither would he be quite suited for the equally arbitrary role of aged King Solomon. Though tempted by Solomon's authority, Scobey's sex life might be hampered by age. Not that he would have been willing to concede that his sex life was fully dormant.

As a side-light to Scobey's pretended adultery, Harding had been surprised to discover that during their two-couple trip to Europe in 1911, Scobey said he had arranged to meet a woman from Nebraska, a talented soprano, with whom he'd had previous contacts. As Harding recalled it, "Scobey confessed to me that he kept six trysts with her in Paris, in the eight days we were there—and I never knew it..." (Affair, 52). There is no way to know whether Scobey was bluffing, as, considering the byplay he and Harding had been having on the subject, he may have been. But, assuming he wasn't, that would give additional bite to all of the ribaldry they shared.

Harding then passes on to his sexist joke that likewise suggests the limitations of age. As indicated, a major aspect of their byplay on sex rests on the irony that it is Scobey, actually four months younger than Harding, who assumed the part of an old roué.

The story has Jeannette Rankin, the Congressional Representative from Montana, and lone female member of the House, interrupted when addressing the Chair and being asked if she will yield to "the gentleman from Illinois." When she replies that she gladly yields to said gentleman, Uncle Joe Cannon, the Chair, offers the aside, "Now ain't I in a hell of a fix at my age?"–to which Harding appends a moral: "Be a King in your youth."[112]

Their self-acknowledged obsession with sex was as much a part of their laughable ignominy as 'dirty old men,' as is the embarrassing fact that there just might be an occurrence at their age akin to Joe Cannon's. Not the least part of the meaning reflected by their jokes—properly the stuff of youth—is precisely how inappropriate they are for older men, made more funny yet because they are enjoying a laugh at their own expense.

Though Harding notes that Scobey is essentially the same age as he is, Scobey was perceived to be older because he acted older, on the basis of which Harding tells him he is "swiftly passing the period when [he has] the capacity to render such efficient service as would be expected of [him]"—an ironic reflection on his guise as philanderer.[113] This was well in advance of the time when Harding would appoint Scobey Director of the Mint, accepted on the premise that Scobey, the supposed wanderer, would not be tied down to his constantly staying in Washington.

Almost two years earlier, Jennings had reminded Harding and

Scobey that, when he compared himself to them, they looked like old "patriarchs [who] are hoary headed and harmless."[114] Several years earlier, Jennings had directed Scobey to tell his wife not to be too strict with her husband, as he was simply an older man pretending he could stay forever young, in effect a Peter Pan.[115]

In sum, what is conveyed by the stories about the hyper-active quest for female company assigned to Scobey is a consistent image: that of men faced with the limitations of age trying to vicariously hold on to their fading virility. Their humor offered an innocuous recognition of the problem, particularly when there was the actual fear that age would become an impediment to opportunistic sex, which was to be secretly overcome by Harding. This obsession clearly whetted the forthcoming excitement over his seeing young Nan in the Manhattan hotel room after a long dry spell.

Meanwhile, if one wonders how the two men could have safely kept from their wives this talk of an unseemly pastime, the answer is that they didn't. This was most obvious with Harding's finding that Evaland Scobey had a frank appreciation for material shared by the men.

Not wanting to be left out of the fun, Florence would, on occasion, become quite as receptive to the off-color jokes. That being the case, there were times when Harding could rib Evaland with the complaint that her offerings were not strong enough. When Harding, first of all, offered to pass on to Evaland stories that he'd rather not send through the mail, preferring "personal delivery,"[116]—and, secondly, when the men were so open about letting the women in on the stories that Harding would want to share with Evaland, transmitted through Scobey himself—-how proper could the stories have been and how could the women have not known about the improper ones?[117]

Additionally, since not many improper stories did actually appear in Harding's letters, and since there was an allusion to Scobey's considerable repertory, the inference is that most of those hidden from view had already been told orally, or were yet to be. When Harding asks Scobey to tell his wife she owes him a letter in exchange for which he'd give her a story—and this after submitting a rather rank tale to

Scobey—one can reasonably assume the women themselves may have been passing on the off-color jokes they had come into—something already observed on Evaland's part. A sport mutually enjoyed in private lessens the offensiveness of the stories.

Regarding the shared enjoyment of salacity on the part of both couples, Harding, on noting that the Scobeys' newly hired servants were French, wrote that he was pleased to know Mrs. Scobey could speak French. It meant that, should they take in a trip to Paris, they would not be left wondering what the show girls were saying about them when they spent an evening at the Bal Tabarin, where the female entertainers were scantily clad, if at all.[118] It was understood that neither of these wives were prudes.

CHAPTER 55

"A Sexist Joke"

THEIR "PARLOR STORIES" WERE INTENDED to be fit for mixed company. But a story Harding looked upon as one of the "parlor" variety had a sexual reference insensitive to the treatment of women, and was based on stereotyping. It was a story of two Jewish men bargaining over a situation in which the son of one (Isaac) had assumedly gotten the other's (Moses') daughter with child. So Moses asks for recompense, and, as Isaac counts out the payment that was haggled for, he hesitates, pointing out that the daughter may actually <u>not</u> be pregnant. To this, Moses, with an eye on the money, counters, "Then I gif your son another chance."[119]

Aside from the stereotyping, this has the Ogre of Greed motivating the barter of a daughter for money; and, beyond that, indifference to the arbitrary use of women as pleasure-pawns—which is the same attitude that occurred in the notion of Representative Rankin's "yielding," as well as in the prospect of a visit to the Bal Tabarin.

Enhancing the fun was the fact that the subjects touched on in these jokes were socially sensitive. The sexism, of course, was symptomatic of the age, and Scobey and Harding were no more, nor any less, representative of men of their time. As for the jokes, it was because they were jokes that social implications were not to be taken seriously—lest they spoil the fun.

Whereas the tale about bartering a daughter was simply a fable told for the sake of a laugh, it offered an interesting contrast to the sentiments that prevailed in Harding's real-life relations with Carrie and those soon to be engaged with Nan. That there was no contradiction in the shift of feeling is discernible from the fact that the real-life situations were miles apart from the realm of barter. His life experience with each of these women was acutely personal, and activated by a starved heart.

Save for the limerick, most of the sexist type jokes predate his relationship with Nan, though they appear in years that coincide with his rocky—and fading—relationship with Carrie.

In any event, post mid-year 1917, Nan had the competitive edge. When Carrie came up in a conversation with Nan, Harding pronounced her a "damned fool," twice in one sentence, saying that, while a "brilliant conversationalist," she hadn't "half the sense of her daughter" (PD, 102, Nan's ital.). By putting Carrie down, he was at the same time putting Nan up. It mattered little how well he knew Isabelle. His intent was to reassure Nan, and savor making small of Carrie, a lady not easily minimized.

Even though the "stories" were not particularly sensational, overall, there still were a sufficient number of allusions to women as sex objects in the Harding-Scobey correspondence. Private man-to-man stuff, this can only be taken seriously, if one disregards the humor of it.

Nonetheless, somewhat compensating is the fact that, as indicated, once Harding assumed the office of President, the written exchange of jokes based on sex came to an end, though not an on-going male interest in such items. As opposed to Harding's maintaining a proper official presence, there was no diminution in his need of a special woman. His predicament was how to deal with the conflicting demands of an allegiance to Florence and an all-consuming romance with Nan, a problem which hung on insolubly.

One significant inference to be drawn from the jokes involving women was that in each case of those cited—the Jewish fathers, Congresswoman Rankin, and the dinner guest—the women were cast in roles of subservience to men. This also applies to Harding's voyeurist entertainment, as with his, for example, taking in the Hulu dancers in Hawaii, Little Egypt in Chicago, and the burlesque theater in Washington, which provided men with the illusion of dominance.

It so happened that in Harding's relationships with Florence and Carrie, he was the subservient partner, subject to their control, their decisions, their whims. With Nan it was different. There was no need of sexist jokes, of voyeurism, of his feeling himself at the mercy of a woman who was close to him. Of course, there was the age factor that put Harding in control, while Nan was content to fulfill a girlhood dream. None of that, however, detracts from the genuineness of their romance. And, to a point it worked.

PART VII:

NAN VS CARRIE

CHAPTER 56

"With Nan It Was Really Genuine"

Warren Harding came together with Nan Britton out of outrageous need, and Nan came to him out of an outrageous dream. Remarkably, their love swept aside the idea that so disparate a couple could have a relationship. His only requisite was secrecy. "From the first he begged me to keep our secret and tell it to no one." He didn't want her to be "taking on any confidantes," like her mother, who, on seeing Harding for a job, got a seemingly casual inquiry from him about Nan (*PD,* 58). His interest in Nan suggests that he couldn't not know of her more than interest in him.

Nan does not date his caution, but mention of her mother means it had to have been early. Nonetheless, Nan might have gotten ahead of Warren on that one, as during their "first sweetheart days," before she had made a "complete surrender," she did have "a longing to talk to someone [she] really loved and respected," and she put her "case *hypothetically* to [Warren's] sister 'Daisy.'" Nan wanted to know "what *she* would do if *she* were in love with a man whom she could not marry, but who might want her to belong to him any way."

Daisy's response was blunt: "Don't do it, Nan; the world is against you; no matter how much you love each other, *don't!*" Nan repeated this to Warren, who, fearing anything that might cast doubt on his sincerity, he emphatically countered, "Anyone would advise you against it who didn't know how much I love you!" (Ibid., Nan's itals.).

The important element here is Daisy's acknowledgement that

Warren and Nan were indeed having a genuine relationship, to be denied by Daisy's family. Daisy was offering Nan a woman to woman admonition that, whatever present good might come of their affair, in the end Warren would have little to lose, Nan everything.

Despite that, Nan decided to toss aside misgivings. She found it hard to conceive of the potential for distress, overcoming doubt in her willingness to accept it. "I tried hard to convince myself that it was wrong to love Mr. Harding as I loved him, that it would mean ultimate surrender, and perhaps sorrow for us and for our families."

Harding did some convincing of his own in those early letters she received from him, one of which she said "particularly took me off my feet." Harding had a gift for writing love letters that had an impact. This one, she continued, "contained in sweet phrasing a picture of his desire for me," and ended with the "parenthetical exclamation, 'God! What an anticipation!' "

Nan doesn't indicate whether the letters she was referring to preceded or followed their first private meeting. Nonetheless, those first letters (the contents of which were shared with her sister in distant Chicago) recalled for Nan the wave of emotionalism he packed into his early declaration of love for her. The way Nan phrased this sounded like she may have been quoting from one of those early letters, possibly the first forty pager. "He used to tell me that just to visualize me as he loved to see me brought pangs that seemed virginal in their intensity and surpassed any longing he had ever experienced in his life " (PD, 46). These sentiments were supported by his sending her a snapshot along with that first forty page love letter.

In its simplest terms, Nan actually went first. Warren fell in love with her seemingly because she had already fallen in love with him. It was school-girl love, but no matter. Each had a reason for the declaration of love. After the recent demise of his relationship with Carrie, Warren needed her eager commitment to him. For her, it was the realization of a dream she hadn't thought was possible.

The lovers' decision to live for-the-moment, precipitated by Nan's adoration, and Warren's need, grew proportionally. Blindly vulnerable, Nan's giving attitude enabled her to accept the unacceptable. As she rationalized, "This intimation of his loving protection strengthened my decision that ours was an exceptional case" (Ibid. Nan's ital). Exceptional too was his indebtedness to Nan, as shown by the insecurity of his repeatedly asking that she say she loved him.

Mutually beneficial as their relationship was, the lovers would, in time, be haunted by the difficulty of attaining closure. As in the loyalty given to members of his Administration, Harding had a way of letting irrational judgment dissipate good intentions, which had been the case with Albert Fall. With Nan, there was another component. The nature of his involvement, both desperate and deep, prevented Harding from considering realistic terms for a viable future, which was probably just as well, since, for situations such as these lovers had, there were none.

They had to settle for the diurnal joy their experience brought them, which was meaningful in itself. Warren's psyche being what it was, unsteady at best with regard to women, there was a life-changing difference in the intensity he experienced with Nan Britton. In the world he enjoyed with her, unlike politics, he genuinely lived what he felt.

As Nan wrote of his confiding how he felt on meeting her privately for the first time in New York in late May, 1917, the desire to absolutely "possess [her] had been born in his heart" and the occasion became equally "enshrined in [her] own heart" (PD, 17). With possession and enshrinement as complementaries, what they had for one another was big. Their ultimately having to come down from that point was commensurate to how high it had originally taken them—on a trajectory which coincidentally mirrored Warren Harding's political career.

Looked at in perspective, what they feared in the beginning of their romance, Fate would award them up to the end, six and a half blissful years later.

On the winter's day that would be their last together, hope drained away, and with Warren coming down with the flu, he saw himself being worn down by cruces he couldn't navigate. His disregard for symptoms of failing health on the westward journey in 1923 would be greatly abetted by worry. Despondent over word of incipient scandal, betrayed by supposed friends, and facing the possibility of a dead-ended relationship with a woman who, too late in life, had become very dear to him, Warren was a psychological wreck.

In sum, a good Presidency declining, its decent record threatened, harmonious love caught in an impasse—his disappointments seemed to indicate a way out would have to be arrived at laissez-faire. By ignoring ill health to the point of physical deterioration he succumbed to a subconscious death wish. His final trip in 1923 had been a journey of 15,057 miles taking him through 15 States and into Alaska. He couldn't yield to a tenth of the demands made on him, but those that he did meet were more than enough. "I need rest," he pleaded, "but at the same time I want to see my country and its people" (Florence, 416).

On evidently receiving word of scandal that he feared would undermine his hard won public approval, Warren was recklessly pushing himself to exhaustion inspired by the enthusiastic crowds who were turning out to greet him at every stop on his journey west. Although the people could allay thoughts of what might await him in Washington, their applause did not make such thoughts go away.

If anything might help him to overcome a negative outlook, it would have to have been a remembrance of the rich experience he'd had with Nan. He, in fact, indicated as much. Unable to walk away from their relationship, he regaled Nan with the vision of a "grand reunion" when they returned from their respective journeys (PD, 152).

On their last time together, he'd made a point of putting her ahead of his political troubles. "Our matter" as he emphasized, "worries me more than the combined worries of the whole administration" (PD, 237). Compared to the other worries, which were beyond his control, the one that arose between the two of them looked like it could be dealt with… somehow.

In his farewell letter, Warren had given Nan his "oft-written" reminder that he loved her "more than all the world" (Ibid. 152). If, on parting, he tried to dispel the sadness by suggesting he wanted them to recover their dream, Nan, could do no less than hope so, difficult as it was. Of course, that was January, 1923. Six months and two major suicides later he would make out a new will and tell his sister Carolyn that he didn't expect to come back from Alaska.

CHAPTER 57

"It Was Also Different"

It is said that no man is a hero to his valet—in lieu of which, enough of Warren's personal correspondence that escaped Florence's destruction offered an extensive enough view of his weaknesses. A prime example was an imploring tone that got into his love letters to Carrie, which, to his own detriment, he had sent back to her. Though embarrassing, there is much in the exposure of his weaknesses that inclines a reader to be sympathetic. Carrie victimized him, much as Florence did.

Mistakes in his relationship with the women closest to him became a fact of life for Warren Harding. Although his time with Nan Britton stands out as the most heart-warming experience in the last years of his life, it arrived too late and had a head-in-the-sand prognosis. His letters to Carrie indicate that they had a great sexual affinity for one another, but the love they shared stemmed mostly from that, and was mostly confined to that.

Compatible as he and Carrie had been, when tested by the need of caring and constancy, she was often found to be wanting. Not that she didn't have grounds for indignation. But her inability to come back from that, while she did came back for sex, identifies her side of the relationship.

By contrast, love and sex did come together for Warren with Nan. They took it as far as it could go, and she gave Warren a sense of psychological well-being. When the Presidency limited their time together, he had a "hunger" for her love letters, and committed their messages to his heart, in compensation for her absence (*PD*, 173). It was as if the letters from Nan made up for the sorrow that followed from his to Carrie.

The happiness he had had with each of his mistresses was framed by negatives. Overall, the kind of euphoria he experienced with Carrie was on and off, and the like feeling he experienced with Nan was unsustainable. What the contrast between the two women comes down to is that there was an essential difference between his having sincerely fallen in love and his equating love with good sex. .

On the other hand, he himself had grown in both relationships. There was a difference, after all, between his behavior as an undisciplined philanderer and his discovery of what he had missed in matters of the heart. In their respective ways, both women had him cultivating monogamous attachment—with a difference. For although, there had been shared love in his affair with Carrie Phillips, it was dashed by her harsh response to his loss of nerve for a divorce.

She never really got over that. Rebuffs were common, and, when it came to Germany, she gave him an opinionated earful. Outside the bedroom, Carrie was too much for him. With her displaying a vengeful character, and an aversion to politics, he was lucky to have avoided an ill-fated marriage to her. It was just that, while they were not a good match for one another in temperament, that did not get in the way of their love-making joy, except that it was ephemeral.

There was a sequence of incidents, but three months apart in which Carrie's callous response to Warren's request for her soothing presence practically set up his overboard excitement on meeting Nan Britton alone in the Manhattan Hotel.

In February, 1917, three months prior to the New York meeting with Nan, Warren was suffering from a deep depression, and he wrote Carrie to bring him out of it. "This is not a man longing for passion," he wrote, "it isn't really at all. I just want you—your presence...*you, you you!* I know I should be lifted up into quite another existence" (*Affair*, 210). As distinct from letters in which he craved to be anointed by her physically, this was a plea for her comforting presence, as such, a call for humanity—some heart.

All it would take under the circumstances was no more than for her to be there for him, a desperate need from a human being in pain. Her reply, as characterized by Robenalt, was "a stinging reproof." Likely upset over his support of the break in relations with Germany, she raised the very topic she knew would drive him "crazy" (Ibid.). Typical of his treatment after she had left for Germany and returned, Warren often met with wrath and ridicule. She liked to remind him—as if he needed reminding—that she never forgave him for voting with the Senate majority for our going to war against Germany.

Not long after this episode, Nan came into Warren's life. He met her hurting for love and found it. The suddenness of it all may have been influenced by Carrie's rebuff. But Nan's adoration actually filled a long-standing need. Harding came into something that grew to an awakening—to wit, that he had life-long been subconsciously needing a true commitment of love, and that Nan, in bringing it to him, brought it out in him. Here was the comfort he had sought from Carrie, raised to extravagance. It was one reason he fell so fast and so completely for Nan, a rapture she was ready to return for her own reasons.

During his separation from Carrie, after the 1911 debacle, Warren wrote her that he wanted her to be his "very own" as he was "hurting to love and be loved." That was the key. It underscored what he most missed. He went on, "I could be tolerably patient if I knew that the next time we met it was to be for keeps. Maybe, who can tell?" (Florence, 106).

This came out following their 1913 tryst, for which Carrie had crossed the ocean to be with him, as much in need as he was of savoring their physical relationship. Renewal following the distance in time and space made it highly rewarding, in fact, magnetic. The reason he was equivocal about "for keeps," was that, based on past performance, he couldn't be certain that the love he'd been hurting for could be sustained with Carrie. His uncertainty suggests there was a subliminal difference between his "hurting to be loved" and love-making. In a line from a verse he sent to Carrie, he stressed what made her most attractive to him: "I love you garb'd but naked MORE!" (Ibid.).

Warren and Carrie had been lovers, and they had also been in love. However, although the sex could be sustained, it did not take much to sour the love that they had had. Just five months after his February, 1917 plea for Carrie's presence, and three months after Warren had been kissing Nan, Carrie was questioning his love and blaming him for the rupture in their relationship (Affair, 258).

She was stranded on their past, when his need was humanly present. Trysts subsequent to their break-up were initiated by Carrie, and they did carry some sentiment as Christmas-time anniversaries of their having fallen in love. However, the trysts themselves seem to have been limited to their undiminished, but transient physical enjoyment.

CHAPTER 58

"And Before? Justice To Carrie"

It was some fourteen years after his barren marriage to Florence Kling that Warren Harding was settled into a love affair with Carrie Phillips, who became a compatible partner for him. Great as his sexual desire was, hers was his equal.

Carrie was the most beautiful woman in town and wife of Warren's friend, Jim Phillips, co-owner of the major dry-goods store in Marion, Ohio. As was the case with Warren, she had not married out of love. But great as their feelings were for one another, Warren and Carrie could not negotiate the moves needed to bring them together legitimately. She would have had to divorce her husband in order to marry Warren, but he couldn't come through with his comparable side of the bargain.

Separation from formidable Florence would not have been easy, and there is some question as to whether Harding would have had the will to get it done anyway.

Francis Russell, as instanced, the first Harding scholar who had read the secret letters Warren had written to Carrie, pronounced her the love of his life. With Carrie, Russell felt that "his sensuality struck depths he was unaware of in himself" (Shadow, 168f.).[120] Other biographers have come to the same conclusion. .

The major source for an account of Warren Harding's relationship with Carrie Phillips is the packet of letters he had written her, and, when returned, was sent back to her as proof of his love. The letters were discovered in a shoebox in Carrie's home in 1954, four years prior to her death. They were taken by a Harding family member (likely Warren's grand nephew, Dr. Warren G. Harding III) to Byron E. Ford of the law firm of Vorys, Slater, Seymour and Pease in Columbus, Ohio. The lawyers arrived at the proviso that letters were not to be made publicly accessible until July 29, 2014.

In 1972, the letters were taken to the Library of Congress, and John Haynes, curator of the LC's 20th Century MS Collection, assured me that no one has had access to those letters there. Hence, prior to James Robenalt's book, half of which dealt with the Warren-Carrie affair, one was left with the bare details of what had been knowable. Robenalt, however, did not intend to publish all, or a major part, of the Warren-Carrie correspondence as such. What he did provide, however, has been more than helpful for an understanding of the lovers' affair.

Meanwhile, as much of Harding's love life still lies appropriately hidden, I draw on applicable evidence from the next best source for such information; namely Nan Britton's memoir, The President's Daughter, which is the only first hand account of that subject. Beyond my coverage of the matter in prefatory Chapters, there is no need to once again set forth the authenticity of Nan's account. As I point out, the subject has been sufficiently debated.

The content of Nan's book had naturally been rejected by members of Harding's family (mainly Warren's brother, George Tryon Harding, III, "Deac") though accepted by others Nan cites, like Warren's sisters, Carrie and Daisy, who were fully aware of their brother's affair. It was as a result of this awareness that sympathetic Daisy gave Nan financial assistance. For reasons already given, I come down on the side of those who, having considered the evidence, accepted Nan's account as essentially true. For this there is the support previously cited. No one was more emphatic about its authenticity than the skeptical H.L. Mencken, who found PD "so palpably true that it convinces instantly" (op. cit., 15).

As for Warren's affair with Carrie, in his correspondence with her, it becomes apparent that a healthy sensuality dominated their relationship. It is rather unique that explicit sexual references would overflow those letters to Carrie. Separation, yearning, deprivation, plus the blockage enforced by Florence increased their need of one another.

A wife easily prone to suspicion, and specifically over Carrie, Florence became all the more tenacious in her grip on Warren, and all the more irritable when suspicious. For a man whose history indicated a large libido, it made no sense for him to be caught in a marriage where sex was assumedly unwanted.

Nor was it smooth sailing for him with Carrie herself, who, as previously observed, could be fully as irritable (and irritating) as Florence. While bringing Warren the satisfaction absent in marriage, Carrie would, over time, distress him as often as she pleased him, finally resorting to bald-faced blackmail. Above and beyond that, her volatile nature was such that Warren could never feel that the love he had for her was commensurately reciprocated.

Interestingly, the periods when she made things difficult for Warren, would perversely intensify his desire for her, which Carrie would exploit, a practice he was experiencing in a different way with Florence. In short, Carrie had the ability to make him feel as much insecure as pleased, and mostly the former. As for the nature of their relationship, it was based a good deal on an extraordinary sexual attraction. For each of them the dullness at home made for splendor away.

The attraction was strong enough that, after they had apparently broken up, Carrie would twice be sailing back across a wintry Atlantic for the trysts they highly prized. Passionate as the experience was for them, what Warren wrote about it indicates that their fulfillment was primarily sexual, and, allowing for companionability on their two-couple excursions, not a great deal more than that. There appears to have been the lack of a lover's tenderness in Carrie's attitude toward Warren, while his toward her was all softness.

Warren's affair with Carrie during its early years had been meaningful, and gave them the desire for a follow-through. In 1910, as Harding would lose his race for Governor, and Carrie was increasingly annoyed by gossip, they wanted to find a way to give their relationship legitimacy. Not that the complication of double divorces and a remarriage could have been easily accomplished in the first place, the greater difficulty being Warren's. Chief among the difficulties was the fact of his never being very good at contesting things with Florence—and winning. Still the early, buoyant period of Warren's relationship with Carrie was so great it lasted a good six years.

Discounting Florence—actually impossibly—he had had reason to imagine a new life with Carrie. With his home state defeat signifying a stunted career in public life and his future uncertain, he would have been amenable to making a new start in a life with Carrie. If accomplished, he would have had nothing to lose and much to gain, beginning with a beautiful Gibson-girl wife and a remedy for the frustration at home. To get a feel for how this played out, it is helpful to revisit a relevant sequence of events.

To begin with, for an indication of how Warren and Carrie's relationship peaked in the early going, one need only have a glimpse at how Warren emblazoned their physical epiphany in a letter he wrote Carrie at Easter time, 1908.

"I wanted to kiss you out of your reserve—a thousand of them, wistful, wild, wet and wandering and I wanted you to kiss as only you can. ... And I wanted to feast my eyes, to intoxicate them in glorious breasts and matchless curves and exquisite shapeliness. ... I'd caress and fondle while I worshippingly admired until you caught the spell and answered kiss with kiss and caress with caress. God! I do love that I am wild about it. Heavens! How I would revel in your matchless charms. I'd pet and coddle and kiss and fondle and admire and adore, utterly impatient until I made you the sweetest and purest and darlingest wanton. ... There is one engulfing, enthralling, rule of love, the song of your whole being which is a bit sweeter—The 'Oh Warren! Oh Warren!' when your body quivers with divine paroxysm and your soul hovers for flight with mine... " (Florence, 87).

It is no understatement to say they had difficulty walking away from this three years later. And it is no irony to say the emotional intensity of their relationship was precarious, which had everything to do with their 1911 break-up. As pointed out above, those 1908 sentiments were relived in the week-end rendezvous in out of town hotels, and were a prelude to that 1909 European tour the Phillipses and Hardings took, leaving February 4th, on which Carrie and Warren enjoyed nighttime trysts on deck.

Memories brought them together, as the opportunities might present themselves, or as they created their own. It was not long after Carrie left for Berlin that they found a way to get together in London's Devonshire Hotel in mid-August. To tide them over the rest of their 1911 separation, Carrie (again, as previously cited) booked passage for a December return to New York, from whence they proceeded on to Boston and then Montreal, where they memorably climaxed in unison with the sounding of the bells that ushered in the New Year.

Again, mindful of their anniversary, Carrie returned in late November, 1912, and they had their December celebration in Richmond, Virginia, during which, as Robenalt rendered it, they had "one of those experiences that stayed with them for the next decade." Warren had measured their experience at "a year of life, yea five of them for one heavenly day in Richmond" (Affair, 76). His love of Carrie had been all consuming, and literally so. Two years prior to Richmond, he had written that his love for her "flames like the fire and consumes" (Ibid., 40).

It would seem incredible that the lovers were unable to use their fiery experience as an incentive to do what was necessary for them to achieve a lifelong relationship. The fact that they couldn't bring it off, however, was the basis for the frustration, and finally disillusionment, which destroyed any possibility of their having another try at it after 1911.

CHAPTER 59

"For Him and Carrie It Was Not To Be"

WARREN'S LAMENT FOLLOWING CARRIE'S DRAMATIC 1911 departure, took the form of 'if only.' Tendered as a lame apology for her going, he wrote her, "How often do I wish I could have you, openly and honored…". For an immediate cause, he blamed the petty gossipers, the 'knockers," as he called them, whom she had said hounded her. Warren tried to treat them as a temporary nuisance, to be gone and forgotten when Carrie would have returned from Berlin, which he then (January, 1913) thought might be in no more than a year (Affair, 47f.).

Not much of a rationale for disappointment, this did not begin to approach their basic issues. An underlying problem for them would have been the inveterate pull of politics for Warren. With him becoming known nationally, it wouldn't have taken that much to get him back in the game. As previously observed, politics, also loved by Florence, was hated by Carrie.

If soberly looked at, their relationship once renewed would have become fiery in another respect. Carrie could not rid herself of pay-back for past hurt. She had been making Warren despondent by writing from Germany that life there suited her so much she wanted to stay, permanently. She was even offering him teasing tidbits about her enjoying the company of German men, who, in fact, interested her.

Compelled to return home by the outbreak of War, Carrie was

so pro-German she would, in time, come up with the threat that should Warren, as Senator, cast his vote for our entering the War and becoming an enemy of Germany, she would tell her husband what his friend had done, and she'd get Warren Harding run out of office by publicly revealing his letters (Shadow, 281). Warren, of course, voted with the majority on the 6 April, 1917 joint resolution that Congress passed for America to enter the War.

Managing to get through that, Warren, instead of immediately breaking it off with Carrie, became anxious on her behalf, concerned over her openly expressing pro-German sentiments which brought her to the attention of the Secret Service. After Carrie had rejected Warren's invitation to come to Washington, (accompanied by her husband and daughter) so he could give her—and them—an urgent awareness of the problem she was creating for herself, and family, he wrote her several times in mid-April, 1917, to no avail. He got back to her in February, 1918, asking that she watch her loose tongue on hearing she was "discouraging young men from entering the service" (Affair, 307).

As Warren explained in a letter to her husband, he was warning her "of impending dangers" and urging "that she exercise great prudence and caution."[121] Warren's appeal proved to be "very futile," earning him an angry retort, the tenor of which was to tell him, in so many words, if he would just mind his business, she'd take care of her own.

Warren wondered half-heartedly if husband Jim could "possibly command her" to take heed, though, as he added, he "frankly," doubted that that could be done (Shadow, 297). This was reminiscent of the times when Carrie's having put him off accentuated the effect of love lost, the result of which would bring him back to her, only to be made a fool of.

If Carrie was difficult, Nan was not. The contrasting treatment he received from Nan had to have added to the impulsive suddenness with which he seized the opportunity presented by this submissive young lady. Once their relationship had been established, there was a decided lapse in his letters to Carrie. They ceased entirely from October to December, 1917 (Affair, 278).

As World War I broke out in the summer of 1914, and as Carrie returned soon thereafter, her unwitting competition with Nan began upon the young girl's coming to congratulate Warren on his election to the U.S. Senate in November of that year. The timing was such that he would by then have had more than a hint that it was best for him to move on from his by then tormenting affair with Carrie.

It did not happen immediately, but the groundwork had been laid. On Nan's visit, which had been encouraged by Warren's sister Daisy, she was greeted at the door by Florence, and, since Nan was interrupting a card game, her appearance should have been brief. Instead, it was unrushed and gave Warren the basis for contemplating future prospects, that being the type of sentiment which, three years later, he would be identifying for Nan as the circumstance that led to love at first sight.

Nan herself knew back then that there had been more than a casual response from Warren. His "smile of genuine appreciation," was assumedly brought on by its being apparent to him that she was "thrilled unspeakably under the touch of his hand," the "pressure" of which she understood to be Warren's "seal of sincere cordiality" (PD, 20f.).

Less than three years later, a scant month after Carrie had been telling him off about minding his own business, Warren would be meeting Nan at the Manhattan Hotel in New York City, telling her that with her "spirit and determination" she was just as he had "always imagined" her to be, implicitly recalling their prior contact (Ibid., 31). From that point on, there was no turning back to Carrie, at least not for love.

Having recoiled from Carrie over her attempt to blackmail him in 1920, Warren, with Nan already there for him, had obviously felt the breech was final. The "cooling" had been underway years earlier. Continuation of a contact with Carrie—the affair well enough known to reach political opponents—could never have survived the onset of a Presidential campaign, any more than a divorce would have.

Though not a vengeful person, Warren could savor pay-back, and, if he needed any confirmation that he'd made the only sensible decision, Carrie gave it to him via blackmail. It was at that time that he would see an enraged Carrie approach him on his front porch in an unabashed effort to get Florence's goat, which it did, bringing her out to throw the feather duster, waste basket, and, finally, piano stool at her—an incident punctuated by Carrie's defiantly throwing Warren a good-bye kiss.

Although there was some relief for Warren in his decisive break with Carrie, nonetheless the final, and complete, separation was still typically achieved for him by members of his Presidential campaign. Until the pay-off finally took effect, he was somewhat adrift in the status quo ante, his only immediately satisfactory harbor being an unsatisfactory marriage that he had neither the will nor means to change (unthinkable during the campaign) any more than he could alleviate the unsettling situation that Nan had to bear up under.

While it did happen that, toward the end of his relationship with Carrie, there had been some overlap in his seeing both women over the same time span, there was a geographical separation, with one being seen in Marion, while the other was being visited, on different terms, in Washington, DC and New York. It is difficult to determine whether Carrie may have actually known Warren had a relationship with Nan, unless she was vaguely encompassed by Carrie's angry charge that he was seeing other women (Shadow, 344).

All that Carrie could have definitely known about Nan was what was generally known in Marion—to wit, that she was a young girl, whose visible adulation made Warren Harding her "hero," and that that was enough for Carrie to look upon Nan with disdain, as a silly child.

Suggesting how dismissible Nan could be to Carrie, that implicit attitude had apparently rubbed off on her daughter, who stopped Nan's sister on the street one day to let her know, for Nan's benefit, that Warren, on a visit, had embarrassingly "sat the bottom out of one of [Carrie's] mother's favorite chairs!" (PD, 11f.).

In the three-way contention for Warren, there was some consolation for Nan in her having emerged victorious; until Florence pushed him into the big time political game. That should have blunted any hope that Nan and Warren entertained about their future. It didn't, and they continued to take as much from the present as was available to them. Whatever their prospects, Nan indicated she wasn't to be robbed of the memories she held to her heart, and portrayed in an account of the happiness she shared with Warren.

PART VIII:

WARREN AND NAN IN LOVE

CHAPTER 60

"We Were Made For Each Other, Nan"

GENERALLY SIDETRACKED BY A MAJORITY of Harding historians, Nan Britton's memoir of her romance with Warren Harding gives us the litany of a man devoutly in love. I have early on addressed the evidence validating Nan's account of their affair. Even if—at worst—Nan's intimate account is taken as her <u>perception</u> of Harding's life with her it still makes a convincing story. It is all the more of one for its having been factually based, confirmed by data derived from the Carrie Phillips letters. Nan, in effect, provides a detailed narrative—call it a factual dramatization, if need be—that goes much beyond what she merely perceived.

James Robenalt, who had questioned Nan's reliability, was willing to concede that she did have the facts. In a statement cited in my introduction, Robenalt noted, "Since so many of her [Nan's] dates and 'facts' are corroborated by the Phillips letters, her story could be true, though not as she has embellished it" (<u>Affair</u>, 347). He is not the first one to suggest "embellishment," but no one cites what that was. Actually, Nan's narrative is markedly straight-forward, and is not given to rhetorical excess.

All of Marion believed in the truth of Nan's book, even if they may have disliked what it revealed. People—among them Warren—knew of Nan's idolizing her 'hero,' for she had done nothing to hide it. In their affair, acknowledged by Warren's sisters, Nan would give the sense that he at last had the upper hand in a relationship. Unlike the kind of arrangement he had with Florence and Carrie, it was a relief for him to know he was the one who made the decisions.

In a superficial sense, he could love her for that alone, but in the attitude which saturates Nan's memoir, his love was profound. On the first occasion of their private meeting it was instantaneous.

More importantly, Nan appreciated Harding's difficulties, and sympathetically abided the claims made on him by both Florence and Carrie. Since her commitment answered his, she stayed fast to him, despite prior claims, his wife's on-going. She was understanding. Warren emphasized that he considered her his true wife. And she knew that great as her feelings were for him, his exceeded hers. They felt they were naturally mated. As he said, "We were made for each other Nan" (PD, 37).

Nan was simply the right partner for Warren, if not quite at the right time. Though she had cause for complaint, especially when it came to their child, her love for Warren superseded other demands. For, in truth, it was Nan, who, more inclusively than Carrie, became the love of Warren's life. It was a giving love that exceeded reciprocation, unique in his experience.

As their romantic discourse expanded, Warren found himself thinking of Nan as his ideal of a prospective wife. Put that way, this idea did not come up in comparable terms in any of the available letters Warren had written to Carrie, though, in Warren Harding biography, his love of her had become the standard for intensity.

Warren's rampant imagination inspired the vision of a new life, in which Nan became his "lovely bride," his new "wife" to be, both names oft-repeated (e.g., PD, 74f., et passim) and jubilantly meant. True, the sudden whole-heartedness with which he turned to Nan originally had much to do with her obliging attitude toward him. True, as well, is the fact that the love was based somewhat on a sense of alleviation, occasioned by comparison with his prior treatment at the hands of Florence and Carrie. But the love which followed from those entrèes was really unadulterated.

Furthermore, not only did his off-color stories cease when he got together with Nan, but so did his adulteries. Though on some occasions he had been in contact with Carrie while pledged to Nan, it was a distanced contact contained in letters. By 1915-16, Carrie had made him aware that she was not interested in restoring the "old feelings" (Affair, 159).

Warren told Nan, that in evading the temptation offered by another woman, "he couldn't ever 'fall for' anybody but [Nan]" (PD, 60). In a sense, his telling Nan she was the 'only one' might seem like what a man would say to reassure his mistress. But, there was more at stake here. If that 'temptation' had been a vague reference to Carrie (who was a temptation) it may well have been that he was signaling that she really no longer tempted him as she had in the past. The whole thing was part of his desperately wanting to make sure that Nan stayed with him. He honestly told her, from the beginning, that, more than just a passing affair, he had an absolute need of her, and wanted her for life.

When Nan recorded his insistently repeating that he wanted her to believe he loved her, he was talking from the fear of losing her, so suddenly had she meant that much to him. Considering the unique—indeed unlikely—nature of their attachment, he wanted to be assured it was securely there for him. He seemed to have come into an attitude that was quite new to him. There is little doubt that he had once had as strong a desire for permanence with Carrie. The difference was that he saw Nan was willing to wait for it, and Carrie let him know she was not.

His stressing, "we were made for each other," cliché that it was, apparently had the same motivation of letting Nan know this was for good (PD, 37). In fact, many of the clichés he used with regard to Nan were also spoken in truth. No matter if the words were stale, the sentiments were fresh. The expressions might be characterized as juvenile, and, as will be seen, that would be apropos. It was an interesting feature of the carefree relationship they grew into.

CHAPTER 61

"It Was More Than Sex"

RESEARCHERS WHO LOOKED INTO THE sexual propensities of men in power have offered several apt conclusions, particularly if their subjects happen to have been politicians. One conclusion was that "Men in politics are much more sexually active than the average man, and this activity continues undiminished to an advanced age." The researchers proposed that, to begin with, "the force of this sex drive is related directly, indeed is indistinguishable from, the power drive...[as] men who get to the top will also have a high sex drive."[122]

On the surface of it, however much Warren Harding may have fit the mold, there was a crucial difference in his relationship with Nan Britton. It began as platonic love, which, for a man used to physical relations with women other than his wife, was rather unusual. As the relationship progressed, Nan filled an emptiness that had exasperated Warren in his married life. Nan took account of this, in her response to Warren's saying that Florence made "life hell for [him]...!" "Knowing this," Nan said she "did all in [her] power to make up to the man [she] loved all his legal wife failed to do" (PD, 74). Florence's 'hell' would have resulted in any of a number of frustrations. Where her dominating personality put him down, acquiescent Nan wanted to pick him up.

He and Nan enjoyed one another to the hilt, and to do so, put off ambiguities, such as a future vaguely hinged on Florence's demise.

Though their coming together was a life-changing event, it couldn't change the facts of Warren's life, which is just what love ignores.

Psychological enhancement was one thing; real life problems another. For all that Nan did to reward Warren's life with her, he did still sustain a life with Florence, who gave him priceless advice, particularly during his Presidency. For a limited time, Warren could well have considered himself lucky enough to enjoy the best of both worlds. Habituated to ignoring reality in other circumstances, he treated his double life as if it were treatable, perchance by fate.

And speaking of reality, before getting any further into the text of The President's Daughter, I should pause for a reminder of the positive reception given it by Harding critics who have looked into the reliability factor. To take it beyond Robenalt's certifying Nan's factual base, there is Phillip Payne's expanded study, for which he acquired access to the Nan Britton Papers at the University of California at Los Angeles. After examining the manuscript of her book, he set to rest one nagging question by establishing that Nan did indeed write the book herself, with the possibility of some editorial help.

Moreover, Payne indicates that, personally, she "does not appear to be the gold digger that Harding partisans would hope for." Holding back from complete endorsement, Payne believed the case for Harding's having had a daughter with Nan "can be compelling." But, based on the near impossibility of getting evidence beyond what is already available, Payne cited "the difficulty of evaluating Britton's story," while conceding that "many readers, however, have found the intimacy and familiarity of Britton's account persuasive" (Dead Last, 245, 154,138). Generally positive, Payne provided the standard historian's view, and a solid one: i.e., based on what can be documented, that Nan was fully believable.

On a more affirmative note, Dean Albertson, Payne's friend and fellow Harding researcher, had written to Nan Britton herself, telling her that, in light of the available evidence, she "was telling a story which actually happened." He went on, "I think you are on tremendously strong ground when you write autobiographically, for when you write in this vein, you are telling a story that actually happened..." (Ibid., 189). Carl Anthony fully accepted Nan's account, as well, writing: "That Nan was an intimate partner of Warren's is hard to deny." He pointed out that her credibility was supported by persons in a position to know about it—i.e., Harding's sister Daisy and his secretary, George B. Christian, Jr., who personally "knew [Harding's} every move and visitor" (Florence, 530f.).

The best case for trusting the overall truthfulness of Nan's book rests with the views of two respected Harding historians, unafraid to take a stand, Robert K. Murray and Randolph C. Downes. After giving an unquestioned recitation of the content of Nan's book, Murray observed that "her claims and descriptions contained enough authenticity to confirm suspicions." Like Anthony, he also indicated the significance of two sources which back Nan's truthfulness: first, the acceptance by Harding's sisters of Nan's claims "that some sort of intimate relationship had existed between herself and their brother," and, second, that George B. Christian, Jr. "admitted many times in private that the Britton story was all true" (Era, 489, 584f., n. 51).

Downes, who had been in personal contact with Nan, was a little more direct: "A historian does not always accept as proof what other people do. Nevertheless I am convinced, and I think most authorities on the Harding period are convinced, that her [Nan's] story is true" The sub-head of the New York Times article reporting on the discovery of the Carrie Phillips letters read, "Harding Letters Tend to Give Credence to [Nan's] Story of Affair with President." This was based on Francis Russell's statement to that effect. He too was positive on Nan's credibility.[123]

There is one piece of information that helps to confirm the truthfulness of some particulars in Nan's account of her relationship with Harding. In an item I have cited in another connection, this occurs in how she worded a declaration Harding made in the course of dictating a specimen letter, after their first secret meeting at the Manhattan Hotel: "I love you more than the world, and I want you to belong to me" (PD, 35).

The first part of this declaration contained almost the exact same wording Harding had used around five years earlier in a poem addressed to Carrie Phillips, followed by the same acute desire for permanence, synonymous with possession. The first two lines of that poem read: "I love you more than all the world; Possession wholly imploring;" (cited by Payne, 173). It would seem that Nan kept pretty good records of what passed between herself and Warren Harding.

Discounting the embarrassing reflection on Warren for repeating himself, it was entirely possible for him to have felt equally committed to each of these women at different times under different conditions. Love-starved as he was, Warren found himself continuously in want of the full emotional commitment from each of these women.

Carrie and Nan had both salved the same deep-seated need, except that with Nan it went beyond physical gratification. Rather conclusive on this point is the fact that Warren made his declaration of love before he and Nan had had their first sexual experience.

Whatever Warren's original motive for setting up the Manhattan Hotel tryst with Nan, since the experience itself happened on impulse, it was either unplanned or subject to a plan that fell apart. Contrary to how a worldly wise friend of Nan's saw Warren's intention, his conduct, as Nan perceived it, was "all too spontaneous, too sincere to have been premeditated" (PD, 34). Surprised that the young lady he'd had an eye on should have been so receptive to his amorous kisses, his towering feelings told him it was love, and he told her so.

It was all so breathtaking that he had to apologize for the kisses, fearing he had gone too far. An amazing turn-about for a man with a history of sex addition. Overall, Warren acted very much like, if he had he come looking for sex (as he might have) it was dispelled by her innocence (how could he?) and heightened by her counterpart yearning. Elated, he apparently realized that she echoed a need of his own. Breaking off his dictation of a sample letter, his "I need you so" emphasized his needing to have his need fulfilled (Ibid., 35, my itals).

Hoping for a sign of something like that after his let-down with Carrie Phillips, Warren entered the bridal chamber anxiously, and Nan's response was a felicitous surprise. Not just lovers in the conventional sense, these unlikely two falling in love like that, gave them the inscrutable sense it was genuine. Feelings keyed that high offered the premonition of a lasting attachment. They started out in love. And sex had yet to come.

Two years into their relationship, they were riding high during Nan's pregnancy. She was picturing their contemplated future: "To marry Warren Harding! To live on a farm and raise children with Warren Gamaliel Harding! What rapture! I put my lips against his and spoke through my kisses. 'Oh sweetheart, that would be too heavenly!'" Looking at Warren, she writes, "A love divine was in his eyes as I spoke" (PD, 82).

Immediately preceding this, Warren has been repeating, "Would be grand, wouldn't it, dearie?" As he looked out the window, his voice "grew stern," and he looked back at her "hard as a man might who is trying not to cry." (Ibid.). Emotions were getting the better of him, but Nan leaves it for us to conclude whether the suppressed tears had to do with inordinate joy or apprehension—or both. Taking Nan's story from its beginning gives us some background for this scene.

CHAPTER 62

"Taking It From The Beginning"

SINCE DEALING WITH THE CONTENT of The President's Daughter has been fairly well avoided, one might want to have a look at it to see behind the curtain of Warren Harding's secret obsession during his final years. Nan's record of a double life, to which, she remained the sole witness, gives us the only close-up profile of what he was like in times of private joy—pre-crisis times when he could lock out external pressures up to, and into, his Presidency. Nan's portrait of events here is self-evidently convincing. Among other things, Harding identifiably echoes the impulsiveness one finds in his love letters to Carrie Phillips, apparent early on.

This comes out in the first major episode in Nan's Memoir. In brief, after having worshipped the hometown hero from afar, she proceeds to the scene of a private meeting with him, which explodes into love at first kiss. Suddenly as this came on, it had been slowly worked up to.

The opening pages of Nan's saga began with the exigent request for Warren Harding to help find Nan a job. After the 1913 death of her father, a small town doctor, and friend of Harding's, she became starkly aware that the family was left in deep financial straits, which made the need for assistance immediate. The request she made of Harding would follow a visit that her mother had earlier made to his office in hopes he could come up with some "Chautauqua work" for her.

On that occasion, Harding had asked about Nan and suggested he might "do something sometime for Nan," which had the girl walking "in the clouds" for days thereafter (PD, 20, Nan's ital.).

So child-like was her idolization that her heart would beat "wildly" simply from a glimpse of Harding when her family was passing by his home on Mt.Vernon Avenue. The greater the distance, the greater the worship, further enhanced by the impossibility that this could eventuate into anything other than a hoped-for acquaintance, plus a job. At that point, such an acquaintance would merely be part of small town neighborliness.

When the opportunity for a personal meeting occurred, Nan was more than willing to be overwhelmed—having already been pretty much so from the anticipation. The "adoration" for Warren Harding, of which she "had been so publicly boasting" (Ibid., 17) had become widespread enough that he couldn't have been blind to what most of Marion knew. At the thought of his coming to New York City with "the sole motive" of seeing her, Nan was feeling that "an inexpressible happiness reigned in [her] heart" (Ibid., 29). Though trite in the expression, her sentiments were real, and made an impression on Harding.

However, in the prelude to their relationship, it looked like Harding's interest may have been aroused by the simple attraction of opportune sex, as he had witnessed enough of the girl's idolatry to fantasize her vulnerability.

So, he comes up to New York to meet her, supposedly about a job, but, no sooner does he have her in the bridal chamber of the Manhattan Hotel than she is in his embrace, and his impulsive kiss is abruptly followed by the apologetic awakening that he has been rashly taking advantage of this young girl, even with no more than a kiss. As he took the situation in, his head was as much in the clouds as hers was.

"Oh dearie," he pleads, "tell me it isn't hateful to you to have me kiss you!"

Embarrassment is swiftly quelled, their feelings are mutual, and, after additional "very ardent kisses," he tucks $30 in her silk stocking. It is money supposedly toward her trip to Chicago to see her sister (Ibid., 33), which a woman less entranced would have considered crass—at any rate, a sign that maybe it had been done before. Since, instead of taking offense, Nan responded that his kisses "surpassed even [her] gladdest dreams of him," the amazing turn of events had them both spontaneously enthralled. Looking ahead, their hearts were aglow with promise, romance dancing before their eyes.

It is pertinent that for their first private meeting, Harding should have met her in the bridal chamber, on the claim it was the only room still available. That may have been true, but as it might not have been the case, it seems clear that, while he may originally have wanted to bed her, what happened under the spell of this girl's contagious appeal produced an unexpected change in Harding's attitude toward her.

As Nan describes the scene, she leaves us with clear inferences to be drawn from what happened in that hotel room. The money in the stocking gesture, for instance, suggests a carry-over of what would have been Harding's initial desire to make use of the bridal bed.

A wholly novel experience for Harding, his change of heart would appear to have followed from his having simply fallen in love with this girl's love itself. As Nan spelled it out, there was little doubt that any prior anticipation on Harding's part had to have been erased by her corresponding response to the emotion with which he kissed her. Brimming with the unexpected, if he saw that there was not going to be any sex in a room reserved for newly weds, his having become overwrought by the kissing alone would have told him, how, for the time being, that much had to suffice.

The key element here was obviously love. The new consciousness set in so rapidly, the upshot for Harding was that on seeing this girl was so much in love with him, he himself, in need of that love, would grow a fantasy wholly different from an original one. He, in fact, instantly began to envision an auspicious future for their relationship, which was to be expressed in passionate letters, imploring her to "belong" to him (PD, 32-35). Letters these were of some length, a few—maybe more—running to all of forty long-hand pages, one of sixty.

When Nan reminded him, during their Manhattan meeting, of an earlier incident when they had had a chance encounter on a street in Marion—an exalted moment for the young girl—he told her that, on his part, "the desire to possess [her] had been born in his heart upon that occasion" (Ibid., 17). She didn't give a date for that chance meeting, but, it was pertinent that—true or not—Harding had said he'd had a desire for her in mind over a number of rapidly elapsed years.

Hence, as a precondition of his mercurial change of attitude, there seems to have been as much of a yearning on his part as there had been on hers. Only his motive had changed. What he told Nan amounted to a reconciliation of his attitude with his conduct. Since he at first could not take things further than passionate kisses, it was appropriate that their relationship should begin purely at the level of romance, enforced by Nan's virgin resistance.

As for the desire of possession itself, this was summed up in the letter he pretended to be dictating to Nan (as an aspiring secretary) in which he spoke specifically of her "belonging" to him. It was in this specimen dictation, which immediately followed their private Hotel meeting, that he blurted out, "I love you more than the world, and I want you to belong to me. Could you belong to me, dearie? I want you…and I need you so…" In wording reminiscent of Carrie, strange as this might have sounded, it was more than Nan expected to hear, and she silenced his dictation "with the kisses he pleaded for."

Moreover, Nan continued, "He would tremble so just to sit close to me, and [she] adored every evidence of his enthusiasm" (*PD*, 35). As the relationship advanced, so did their closeness, hastened by events. When he knew she was going to be having his child, for example, he bought her the ring she wanted, and, Nan reported that they "performed a sweet little ceremony with that ring," which included Harding's declaring that Nan "could not belong to him more utterly had [they] been joined together by fifty ministers" (*PD*, 87).

Quite as important as having Nan voice her love for him was his counterpart desire for possession, also sounded several times over (e.g., "I want you to belong to me,…I need you so," *PD*, 35, et passim). In his two prior relationships, *he* had been the one who got possessed, which more than anything re-emphasized an otherwise subconscious void in Harding's inner world—to be filled and overflowed by the only woman who gave Warren G. Harding her complete and unqualified love.

Nan dates their first meeting as having occurred in late May, 1917. She goes out of her way to emphasize that there were "no intimacies" in the bridal chamber "beyond [their] very ardent kisses." On the other hand, she shortly makes a special point of setting down the date when she "became Mr. Harding's bride," which, as she says, was the name he assigned her to celebrate the consummation of their relationship on 30 July, 1917.

Unlike anything from prurient Warren's past, they had been in courtship as a pair of innocents for a bit more than two months before having sex. As they both saw it, she was not just comparable to a wife; she was more of one than the wife he had. The effect on Harding was profound.

CHAPTER 63

"Their Love Child's Play"

WARREN HARDING'S RELATIONSHIP WITH NAN Britton was a second childhood, dream-like, unreal, and dangerously adulterous for a President. But, considered for what it meant to Harding, it was heaven-sent, an emotional break-out, pure in its way, naïve, and devoid of adult consciousness. Kids tend to do foolish things. Harding had called Carrie "foolish," but clearly the same could have been said of him, to say nothing of how clever Florence looked for marrying the handsomest man in town, with whom she was disinclined to share a bed. There were mistakes made all around.

The love Harding found with Nan Britton rejuvenated him, quite literally. He and Nan indulged in the joyful antics of childhood relived. They had a closeness that resembled the friendship ties that kids have. Nan had to confess, "I was becoming so growingly dependent upon his love and support in every way as to make it inconceivable for me to do without him," (PD, 102f.)—which duplicated Harding's sense of what she meant to him. Nan dated those feelings back to when she "first saw him in Marion when [she] was a child" (PD, 103, my ital.). It seemed a child's fantasy when she found that his love was the equal of hers.

One aspect of the psychodynamics of aging politicians whose sex drive was activated by their position is that there is the resurgence of a youthful stage in their lives; in effect a reversion to adolescent behavior. As Janus and his colleagues put it, "The self-seeking idealism which characterizes so many politicians is also typical of adolescence, and indeed such men can be described as fixated at that stage of development" (op.cit., 5).[124] In keeping with the youthful effect of love newly found, there were no more sure indications of Harding's adolescent response to his budding relationship with Nan than the type of behavior she discloses.

As evidence of sheer puppy love, on that night when they over-stayed the time of her permissible presence in his Senate Office, the reason Harding gave for why he so much liked having her there was typically adolescent. Her presence invested the place with such "precious memories" that "he could visualize [her being] there during the hours he worked alone" (PD, 75).

Another such instance of adolescent fervor was his explanation for why the salutation of his letters was different from the penmanship in the body of them. He said it was because he was so consumed by day-dreams of her that he often wrote his love letters "on memo paper during legislative discussions in the Senate Chamber," and, having shut out adult matters to write them, he added the salutations later (Ibid.).

These letters were unusually long. An early one—accompanied by a photograph showing him probably at the Capital steps—which was received in June, 1917—would run to forty pages (Ibid., 59) its length likely inspired by his unburdening himself over their being separated, hardly a month after the beginning of their pre-sexual love life. In its early stages, they were moon-struck. These were letters being written by a middle-aged man, over fifty years old, playfully doing a time-warp retreat from his official position in the United States Senate.

Although Warren and Nan decided on the prudence of destroying their love letters, it was so difficult for them to part with them that, like children, they preciously clung to the latest as long as they could, for re-reading, so they could feel reunited when apart (PD, 77).

Typical of that mood, the letters contained such "heart-revealments" that Warren admitted he had never read "anything comparable to [their] love letters" anywhere, "except in French" (Ibid.). Appropriately enough, there were times when, contemplating Florence's death, he would dreamily speak of their finding a place in the country, where, as in fairy tales, they could live together in blissful freedom, and—in their bridal utopia—live, yes, happily ever after (PD, 74).

On one occasion after the other, he would compulsively plead with her to believe that he truly loved her, as he did after proudly getting her an interview for a job with none other than Judge Elbert Henry Gary, head of U. S. Steel. His love-sick attitude was underscored, yet again, when, exiting the taxi, he tripped, prompting a superfluous reassurance: "You see, dearie, I'm so crazy about you that I don't know where I'm stepping!" (PD, 37). Like a moon-struck adolescent, he didn't know 'where he was stepping' and didn't care that he didn't.

This scene was followed by Nan's recalling their return to the Manhattan Hotel bridal chamber, as a nostalgic reminder, which had Harding redundantly expressing his love for her and adding, typically childlike, that they were made for one another (Ibid.).

Warren's passionate outbursts were so overboard they sounded a lot like desperation, which they, by and large, were. They also betrayed their felicitous surprise at finding one another; the first-love syndrome. They were, after all, one another's faithful "sweethearts." But every now and again a touch of reality would escape. As Nan observed "There was something pathetic about watching [Warren] at play," which was what a friend of Nan's had noticed about their little child "at play" (Ibid., 102).

Since Warren came on so euphorically to Nan, and she had been cultivating a school girl crush on him, they seemed to have naturally slipped into an adolescent mentality. Typically, they shared a kindred feeling. One of the requests he made of her, very early—and continuously thereafter—was that she tell him she loved him. His perseveration was symptomatic of a man so overwhelmed that he couldn't trust the fact that this intense experience was really happening, which bolstered the need to have it asserted and reasserted that it was.

For inundated Warren Harding, there were times when his boyishness brought them simple joys. On one of Nan's trips to Washington, for example, after they had spent the morning at her hotel room, Warren took her out in a hired touring car for a sight-seeing excursion, "about the city and out along the Potomac." She enjoyed his "boyish enthusiasm in playing host" as he "pointed out places of interest to [her]." She found it "delightful," and knew she was "a most appreciative guest" (Ibid., 69). Saturday being date-night, there were occasions when Warren took her to a Saturday night play.

Ignoring the high stakes consequences they were courting, he and Nan carried on as if they were playing a child's game, children absorbed in play being oblivious to risks. Scandal ignored, the adult children seemed to relish the fun of treating their world as non-conforming to the external one.

As Nan spelled it out, the experience they shared was unique. "So potent was the spell which we had for each other that for whole evenings we were its willing prisoners, living as in a dream, neither of us coming out from the intoxication of each other's presence until long after the separation. Often then we wrote to one another about it. If we were in a taxi, we would become so oblivious to the entire world we would both be amazed when we reached our destination" (PD, 67).

CHAPTER 64

"Nan In Relation To Concurrent Events"

THERE WERE COLLATERAL EVENTS SURROUNDING the time of Warren Harding's coming together with Nan Britton, events which influenced decisions he contemplated, and some that he made.

First of all, since the opportunity for seeing Nan had been on Harding's mind before the Manhattan Hotel meeting, it coincided with a fall-off in his allusion to parlor stories. Nan was a fresh start; the stories were an antidote to middle-aged boredom. She also happened to reach Harding at a time when he was in need of having his battered ego soothed from the treatment meted out by Carrie Phillips.

Following the time of Carrie's return from Germany in 1914, her relationship with Warren had been on-again—off-again, which left him uncertain as to when it was either. At the end of 1915, he was left wondering if they could restore old times. He doubted it, but clung to the hope that restoration might still be possible. In January, 1917, he was writing Carrie that he was "blue," adding, "hope doesn't brighten where I most wish it might." He ended the letter saying he was "in the depths and will await some ascent."

In his letter of the following month (previously cited) he wrote that he was no better off, and appealed to Carrie for help, to no avail. All he wanted was to "be lifted up" by her presence. (Affair, 159, 204).

On 11 May, 1917, Nan would be writing Harding for a letter of recommendation, and a few days later she received a hasty response. This innocuous exchange, however, provided an occasion for the awakening of an interest that he said went back to their supposedly prophetic encounter on the street years earlier (PD,17). Interestingly, it was in a 7 May, 1917 letter to Scobey (quoted above) that Harding had been playfully emphasizing the need to observe propriety in connection with the stories he'd been sending through the mail. He insisted that he would maintain his virtue "at all hazards."

Put on for the fun of it, that virtue would assume another dimension for Warren, actually another sense, when shortly afterwards, Nan would be propitiously coming into his life. This, after he had sent Scobey in the preceding month his tale about Representative Rankin's "yielding," a letter he concluded with the out-dated advice for Scobey to be "a King in your youth." Behind the scenes, "yielding" was to take on an interesting connotation for Warren and Nan. On their discovering one another, contrary to the sexual overtones of yielding, they were more than content to yield to platonic love. As indicated, Warren's reversion to youthful antics had a regal equivalent.

There were certain effects that ran parallel to the growing relationship with Nan. It was in October, 1917, with their relationship in its discovery phase, full of wonder, that Harding would for the first time dismiss his ambition to run for President. That possibility had initially arisen on his election to the Senate in 1914 by a substantial plurality. The ambition had grown from there, and three years later it stalled.

While one can't necessarily say post hoc, ergo propter hoc, it is not without significance that, so shortly after a rapturous encounter with Nan, he would be writing Scobey that, in humble comparison with TR, people who would think of him as a candidate were "foolish." True to his new attitude, he continued," I never fool myself. I am neither fit nor capable" of running. The only supposed "lure" he jests was the wish to give Scobey "a party at the White House."[125] At the time, he was enjoying an emotional party of his own.

His joking about a run for President suggests there was something else on his mind inconsistent with the pursuit of public office. An interesting sign of his wanting to pull himself out of contention for the Presidency in October, 1917, resides in the fact that, a year earlier, the restraint imposed by TR had not been a deterrent to his then considering the Nomination a viable ambition. It had, in fact, been entertained with careful forethought as to how he represented himself to the Party—and public.

As noticed by William Allen White (mentioned above) Harding, being keynote speaker at the 1916 National Convention, had shown himself to be "tiptoeing…into a national limelight," with "the circumspection befitting a potential candidate, so much in earnest had he then entertained the idea of making a run for it" (Masks, 394f.). Since his wanting out in 1917 would occur to him while his thoughts were consumed with Nan, it is as if that—call it nascent love—would have made him willing to set aside aspirations, which otherwise were never lacking in importance to him.

Of course, his aspiring to run for President became a love-hate proposition for Warren. When hated, it could be abhorred. Having emphatically rejected early efforts by supporters like Kansas City journalist Mont Reily to make him a Presidential candidate, he indicated that the thought of it intimidated him. That was shortly after the death of TR in January, 1919, which left the field wide open to him. That month was likewise a high point in his relationship with Nan, their intensity leading to the conception of a child.

Once Harding gained the Presidency, he told Reily off, writing him that he could kill "Harry D and [him] for getting [him] into such a mess as President... as it is all grief and no joy" (Shadow, 313, Frances, 414). Having begged off in the anticipation, Warren could look back in envy at his having found love with Nan a better alternative than fulfillment of the aim that would end up giving him grief and joylessness.

There is an additional incident that may have been subtly influenced by Nan's having come into his life. The June, 1920 Nominating Convention took place nine months after Nan had given birth to their daughter. Greatly disheartened by the meager showing he had made in the vote count during the early stage of the Convention, Harding was discouraged to the extent that he was all for giving up his bid for the Nomination. He thought of making it decisive by filing to run for re-election to the Senate. Even Florence, his strongest and most sympathetic backer, was disheartened, at that point, claiming he didn't have a chance.

On telling Nicholas Murray Butler that the Convention would "never nominate" him, Harding not only didn't reactivate his filing for re-election to the Senate, but he went on to tell Butler, "I am going to quit politics" (Adams, Incredible Era, 143). This was a remarkable decision on Harding's part.

His dedication to Party being ingrained, it took a force equally as strong as that—his dedication to Nan—to strengthen his desire to pull out of contention for the Nomination.

It would seem like Harding was banking on a climactic farewell to politics when he had Nan deliberately sitting out there in a seat he had given her at the Chicago Coliseum in1920. This had to have had something to do with a hidden decision to severe ties with that arena. For one thing, he was not concerned if it was discovered who had put Nan there, an unconventional placement, subject to question. Of no concern, if he was to be pulling out anyway.

Just as he would be thrust back and forth in his relationship with Carrie, so had Warren been ambivalent about going for the Nomination. Since the Convention seats had to have been assigned early, the reservation would have been made in his wanting-out phase. Regardless of its being questioned, Nan's sitting there would have constituted a secret celebration of Warren's decision to take his life in a new direction.

As with Carrie, Warren and Nan both had to know the Nomination might become a barrier to their dream. Based on past behavior, Carrie could not have accepted a return to politics. Nan, to be sure, had little recourse, other than to trust that the strength of their relationship was going to see them through. Counting on Florence's death, Warren had told Nan, "You'd make such a darling wife!" (PD, 74). During that 'wanting-out' phase, he incredibly went so far as to put wife-Nan ahead of an adamant dedication to Party.

There had to be reassurance in that. Nan, after all, had come into Warren's life just three months after he had a second time written Carrie about his depression, and, wanting nothing more than her caring presence, he instead got her "stinging reproof." Then, come May, and all of a sudden there was Nan. Then, three years later, what also came was a pair of situations that would reverse Warren's inclination to pull himself away from politics.

First, Florence decided to put him back into the fight for the Nomination, and Warren went along. That did not mean he would get it, but it got him to thinking he didn't have to sacrifice Nan for politics. However much this may have dimmed the lovers' dream, it did not result in a falling off of their devotion. Besides, as the Convention went through one fruitless ballot after the other, Warren could reasonably assume there was little chance the Nomination might fall to him.

However, there was an additional reason for him to hang in and hope he might be chosen after all. As Randolph Downes has pointed out, his having to turn around and maintain his candidacy for the Nomination was not just a personal choice. "There were hundreds of Republicans…throughout the state [of Ohio] whose tenure depended essentially on the Harding organization helping them against the threat from the [opposition] Hynicka-Brown faction" (Rise of WGH, 346f.).

Recognizing this problem, that was the same Warren Harding who would at one point break out with a guilt complex in telling Nan, he'd "rather die than disappoint the Party" (PD, 240). In context, that reminder came out of nowhere. Its source, however, was the same as that for his reviving his Candidacy. So a significant motive for his rethinking the matter and wanting to get back into the running had to do with his need to preserve his political status as a force in Ohio, where numerous office holders were depending on his support.

As things simultaneously progressed in his relationship with Nan and his pursuit of a political future, it should have become clear to the two of them that his being elected President (a far cry from his frivolous Senatorship) might be toxic for their future. For one thing, a husband in high office would activate Florence. And a Florence sidelined by illness was one thing; her as an aggressive political strategist was quite another. She knew she could make a President of this indecisive candidate; to her a bowl of gelatin that she could stabilize.

Florence's tendency was to wall off all that might get in the way of business, and at least part of the reason Warren seemed inattentive and let her get away with running political affairs was the pleasant distraction he had with Nan. That would be the good side of his not getting the Nomination.

But the Presidency? Ignoring a high-stakes risk, Nan regularly made visits to their favorite nook in the ante-room of the White House, perhaps weekly, if clear. Politics might interfere with their relationship, but their relationship didn't interfere with politics. That's why Warren would supposedly have had no difficulty answering a query put to him about potential embarrassment before the Nomination would be handed to him.

Whatever limitations the Presidency might impose on Warren and Nan, they seemed bent on hedonistically seizing every opportunity for togetherness they could create for themselves. As Florence's fragile health meant she could die any day, they felt things would work out for them. Nan abided the times he 'couldn't have her' in exchange for those that he could.

It wasn't easy for them. As plans hung fire, there were times when Nan's "sense of unfinishment" had to be "banished," and she "clung to visionary hopes and to Mr. Harding's oft-repeated statement to [her] that in his 'sober judgment' he felt that [their] relationship was 'predestined'" (Ibid., 203f.).

Apparently putting their trust in predestination, Nan and Warren weren't prepared for having the Presidency compromise their opportunities for togetherness. Disregarding the limitations it imposed, they seemed bent on seizing whatever opportunities they could avail themselves of.

Why not? Florence's fragile health meant she could die any day. Looked at from the perspective of how things did end for them, it was probably just as well that they enjoyed what they had while they had it.

CHAPTER 65

"Nan Vs Carrie; Meeting Warren's Need"

WITH ALL OF WARREN'S PROFESSIONS of love that were reported by Nan, and all of the same that were mentioned in his letters to Carrie, the question arises as to whether there was a distinction between the commitments he made to each. More explicitly, since Nan meant so much to him, how genuine was it in light of what he had felt for Carrie?

For one thing, the relationship with Nan lasted and remained steadfast until it couldn't go any further, and broke down. It seemed that it was only a question of when Fate would catch up to these lovers. As for Warren's relationship with Carrie, it hit a road-block of its own. Carrie walked out on him and put an ocean between them. Carrie's patience gave out; Nan's was tested, and held fast.

The Carrie relationship deteriorated over a number of years, and, in the process, it made Warren miserable. As the Carrie affair descended, it was avidly supplanted by the ascending one with Nan. It becomes apparent that, unlike prior relationships, the one with Nan was based on her having been swept away for him, even though, first-off, he fell head-long for her. Much as he had sought a comparable experience with Carrie, Warren found himself being the partner who on pledging his love, hoped it would be returned. When it was, it was mainly on Carrie's terms, and in bed.

Nothing speaks more acutely of the difference between the two mistresses than their respective attitudes toward politics. Carrie had no use for it at all. For her, it was an unneeded distraction that would take time away from her (Shadow, 249, 254). In 1920, Nan, by contrast, was eager to return to Marion for the November 2nd election night in hopes of getting to be with Warren then. Because, out campaigning, he hadn't been with her since June, he wrote that he was "hungry" to see her.

Jim Sloan, their Secret Service go-between, brought them together, and a remarkable scene ensued. After repeated kissing, Warren had an astounding response to her exclaiming, "Oh, sweetheart, isn't it wonderful that you are President!" She repeated her exclamation, following which, as she wrote, "he looked at me some time before he answered. Then [came] his 'um.....say dearie, do you [ever] love me!'" This, Nan continued, "showed me that the glories of a victorious hero were submerged in the grander glories of a lover's delight in being with his woman."

This was a clincher: Harding, the politician par excellance, was putting Nan above his winning the Presidency: "This," he declared, "is the best thing that's happened to me lately, dearie." (PD, 146, 149, Nan's itals.).

Harding had been very much taken with Carrie. Going back to their rocky years, it had surely been more than a bruised ego that would have sent him back to Carrie in 1916 following her rejection of him because he stayed on in his marriage. Also hard for Warren to deal with was her combative sensitivity regarding Germany, over which she had charged him with low-down hypocrisy for a campaign speech in which he tried to make himself appealing to Cincinnati Germans.

She had told him as early as 1911 that her love had begun to change, and he, in the next year, felt she had gotten away from him, and was beyond reach. By 1913, there was a definite "cooling" between them (Affair, 242, 185, 58, 62, 100). Nevertheless, none of that would prevent their coming together for steamy sex in each of those years.

One can only speculate on what else beyond sexual attraction could have motivated Warren to keep telling Carrie how much she meant to him, how much he, in fact, loved her. She surely loved him, as well, but she could rather easily be put out with him. She would chide him, for example, over the seemingly small matter of his having gone to Hawaii with his wife in January, 1915, when he and Carrie had themselves once dreamed of going there together (Ibid., 136). The simple fact was that Carrie hated Florence as much as—perhaps more than—she loved Warren.

Significantly, with the beginning of his spirited relationship with Nan—a sort of revenge on Carrie—there were a number of instances in which Warren was supposed to meet Carrie, and offered excuses for his having been unable to do so. The real reason was that he preferred being with Nan—a relief from Carrie. This was particularly the case in late May, 1917, shortly after he had started seeing Nan.

On May 24th, for example, Carrie had let Warren know that she was looking forward to meeting him somewhere in the East, and he indicated that he had been indisposed for a while, in no shape to see her. The truth then was that he had gone to New York to see Nan before she left for her new job with U. S. Steel in Chicago (Ibid., 248f.).

There was a similar situation next month (June, 1917) when Carrie had had an expectation that they'd have a meeting in New York. Regarding that, she had sent Warren two letters, and had even telephoned him at the end of May. As she hadn't received a response, to save face, she had to break off the possibility of a get-together.

Preoccupied with Nan at the time, Warren, instead of setting up a meeting with Carrie, was making arrangements to meet Nan in Indianapolis, where he would be giving a speech (Ibid., 251f.). On that occasion, he incidentally registered Nan at the Claypool Hotel as his 'niece' (PD, 40).

Typically, it was not a problem for Warren Harding to be alternately courting both women, still needing a recovery of love lost with the one, while deeply engaged in a new-found love with the other. However, it seemed like the old attraction would die hard. Again in June, 1917, partially as a result of the missed appointment, Warren had felt it was all over with Carrie. But, a touch more than half a year later, he and Carrie had apparently had an intimate meeting in February 1918, following which Warren wrote her, "There is no other like you" (Ibid., 307). Sex, in other words, did not restore love; it temporarily sublimated her unloving treatment of him.

The tie with Nan, had other ramifications. For one thing, the child-like benevolence fostered by Warren's love for her was an extension of his being essentially good natured. Although Warren's benevolence existed alongside indecency in his private life, there was personal decency in his public life. He was, in fact, known for that. Herbert Hoover made a point of it in his Memorial address, describing Harding as "a man…of sympathetic heart, of transcendent gentleness of soul…who reached out for friendship…who gave of it loyally and generously…" (Memoirs, II, 53).

Harding's oversized libido aside, the love that was considered morally tenuous in his private life shows up in his having a heart for others, eminently illustrated by the pardons he granted almost instantly upon his assuming the Presidency. His freeing Eugene V. Debs, no friend of the Republican Party, and wanting him to be home for Christmas dinner, was motivated by Harding's instinctive kindness.

The spirit of good-neighborliness came naturally to him from the culture of his rural upbringing. In his political dealings, no less than his social ones, he not only had a soft spot for people in need, he was even charitably disposed toward some crooks in his Administration.

The "Prince of Normalcy," he brought a kindly presence to the Presidency. In the aftermath of the "Great War," he dedicated himself to avenues of peace. He convened an international Conference on Disarmament, advocated a World Court, and got Congress to finally pass a resolution ending the War with Germany and Austria.

On a more personal basis, his kindliness was exhibited on the job, as with the face-saving exit he gave to thieving Charlie Forbes. As Robert Murray has pointed out, Harding's sensitivity went so far that he "did not publicly disassociate himself from Forbes or expose his crimes" (Era, 430). After all the corruption Forbes had heaped on Harding, he was allowed to inconspicuously leave for England on the pretext that he was going there to visit British veterans' hospitals.

Non-vindictive, Warren not only refused to harbor any ill-will toward rogues in his Administration, he was equally magnanimous with Carrie following her blackmail. Post-election, he indeed had her comfortably situated in Geneva, where he had assigned her husband an obscure embassy post (PD, 261).

Warren was not only in the habit of soothing others, he needed to have his own psyche soothed as well. This would emerge in his relations with two women who helped to dispel the emptiness he felt after a Christmas-time spat with Florence, which, as noted, couldn't have been an isolated event. As he superfluously "confessed" to Nan, "it had been many years since his home situation had been satisfying" (PD, 44). Which didn't mean he was unloving toward Florence.

The President who had a care-worn expression and a soft feeling for others was frequently in need of some softness for himself. Which was where Nan Britton came in.

CHAPTER 66

"A High Point Precariously Enjoyed"

NAN HAD GONE THROUGH A number of disheartening events with Warren, none more poignant than those in which they let themselves think that their destiny seemed within reach, if only they would just recklessly grasp it. During her 1919 pregnancy, occurring in Warren's Senatorial days, when he contrasted Florence's abhorrence of having children with the expectation of Nan's having theirs, Nan found him "filled ...with the first real longing he had known to have children"—not just this one, first child (PD, 80).

Nan said this critical meeting took place in, roughly the "thirteenth week" of her pregnancy, which she put at either late March or early April. However, since she records conception as having taken place in January, 1919, and states that "the latter part of February" gave her the confirming sign (Ibid., 78) that likely being the fourth week, the thirteenth would doubtless have come in late April, when the cherry blossoms would still have been in bloom. The beautiful springtime in Washington was in itself enough to lift one's spirits, as it did for Nan and Warren.

It was the time that appropriately had Warren thinking about being "finished with politics," and his rehearsing the "old story" about her being his bride, with them settled down on a bucolic farm with their dogs, horses, and chickens, a regular barnyard. But it was by virtue of his very exuberance that it brought out a concealed uncertainty, latent in his very yearning for the good life that might await them. As this began to take form, Warren made use of the conditional modifier, "would," and he used hypothetical phrases like "if we could only," applied directly to their having their "child—together!" As Nan described it, this reverent moment becomes a dramatic scene, emotion packed.

In giving his response to this hope of shared parenthood, their feelings burst out in such raw, unalloyed rapture, that Nan said his words came forth as a "hushed exclamation, almost a prayer, scarcely audible. The yearning of a heart laid bare! [She] nodded wordlessly. The very air seemed sacred." The reader is left to assume an unrecorded silence, and Nan observed that "when he spoke again," on recovery, "it was as if he had returned to stern realities." Even when their spirits were so high, and all the more so when a wished-for future was so openly and emotionally contemplated, the prayerfulness suggests an undercurrent of doubt.

It was for the very reason that, since what could be might very well not be, that a taint of realism intruded and had to be confronted, eventuating in a heart-wrenching pause (82). Coming out of it, he smiled at Nan "sadly," saying, "Would be grand, wouldn't it, dearie?" Overcome, she wrote, "I could not yet safely answer, but I nodded." In ascending hope, the air was "sacred," and, in a coinciding descent to earth, tragic. Star crossed lovers that they were, their "Romeo and Juliet" trauma was not lessened by the metaphoric nature of the dying.

The impact of this scene was all the more heightened because it was a reminder that the unresolvable problem hanging in the background, the invisible elephant in the room, had almost everything to do with the emotion that was being so starkly evoked. Nothing would have more imperiled Harding's official life, to say nothing of his name, nothing more than an illegitimate child—not yet actually disowned, if disowned she could be. So settling his problem on terms satisfactory to a union with Nan would require his addressing more than the issues of politics and Florence.

Ironic undertones there were aplenty in this scene. Over and above a springtime mood, the place of their meeting being the New Willard Hotel, that would provide the comfort of familiar surroundings. But, ominously, Harding had arrived with a wet forehead and "other signs of nervousness" (79). His taking her on his lap, was meant to sustain the atmosphere of comfort, an effort to shield Nan from his underlying ambivalence about her having their child—thoughts it was difficult for him to put into words.

So, knowing how Nan felt about the pregnancy, he came up with soothing remarks, like his having no fear "for the future, after the child comes," and his "wistfulness" over the fact that he had "never been a father." That encouraged Nan to go overboard and assume—even though "mockingly"—that, "as he had always had such a desire for children [she'd] have to raise a family for him" (80). A ripple of humor tides them over.

Warren found himself in a tangle. Not really wanting the child (revealed in his having offered Nan several means of avoidance) though fervently wanting, at the same time, to keep his "sweetheart," as he put it, "enshrined...in his heart," he had had to yield to her unsubtle resistance to all thought of ending the pregnancy. Hence, whatever the optimism he'd had about a future with Nan, there were suppressed feelings of uncertainty, even when they wanted to maintain their relationship at its height. In fact, though fully aware of the difficulty posed by a child, both seemed to be intent on keeping up a brave front.

There were other, later times when Warren would inadvertently disclose his misgivings, as when he unambiguously lamented, "If [only] you had been born earlier, Nan!" (Ibid., 225). But their delicate problem—more like his—could as little be dismissed as articulated, free of emotional damage.

Having given more than a hint of his desire to be "finished with politics," as a prelude to their idyllic life (Ibid., 80f.), in 1919 the ideal prognostic had seemed to be in sight. The possibility of his being liberated from an inhibiting political life was at that point very much there, as was the right state of mind for severance of his tie to Florence. There remained the forthcoming birth of their child, a problem, but not an insurmountable one, should the chief impediments to disclosure be out of the way. "He spoke [to me] often" Nan wrote, "of the 'reverential love' he felt for me as the mother of our coming child" (Ibid.).

The child arrived on 22 October, 1919. Less than a year later, prior to the 1920 Nominating Convention, with Warren Harding's chances of getting the nomination remote, they again talked about disposition of their daughter. After considering, and dismissing, the chance of placing her with either the Scobeys or an institution, a very significant declaration from Harding followed, in which he incredibly took the hoped-for resolution of their problem right up to his forthcoming residence in the White House:

"It was then that Mr. Harding first discussed with utter frankness the probability of Mrs. Harding's death far in advance of his own, in which event he said with undisguised enthusiasm, 'I'd take the baby myself and make her a real Harding! Later he repeated that statement very emphatically to me in the White House, telling me how he wished to make Elizabeth Ann a 'real Harding.' Of course that plan met with a hug and a kiss from me and much worded enthusiasm. But Destiny thwarted the plans Warren Harding had for his child, although during those days we were completely oblivious of its presence" (Ibid., 130).

With his contemplation of Florence being gone, Warren apparently renewed the impossible, head-in-the clouds assumption that his marrying a mistress who had borne him an illegitimate child would not have created a scandal big enough to chase him from office. (Carrie had thought her own disclosure would have done it.) No need for Teapot to come along and blacken his name. With them lacking a consideration of contingencies, as Nan sadly observed, Destiny would take over.

It all goes back to Warren's inability to seize the moment, when it was there for him to seize in 1919, on the arrival of his daughter. But Florence kept inconveniently showing how she could defy death. With the passage of time, inertia would return Warren to real-world sobriety, when he found himself facing the difference between a Presidential verses a pre-Presidential affair.

Looking back at the adolescent consciousness Harding developed with Nan, one wonders whether the unreality of it might have figured in his letting decisive action elude him. Being drenched with euphoria, their ability to live the dream life had its liberating effect. The unfortunate part was that it liberated them not alone from sanity. In any event, in retrospect, it seems as if what had been so good for the two of them contained the seeds of what would go bad.

Since they had had the joy of living their love life to the hilt, for the time being, they had no incentive to abandon their other-world for the diurnal one they could evade for just so long.

PART IX:

CRISES AND AFTERMATH

CHAPTER 67

"The Saddest Moment Of Their Lives"

WHILE 1921 HAD BEEN A good year for Warren Harding's Presidency, a typical political "honeymoon," 1922 was proving to be more difficult and creating worries of another kind.[126] He, for example, had to deal with an economic down-turn, a rise in unemployment, and a sharp decline in exports which promoted the discontent of farmers, whose dwindling income had them calling for lower freight rates.

Worse yet, these problems were to be topped by the coal miners' strike, that erupted into bloodshed, and would be followed by the railroad workers' even more menacing strike, which brought on the infamously drastic injunction invoked by Federal Judge James A. Wilkerson (a Daugherty appointee) that was used to break the strike. The injunction had been petitioned—more like urged—by Daugherty, whose role, seen as a high-handed maneuver, was strongly criticized by other Cabinet members.

So disharmony broke out within the Administrative Family. Then there were the Republicans' congressional losses in the mid-term election, their majorities in the House of Representatives being reduced to five, and to eight in the Senate. The dismal showing by Republicans looked worse when the loss was counted in total numbers. In the House, for example, the reduction was from 299 seats to 222.

Whether or not the troubles were directly ascribable to the President, they landed on his desk anyway.[127]

Hence, with the responsibilities of Harding's Presidency becoming increasingly more demanding of his attention, Nan realized yet again "there were times when he could not have [her]" (PD, 228). She had to decamp for Chicago, where she could be near her daughter, who was being cared for by her sister and brother-in-law in the guise of adoption. It was not the most satisfactory arrangement for Nan, and one that was far from welcomed by her brother-in-law, Scott Willits. Warren, knowing of the brother-in-law's hostility, made provision for him to go to Prague and study with violin master Otakar Sevcik.

Warren was aware of the galling discomfort created for Nan by the child's ambiguous status (who was she to regard as Mother?) but he saw pseudo-adoption as a stop-gap measure that would relieve him of that worry during his term in office, and a situation Nan would be relieved of once he had left office.

Nan missed Warren, but what she also missed, in her absence, was news of a near-death recurrence of Florence's kidney disease. There had been a severe blockage, from which one of Florence's several eminent physicians declared she had little chance of recovery. Warren had been convinced she was dying before his eyes, confirmed by another of the knowledgeable doctors, who said outright, "Dying now, I think."

Evalyn McLean, whom Warren had asked to be there on his behalf and Florence's, saw him physically collapsed in a state of total despair, and, on her looking at Florence's discolored face, Evalyn thought she was already dead. With the Hardings' inconsistent physician Dr. Charles Sawyer opposing an operation on grounds that her heart couldn't endure one, there seemed little chance of Florence's surviving. Nor, as things turned out, would her chances have necessarily been enhanced had an operation been needed; for, miraculously, she did once again surprise everyone by coming through (Shadow, 549f.).

The traumatic effect on Warren posed the problem of how he could inflict further, possibly fatal, harm on this woman who had stuck by him and done so much to help him make a good showing as President. Nan had remarked on his capacity for sympathy in small matters, such as stopping to give a blind man a coin (PD, 97), but his wife's condition aroused his great capacity for sympathy—and guilt. It was easy enough for him to report ("calmly") that his wife would not survive another urinary attack; but it was something else to witness her going through one.

There was neither a need, nor a desire, for him to impart how distraught he had been, for, when Nan came to see him in January, 1923, Florence had just had yet another recurrence of the crisis she had gone through but four months earlier. The Press reported on the severity of her condition, but, by the time of Nan's arrival, Florence had remarkably pulled through the worst of it, one more time.

This prompted Nan to recall that Warren's wife had been ailing most of the time. She brought to mind an occasion during Warren's Senate years when his wife was so gravely ill that he, even then, told Nan "very calmly that they had been 'sure she would die'" (Ibid., 234). Clearly, that had to have been a back-of-the-mind reason for Nan to bide her time, plagued as she was by uncertainty during the period of her separation from Warren.

Warren was himself not in the best of health when Nan arrived at the White House on that fateful January day in 1923. He had had a heavy cold that was more like the flu, which, along with other ailments, was about to overtake him that spring. The illness got so bad that, according to Daugherty, he was finally put to bed "in a very weakened condition" (Inside Story, 267). The Warren Harding that Nan saw was already suffering from high blood pressure—in the 170-180 range—and was showing signs of an encroaching upper-respiratory illness that he wasn't doing anything to alleviate.

Worse yet, in his greeting, there was none of the brightness of expectation that Nan was led to believe awaited her. After Nan's great anticipation and the "elaborate" preparations she had made for the visit (including purchase of an "orchid neglig ," ostrich-feathered mules, a lovely hat, and "stunning gray" dress, (PD, 234f.) she was in for an enormous let-down, which would have been all the more destructive had she known that this was to be the last time they would ever see one another. What followed was devastating—and poignant.

Warren's mood differed from that in the optimistic letter Nan had received, in response to her wanting to see him about enrolling at Northwestern University. The tone of his letter had had her looking forward to an exciting reunion. But it did not take long for her to be struck by the revelation that her Love was suppressing the realistic conclusion that their dream probably could not be realized.

As she soberly put it together, instead of the possibility of recovering their "old sweetheart days," she began to see that his "high hope…was really a dreamy lapse on his part into contemplation in writing of what he would <u>love</u> to do, rather than what he <u>could</u> do" (Ibid., 235, Nan's Itals.).

As the scene unfolds, the shock of disillusionment that falls upon Nan is practically instant. The worries Warren mentions are exactly the concerns that she sees distancing him from those of her own. Rejecting her request that he go to bed and rest out his cold, he says: "Can't do it, dearie…why right <u>now</u> I am the cynosure of the whole world—'the President of the United States, with a sick wife'!" (Ibid., 236, Nan's ital.). He would inappropriately come back to the same point later in the conversation, saying, "Nan, I'm tied. I can do no more. And I cannot desert my party!" (Ibid., 240). Nan does not comment on the priority of allegiance to Party at such a time.

What Harding's strange response does is not only to increase impediments to normalizing their relationship, it wholly ignores the problem of maximum importance to Nan—their child. Of all things, the Presidency and Florence (who refuses to die) are taking precedence at a time when Nan feels her problems "eclipsed those of anybody and everybody" (Ibid., 236). On top of that, there is the sudden absurdity of a concern for Party.

As Nan begins to gather what "the real situation is with him," compared to what he had led her to expect, it breaks her down "into a state of weeping, [and] a bitter railing against fate," unlike anything she had previously allowed herself to say to him, "no matter how low [her] spirits had been" (Ibid., 235).

Composing herself for a moment, she thinks she has to offer the obligatory hope that Mrs. Harding would get better (with the additional hope that, on recovery, she'd be "able to go to Florida") and he has to say that he too hopes she would recover (Ibid., 236). This provides a temporarily break in the tension.

Coming back to their core feelings, Nan, as she writes, is struck by how, during this their very last meeting, her let-down was deepened by Harding's desperate efforts to bring her out of it. His sad attempt to cheer her up ("a failure") climaxed a sense that stern reality was bearing down on them as never before, leaving her fairly crushed: "In truth, the whole atmosphere of that visit was one of finality," which struck so deeply that she "felt a presentiment of much evil" (Ibid.).

It was a situation in which, even with the best will on Warren's part, nothing could go right. Since it was also the wrong time for things to go wrong, it took no great insight for Nan to see she was facing inevitability. She was looking right at it in the very image of Warren himself, whose "drooping body expressed a dejection which was shocking to see" (Ibid.).

Heart-sick, as he was, with more than a cold, that 'drooping body' encapsulated the grim sense of finality which hovered over this scene. He laments, "I'm tied." For a moment one thinks Nan may have misheard his saying, "I'm tired." But no; tired as he was, he was at a stage beyond tired, and beyond all else, which "tied" tersely summed up. Immobilized he was, with nowhere to go from there.

After telling Nan "our matter worries me more than the combined worries of the whole administration," Warren, well-meaning, inadvertently comes out with his inner glance toward finality. He emphatically promises to make provision for her and their daughter for "as long as you both live" (Ibid., 237, Nan's itals.). For Nan, this re-emphasizes the bleak hopelessness that brooded over them, the state of their relationship nearing bottom. She acknowledges that "the disillusionments suffered in the Presidency of these United States were cruel." But, as she breaks down over the disappointment they personally suffer, she has little use for his senselessly suggesting the anodyne of "work."

She can't resist letting him know the extent of her hurt, in a rare, challenging objection: "There have lived some men who have given up *everything* for their sweethearts!" She stands "away from him with head held high" (Ibid., 239, Nan's itals throughout this scene.). Having just scorned his inane advice that she bury her troubles in work, the sheer painfulness of it all forces her to stand up and have at him with the only severe upbraiding she would ever voice:

"But I *do* work! I want *you*! And I want our baby as *mine*!" she cries in righteous indignation, adding, "And I don't believe I can ever have you again in the same way. I can't stand it, darling! It is breaking my heart. My baby lost to me, and the world has my sweetheart!" (Ibid.).

On getting it off her chest, it is as if she couldn't really trust the promise he comes out with that he'd absolutely take the child once he was out of office. In his saying so, what she suspiciously noticed was that "his attempt at a smile was pathetic." In other words, the promise was a futile gesture, sincerely as it might have been intended (Ibid., 237).[128]

He had just told her he worries about their "matter" to the point of practically losing his mind. To this, she counters "with rather a spirit of resentment," that she worries too, as she puts it, out of "the daily ghostly fear of living the rest of my life in such unhappiness as that adoption had brought to me." They get it off their chests, but the result, far from being therapeutic, ensures pessimism.

At the end, they stand there emotionally drained. Unalterably beloved, they steadfastly cling to one another in a wet-eyed "farewell embrace." On his heart-wrenching request for her to tell him that she is happy, she "bravely" lies, "I am happy, sweetheart" (*PD*, 241). The poignant conclusion to a foredoomed romance, with their love forced to its painful strongest, this became the saddest moment of their lives together. It was the last time Nan Britton ever saw her Sweetheart (Ibid., 242).

CHAPTER 68

"What Killed Warren G. Harding?"

PRIOR TO JANUARY, 1923, WARREN Harding had been distressed over suspicions aroused by news that Chares Forbes was being forced out as head of the Veterans Bureau. Then there was the suicide of his second in command, Charles Cramer. The shock of Jess Smith's suicide had raised even greater suspicions. Surrounding all of that, Warren had to be wary of consequences for himself. For the time being, a separation from Nan was the necessary thing to be done.

When Nan coincidentally learned of an Armstrong Tour of France, Warren was more than willing to pay for it. On her leaving for Europe, Warren, in his farewell letter, wrote her that he probably wouldn't be there for her return, but there was no hint that this meant anything other than scheduling.

Assumedly their respective trips would offer a necessary distraction from the depression on which they had parted. Dear as he remained to her, she had to have derived some comfort from his writing that he envisioned a "reunion," in the fall—also to be "grand" (PD, 252). Holding on to one another for support at the end of their last meeting, it was as if they were unable to let things rest on so bleak an ending. If Warren's unanticipated death put that to rest too, Nan's love remained strong enough for her to put evidence of it into her book.

When she visited Marion in September, a month after the death, Nan met with Warren's sisters Daisy and Carolyn, and learned from the latter of her brother's answer to her surprise over his having suddenly made out a will. Carolyn said he told her, "I don't expect to come back from Alaska." (Ibid., 253). For Nan, that remark, given in what seemed an off-hand manner, took her back to the tone of despair that had crept into his farewell letter. Had he, then, on a brooding second thought, been contradicting the expectation of a reunion? Warren was not a well man even before he started on his cross-country train trip.

Perchance, as he contemplated that they were about to be separated by an ocean, plus the upcoming length of a continent, Warren might well have been thinking that vindication had to take precedence over an unrealistic love affair. He seemed to be hoping he'd still have Nan, plus vindication. Conceivably, such possibilities would leave him in a quandary. Then there was his health.

Though he seemed close to the brink as his trip wore on, one could not say that a death-wish would translate into a self-fulfilling prophecy. Toward the end of his trip, there were moments when Warren did seem suicidal. However, as he became upbeat over how people responded to him, there was reason enough for a return, despair notwithstanding.

Adding to Warren's confusion, was Harry Daugherty's coming west to brief him on the latest from Washington. Bad as Harry's news had been, for Warren, the presence of his campaign manager increased it, adding uncertainty. It made him recall that he was on record to run for a second term. If he was eager for something on the positive side, re-nomination could serve as a means for redemption.

However, since, in May, he had known enough about boodle in his Administration to tell Jess Smith he was about to be arrested, the news from Daugherty had to suggest that he didn't have to wait for a second term to seek redemption. In fact, the "Journey of Understanding," which he did not want to seem like a political expedition, had precisely been set up as a built-in opportunity for him to shore up his image on the stump as he traveled the country.

There were several conjectures about what killed Warren Harding. Warren had told Nan that he wanted her to be free from worry, saying, "worry kills" (Ibid., 92). And worried he was. The image of his "drooping body" caught him at an epitome of worry. But, point blank, the obviously most immediate cause for his subsequent collapse had to have been that he over-extended himself in his frenetic effort to connect with the people, a typical ploy of Presidents in trouble. In Warren Harding's case, the people constituted his last best defense against disaster. He had told Nan on their last meeting that he could "do no more." On that trip west, he unfortunately tried to do a good deal too much more, sick as he was.

Both Nan and William Allen White had been visiting Warren in about the same time frame (in January, 1923 for Nan and in "midwinter" of that year for White) and both had noticed he was in obvious bad health. White saw him just after he'd been sick, and Nan while he was in the midst of getting sick. Both were struck by how poorly he looked physically and sensed how low he felt psychologically. He was indeed suffering from a double blow, as it was just then that he had told White about something that was heavily on his mind: the "friends" who kept him "walking the floor nights" (PD 236; Autobiog. 619).

That Warren had more than an inkling of behind the scenes connivance by members of his staff was indicated by his having told his campaign biographer, Joe Mitchell Chapple prior to his westward trip that "someday the people will understand what some of my erstwhile friends have done to me" (Life and Times, 213). Though Chapple was vague about the date of that remark, it exactly coincided with what Warren would tell White about the reason for his walking the floor at night.

As things stood, there were niggling side effects, which, small as they were, constituted just the kind that would aggravate Warren's dejection. Charles Cramer's suicide, for example, reminded the Press that it had occurred, in the very residence where the Hardings had previously been living. Jess's provisioning Warren's poker parties with illegal booze showed the President's willingness to take a pass on legality.

He had to take heed that the Anti-Saloon League was gathering political pressure. Likewise suspicious was Smith's having burned his papers prior to committing suicide, thereby indicating that they had been incriminating. Underlying, the tendency to place blame at the feet of the man in charge, Republican losses in the past election naturally rubbed off on their President.

Whatever else had a bearing on Warren's demise, the most significant issue was how that big trip delivered cumulative blows. Prior to his leaving, Daugherty had witnessed how Warren's distress was marked by "night attacks of difficult breathing." He had ironically insisted on Warren's "dropping everything," and his, by all means, taking that trip to Alaska, since it was sure to be therapeutic. He claimed (defensively) that he advised Warren "not [to] overexert himself" and just stick to the limited speaking engagements they had agreed upon. However, appalled at the itinerary Warren actually showed him, Daugherty tried to shock him back to reality by threatening it would kill him (<u>Inside Story</u>, 267-269).

The uplift that Warren, at his Presidential best, derived from cheering crowds tempted him to take on more of the same. As Daugherty summed up Warren's basic ordeal, minus free-lancing: "From June 20 to July 31, he made eighty-five public speeches! An average of more than two a day through the hottest days of one of the hottest summers on record." In addition, the President was daily besieged by an "army of newspaper men," and he had to "attend banquets and shake hands with thousands of people" (Ibid.). A suicidal schedule this was, even for a healthy President.

CHAPTER 69

"How Did It Actually Happen?"

WARREN HARDING'S POOR HEALTH PRIOR to departure was reminiscent of a similar situation years back, when, at the young age of twenty-four, he had come down with a condition of nervous fatigue and exhaustion. This resulted in his going to Dr. J. P. Kellogg's Battle Creek Sanitarium for a therapy that would be repeated a number of times thereafter, once less than a year prior to his marrying Florence. He had, in a letter to Evaland Scobey (of 8 March, 1918, cited above) related that he had experienced a spell of heart trouble which hung on for all of two to three years. Though that was touched on lightly, and only mentioned in an effort to comfort Evaland, if true, an ailing heart might have been part of what had been diagnosed at the 'San,' but misdiagnosed by the family physician, erratic Charles Sawyer (at times, taken up with his own philandering).

Whatever his health record in the past, assuredly Warren was not in the best of health, or spirits, when his train left Washington on 20 June, 1923. On his meeting William Allen White in Kansas City, White made note that he was looking at a sick man, visibly in a bad way: "his lips were swollen and blue, his eyes puffed, and his hands seemed stiff when [White] shook hands with him" (Shadow, 576). A woman who saw the President at the Postman's Meeting in Portland, Oregon, on the 4th of July, reported that his was "the saddest, most careworn face [she] had seen for years" (Honesty, 362).

Reporters had noticed that the President was "entirely exhausted," a level beyond being "just tired or worn out" (Murray, Era, 447). Warren Harding was less than a month away from death, and he looked it.

Having insisted on giving speeches at stops he wanted made along the way, Warren expanded his itinerary. Spontaneously greeting the hosts of people who came to see him, he put himself into the sorrowful state in which he greeted White. Though buoyed by the crowds, his insistence on ignoring the physical strain of the trip itself did nothing to help him survive the health problems it posed, such as an unrecognized heart condition.

Unable to sleep at night, he would stay up late wanting to play cards to take his mind off things. Any diversion would do. While scaring up a fourth for bridge, he acted as if he could have predicted that more bad news was on the way.

On ship board, he received a coded message from Washington, the unrevealed contents of which were disheartening enough to induce a physical collapse, on recovery from which he would be muttering thoughts of what a President should do about friends who were false to him (Shadow, 587). When Warren's ship the Henderson collided with a destroyer in the fog outside of Vancouver harbor, he hoped that his ship would sink (Ibid., 588).

Warren's depression affected physical problems that plagued him prior to, and on, that wearing trip. As Herbert Hoover remarked about his death, "People do not die from a broken heart, but people with bad hearts may reach the end much sooner from great worries" (Memoirs, II, 51). Hoover had been with Warren on that last part of his trip, when he returned to California from Alaska. He was one member of the party who had been prevailed upon to be a fourth for bridge in games that began in the morning and, with breaks for meals, would last well past midnight (Ibid., 49). His condition deteriorating, Warren kept exacerbating the cause.

Preceding the discouraging events on his "Journey of Understanding," over a month prior to departure, Warren had gone through a period when, plagued by what friends (like affable Charlie Forbes) had done to him, he needed an outlet. He had specifically wanted to disgorge his troubles by getting the ear of a trusted friend, like Nicholas Murray Butler.

Butler recounts how one Sunday in early May, 1923 (the 4th) Warren, consumed with a congeries of worrisome problems, had asked Butler to come to the White House. He indicated there were some grave matters he wanted to talk about. Over the course of an entire day (morning, afternoon, and evening) Warren seemed to have been on the verge of coming out with what he needed to unburden himself of. But, being unable to bring himself to the point of confession, he bottled it up, as if all that gnawed at him was too overwhelming to be addressed, no less put into words.

Warren stopped Butler, even as he prepared to leave. Seemingly, he was finally ready to come out with it, but he hit a wall, while still desperately needing to open up. Butler concluded that Warren "had some premonition that he would not live out his term and that things would not go well during his administration" (Across the Busy Years, I, 411f.).

A reason for Warren's having been blocked up clearly indicated he didn't know where to begin. There were: the obstacles to his coming together with Nan, insurmountable when faced head-on; the difficulty of his having to abide by a chronically ailing Florence, whom he couldn't leave; the sudden revelation of scandals that hurt irreparably; the predicament over his running for re-nomination, which would fracture his relationship with Nan, whose love had brought him solace; the problem of how to treat Daugherty's announcement that he would be running for re-election, when, he should advisably decline to go through with it, even if he really wanted to run.

Dilemma after dilemma. The stress Warren was suffering from tells its own story. Jess Smith's haunting suicide, occurring in the late May aftermath of Warren's blocked confessional to Butler, would climax pre-departure worry, which he couldn't disgorge himself of.

If Warren was to open up about what was eating away at him, it had to have come out on a spur of the moment occasion. And there was one occasion on which that happened, as Warren was nearing the end of his journey (literally and figuratively) when he broached a touchy subject to Herbert Hoover. Having heard "some rumors of irregularities centering around Smith, in connection with cases in the Justice Department Harding asked [Hoover] for advice: 'If you know of a great scandal in our administration, would you for the good of the country and the party expose it publicly or would you bury it?'"

Hoover advised that he should by all means publish it and get credit for the "integrity" of his doing so. Warren reneged, unable to accept the picture of his record painfully unraveling in plain sight of the public. He thought publication would be "politically dangerous," refusing to see that avoidance would be more dangerous yet (Memoirs II, 49).

He simply couldn't bring himself to publicize the painful disclosure that he gave to Hoover. Though unmentionable, Smith's blatant graft had by that time likely become pervasively known within the Justice Department, and beyond it. Smith's ex-wife knew. Here was Warren, toward the end of July, almost two months after Smith's suicide, feeling he had to suppress a verification of what was already out there.

There were critical ironies here. If almost everyone in the Administration had a notion of why Smith killed himself—that sort of thing gets around—Hoover, the prince of discretion, couldn't have not known about it. Therefore he was giving Harding good advice based on what he knew. Had Harding had his wits about him, he would have come out and made a clean breast of it, a move therapeutically and politically sound. As Hoover tried to point out, exposure could have been rewarding for Harding. He would have put himself on the side of the graft hunters, instead of becoming the hunted. His image would be that of the good guy going after the bad guys.

Instead, there stood President Warren G. Harding glowing at his chance to meet the people, and get their applause, an experience that came so naturally to him. His reception everywhere on the trip showed that the people still loved him. It turned out to have been a fatal lure. How could he avoid letting them down, and, avoidance being impossible, how, considering the course he took, could he live with the let-down?

Daugherty had unexpectedly come to see Warren in Seattle, and after he conferred with him, Warren was once more severely shaken. He stumbled through a speech in which he called Alaska Nebraska (Chapple, 283) and fell into near collapse. The stress was mounting. Sleep deprived, Warren had already been experiencing physical deterioration, only to have it compounded by unrelenting bad news.

He had to have known he couldn't go on like that, with no relief in sight. In effect, Warren Harding would go to any length to redeem his good name, if it killed him. He could sense that the vultures were about to be circling.

Regarding Seattle, it was on 27 July, a week prior to his death, that he had gone before an enthusiastic crowd of sixty thousand cheering people to give the speech on Alaska, and, as Hoover described it, halfway through he "faltered." Hoover's term put it mildly.

Within a few days after his arrival in San Francisco, the President's health markedly failing, and doctors being uncertain of his problem, Warren Harding died in his sick bed, of what Dr. Sawyer claimed was a stroke of cerebral apoplexy, which he had initially also misdiagnosed as food poisoning. According to a medical specialist, the cause of death was more likely to have been an attack of "acute coronary thrombosis" (Ibid., 589f.).

But three months shy of his fifty-eighth birthday, President Warren G. Harding was gone.

CHAPTER 70

"The Aftermath Considered Pre-Aftermath"

THERE WERE A NUMBER OF issues in Warren Harding's life that, after his death, would be stranded in the same limbo that had preceded it. Chief among them was the question of what became of his promise that adequate provision would be made for Nan and their daughter, Elizabeth Ann. It sounded like they would be taken care of by testimonial instrument. In their January, 1923 meeting, at which they had a dreary premonition of what might lie ahead, Nan, as noted, quoted him to be telling her that he did "expect to provide amply…for you and our little girl as long as you both live" (PD, 237, Nan's itals).

In January, 1921, prior to his assuming the Presidency, Nan's sister Elizabeth Willits had gone to Marion to confront Warren on his responsibility to Nan and their child. He had agreed to make financial provision for Nan and to offer the Willits couple a $500 monthly allowance for their adoption of the daughter (Shadow, 429). Warren had presumably been following through on this promise, or he would have heard from Nan's sister.

Just before embarking on the Alaskan trip, Warren arrived at a last minute decision to have Daugherty make out that new will. While it created a detailed distribution of his estate to Florence, as well as to his father, and his brother and sisters, among others, there obviously couldn't have been a mention of Nan and Elizabeth Ann. Nor could he have managed a separate testament for them without the disclosure he had so zealously guarded against. Surely, Daugherty—skilled at evasion—could have drafted an alternative way for Warren to care for Nan and their daughter, via a trust, with Daugherty serving as buttoned-up fiduciary.

As that did not happen, it meant Warren didn't want to enlighten Daugherty beyond what he may have already known about his relationship with Nan—to say nothing of an illegitimate child. Leery of how the corruption he'd been informed of might reflect on his legacy, Warren couldn't afford the possibility that details would leak out of a potentially explosive personal involvement which he had, to the end, kept out of the public eye.

At any rate, pre-departure, Warren, despite poor health, was consumed with plans for his forthcoming trip, along with complications arising from the suspicious suicides by members of his Administration. He wasn't in a state of mind to think about what he could do on Nan's behalf without making greater trouble than if he painfully did nothing. For one thing, he confessed to Nan that he was $50,000 in debt (Ibid., 238) besides which, he had apparently incurred unspecified stock market losses of up to $90,000, though, on examination, the two debts were probably different versions of the same debt.[129]

There was so much on his mind over and above the matter with Nan that he told her, "Really, dearie…my burdens are more than I can bear!" Filling out the gloom, she gave a vivid picture of its effect on him: "[His] tired face was lifted to the window [of the Oval Office] and the tired eyes gazed wearily at the wintry vista outside" (Ibid.). It was also quite wintry inside. Stressed to the limit, Warren found himself in a situation that resembled his stalemated effort to unburden himself to Nicholas Murray Butler.

Nan had previously recalled what must have been a common enough exasperation response that Warren had had to such situations: "he shook his head in the I-give-it-up-it's-too-much-for-me-to-solve way" (PD, 241). The event which had brought on the helplessness syndrome happened to have occurred when Warren was talking of his disgust with doctors, whose advice he distrusted—in time, fatally.

There was much for Warren to be concerned about prior to his prophesying that he wouldn't return from the Alaska trip. On coming to terms with political realities, always a wake-up call, there he was floating the case for political vindication by means of a second term. As had happened with his being thrust into the race for the 1920 Nomination on the blind, once again, in March, 1923, three months before he was to leave on his trip, Daugherty had put out word to the press that Warren Harding would be a candidate for re-nomination (New York Times, 18 March, 1923, p. 1).

Daugherty doubtless had the aim of foreclosing the opportunity that other aspirants might have to capitalize on the President's being out of town. He didn't want to be blind-sided by the likes of Henry Ford, an unlikely threat, but nonetheless a threat, who was riding a wave of sudden popularity.

How far he was prepared to go regarding his political future was expressed on his behalf by Daugherty in a meaninglessly open statement. To wit, "If the present administration makes good, there cannot possibly be any doubt about renomination. If it does not make good, there ought to be no renomination." (Shadow, 564). Since it was self-evident that the "present administration" was losing ground, the alternative seemed pre-determined. Warren himself already leaned more toward the skeptical side, for, as he discussed with Hoover the initiatives he might undertake in future, he offered the qualifier, "if we are reelected" (Murray, Era, 447; my ital.).

Considering Nan, he had to leave himself an out. However, an 'out' had its side-effects. For, should his run for re-election materialize, what could have prevented reporters from finding out about Nan, plus an illegitimate daughter? It was a perilous scenario that might well have ballooned into a greater scandal than those that did come out. Fortunately, the second term idea was not a prospect known to Nan before Warren's death, and, as no money was raised in the anticipation, it had nothing to do with the lingering problems she had to face after his death.

Still, among Warren's quandaries, the immediately important one to be faced was how he might deal with the future of his emotional commitment to Nan. An outcome of his helplessness syndrome was to jump at the idea of sending her eastward on that Armstrong Tour of Europe while he was on his way westward toward Alaska.

On the one hand, a European tour was the classic way to dispose of a delicate relationship that wasn't intended to be resumed. However, for Warren and Nan, it was more like a necessary intermission during which they could catch their respective breaths before coming to terms with feelings that could not easily be disposed of—if at all. His motives were quite genuinely conveyed by the tender farewell letter he wrote to Nan.

Whatever else their separation imparted, it put them back in the wearisome waiting game. For the time being, Nan was being given an enjoyable diversion, and Alaska was looked upon as a sorely needed diversion for Warren. Though Love is generically impatient, Lovers separated, find their feelings enhanced by the memory of what it was like when they were together. A quality given extensive treatment in The President's Daughter.

The aftermath moved in two different directions for Nan. It began with practicalities, a recall of what was promised by Warren as he looked ahead toward contingences. This was followed by a nostalgic recall that mellowed their separation. Thereafter, in defending her claim to assistance from the Harding family for raising Warren's child, Nan was prodded back to the practical side, shockingly to eventuate in shock.

For, carried away as she was by nostalgia and the degree to which she idealized the love she had had with Warren, she was setting herself up for the disillusionment of her naïveté. But first, she was not to be robbed of romantic indulgence relived.

One of the most touching scenes that Nan described (its sentimentality notwithstanding) was her tearing up Warren's farewell letter which she read on shipboard. After reading it over slowly, she kissed it, tore it in bits, tossed the bits "out upon the billowing waves," and watched "the little white floating pieces" recede as the ship sped on. The few sentences she quoted from Warren's letter went back to what he had excitedly told her on their first private meeting: "I'd love to go to the end of the world with you. …I love you more than all the world." (PD, 253, 252. Hereafter, self-evident PD references will be cited by page alone).

Obviously, their situation placed a special meaning on those words. The letter included a desire to relive their first meeting in the bridal chamber of the Manhattan hotel, and a wish that they could come together again, implying 'if only.' In fact, he wished that they currently were. He wrote, "How I wish I might be going with you!" This included not only "spending the days [with her] in glorious idleness," but also "holding [her] all through the nights in [his] arms."

It was a rich farewell letter. Dropping those pieces of it into the sea reminded Nan of a parallel feeling she had had, when she had torn up a letter of his in a grove of trees in the summer of 1919, when she was awaiting the arrival of their child. After reading and rereading his "precious love letters," back then and scattering the scraps, which contained words like "darling," "bliss," and "ultimate," she would recall an "entire sentence of endearment to [her]."

With her "dropping his last letter into the sea, [she] thought that the sea, like the grove, would always seem sacred to [her]" (254f.). When she returned from Europe, with the impact of Warren's death still upon her, she was possessed of "the divine nature" of their love. Losing him not only magnified her love, beyond its prior magnification, it took her remembrance of their relationship into the realm of the beyond.

On an evening she spent with the Votaws (Warren's sister Carrie and her husband, Heber) their conversation drifted into religion, Heber's vocation. During Nan's reminiscences of Warren, her emotions welled up, as she mused that, though she had been brought up in "an atmosphere of strictest convention, [she] found with Warren Harding that the realest [sic] happiness is of the spirit, and far transcends in its sublimity the exquisiteness of physical rapture." She felt that her love for Warren was "the most God-like instinct [she] possessed—a thing not of this world."

Nan was not clear as to whether she exactly brought this out during her conversation with Heber. But, what she wrote that she did say was to call Warren Harding "a spiritual, almost an immortal" person. Though not an especially devout person, Nan may have been trying to impress a minister who was. Since Heber had been well enough acquainted with Warren Harding to know his faults, he was quick to bring Nan down to earth. "Warren" he retorted, "was as material as any of us" (337f.).

Heber had, after all, been part of the Administration. His attitude was but a forecast of his prevailing on a sympathetic wife (Warren's sister, Carrie) to join him in rejecting Nan's appeal for a settlement on behalf of the child her brother had fathered. That became an enormous disappointment to Nan, who had witnessed how really sympathetic Carrie was before being interdicted. When Carrie had been able to speak freely from the heart, she told Nan she knew how much Nan had loved her brother. Carrie and Nan were home-town friends, and Nan had an even closer friendship with Warren's sister Daisy.

Nan, the inveterate dreamer, was of a mood, post mortem, to treat anything related to Warren symbolically. She tended to frame her remembrances in memorial tones, which, though exaggerated, she held onto as solace. To compensate for loss, she would continue to think of their love as lasting—permanently in her consciousness. The tender feelings she had had while casting those specimens of his yearning out onto the eternal sea suggested that what was lost could not be gone. By his having expressed his love in terms that also carried overtones of eternity ("the end of the world") Warren had made a complementary reminder that what was gone could never be lost.

Additionally, Warren's using the exact sentiments he had used on their first meeting returned them to their experience of the pure, pre-sexual, love with which their relationship had begun. However, after reading his postscript of that last letter, which was "sweet, and fairly long," Nan "could not...help feeling an inexplicable tone of finality [in it], of foreboding, unconsciously expressed." Plainly, he was not referring to the end of their relationship alone. Their love, idealized as eternal, would be passing only physically by virtue of his contemplated death. As if afraid to think his death might actually occur, Nan had a dire intuition, asking: "Was it's over?" Then, retrospectively, she added, "How could I know?—-then!" (253, Nan's ital.).

Subsequent to his writing that last letter, Warren coincidentally did seem to have given thought to what would become a climactic follow-up, unwelcome as it might be. He was considering his death as a real possibility. Evidence of this premonition was his making out the new will and selling the Marion Star, both apparently done on a last minute impulse.

It seemed that a variety of ominous worries—including his loss of Nan—had led him to believe he wouldn't return from the Alaskan trip because he couldn't, since he'd be unable to deal with what awaited him. That had to have been part of what lay behind his telling his sister Carrie, that, regarding his new will, he flatly didn't expect to return from Alaska (Ibid.).

Ironically, from the nostalgia embedded in his last letter to Nan, what seemed a sweet remembrance, before it was lost, seemed as well to suggest that he was equally yearning to come back to her. For, prior to that letter, he had expressly told Nan he wanted to have "a grand reunion [with her] in the fall," after they had returned from their "respective jouneyings" [sic], (252).

He had indicated that it would not be possible for him to see her on her return from Europe because the expected dates of his own return were around August 26th or 27th (Murray, Era, 441). If Warren was uncertain about a return, it was not because his love for Nan had passed. Rather their love—indeed his life—became a casualty of Warren Harding's fear that he would be discredited.

CHAPTER 71

"Nan's Reaction to His Death"

GREAT A BLOW AS WARREN'S death was to Nan, her grief took an interesting turn. She did not in her published memoir come out with any sustained mourning, much as she mourned his passing. Nor did she write of instant lamentation, though she was shocked on first being hit with the news that he had died. She was stunned, and, her mind "in a daze," she was overcome by a feeling of "emptiness and gnawing pangs."

The blow was all the greater because she had just a day earlier been elated over a newspaper headline which proclaimed that Warren Harding was recovering. It was when her thoughts drifted on to the fate of her daughter (but four years old) that she broke down: "I found myself quivering anew from head to foot and the hot tears [were] in my eyes. I was now really crying!" (PD, 274, 275. Again, remaining references, if not otherwise identified are to PD.)

However, in the aftermath itself, instead of grieving, as before, she moderated her loss by elevating the moral stature she gave Warren, as part of her desire to expunge any thought of sordidness attached to their relationship. She used words like "divine" and "spiritual," to characterize the love they had shared for six and a half joyous years. In the course of her memoir, Nan had told of such redundant instances of Harding's reverent declarations of love that Nan's own allusions seemed to reflect the same reverence she had aroused from him.

Nan was mainly obsessed with two things after Harding's death:

1) Celebrating, by way of defining, the sacred quality of their love, proposed as vindication of their adultery, a term never used, and 2) The need to convince the Harding family that they had to assume financial responsibility for the upbringing of Warren's daughter. She herself was broke and over her head in debt. Where, for example, was the rent money to come from? She was already behind in so much else, and owing money to friends like Jim Sloan.

Writing Harding's sister Carrie and her minister husband on 18 October, 1925, Nan was not shy about underscoring what she felt was the character of the love she and Warren had shared, again taking the cleansing, religious tack. "I think," she wrote, expanding on sentiments already expressed, "there is no place in the Bible where such love as ours would go unsanctioned or unblessed, for it was God-given" (362). She had told Daisy the whole story of her relationship with Warren, which Daisy was to pass on to Carrie.

Nan thought the Votaws would be understanding of her feelings. In fact, prior to her upcoming disillusionment, she was counting on them—surely Carrie—to support her contention of a relationship with their brother. That much conceded, the thorny part would be support for bringing up his child, her estimate being $50,000.

There hadn't been any thought given to that item when Nan, on her return from Europe, went back to Marion to visit the Harding family, including Warren's father. Nan had very much enjoyed a motor trip from Marion to Washington, on which she had been invited by Carrie to join her and her friends. Nan said the trip was a "lark." She, along with Carrie and the other two women were, as Nan recalled, "a jolly four, singing songs, reciting pieces, and talking about everything—everything except those things which lay nearest to [her] heart" (332).

Not since the days before Harding's death had Nan enjoyed such complete "relaxation." She "drank in every move Carrie Votaw made and thought, 'What a wonderful family, these Hardings!'" At an overnight stop, Nan shared a room with Carrie, and they were delighted with one another's company (333). And there was much more, over and above delight. A "charming hostess," Carrie "did many things [Nan] was sure were done just to please [her]" (335).

Carrie was so taken with Nan that she wanted her "to come down and live with [the Votaws]" where she could be of help to Carrie "in a secretarial way to write up her many experiences in Burma." She treated Nan as family, which, in addition to making her feel "quite thrilled," gave Nan thoughts of bringing Carrie's "brother's child" with her as a way of introducing her "into the household along with [herself]" so they "could all share her." Carrie had talked much about "wanting a child." The atmosphere was so conducive to hope that Nan had visions of bringing "their beloved brother's own child into their homes and into their hearts as the child of their flesh and blood" (Ibid. Nan's ital.).

Nor was that quite all. Good feelings, in fact family feelings, flowed to the point that on Carrie and Nan's arrival in Washington, husband Heber was up waiting for them, even though he had recently been "very ill." On meeting him again, after having seen him briefly in her high school days, Nan thought him good looking and "liked [him] immediately."

On another evening, he stayed up talking to her until one o'clock, well after Carrie had gone to bed, their conversation having drifted into religion, taking in "the pro and con about this phase and that." Obviously, Heber found an interested listener and enjoyed sharing his thoughts with her, in fact, quite extensively (Ibid., 334, 336). Throughout her time with the Votaws, Nan had been riding high. She probably should have had a premonition that it could not last, but, for the time being, it seemed like it could.

Meanwhile, Nan, on her own, had sought other means of financial support, and in January, 1924, on the promise of aid, she became engaged in a mariage de convenance with the Norwegian Sea Captain, Magnus Cricken (Nielsen in PD). Well received by the Harding family at large, Nan seemed to have been accepted primarily as an old-time Marion neighbor. She signed her letters "Nan Britton Nielsen," which temporarily helped to distance her from Warren.

Since Florence died in September 1924, Nan would not press her case for the child's support until a year later, when she spelled out her financial problem to Daisy. Just prior to that Nan confided that her "heart was full of gratitude" over the visits she had had with Daisy in Marion and with Carrie in a suburb of Washington (341).

While the Harding sisters were aware that Warren had had an affair with Nan, they had to have suspected they were not going to have much leverage with the Harding men. For, when it came to the men's dealing with the settlement issue for Warren's child, beginning even with identity, Nan's dreams blew up. How was one to know he had fathered the child? Where, for example, was the proof of that? But those tidings were yet to come.

When Nan, shortly after May, 1925, secured mutual agreement to an annulment of her marriage to the Sea Captain, she, already in debt, was really hard pressed for financial help (217f.). As the Captain was unable to produce the large sum that had been promised for her child, Nan concluded she simply had to make an open appeal to the Hardings themselves, beginning with Daisy.

Questions of the kind that would be put to her by brother Deac had not occurred to Daisy. She had been an instant believer, keenly stirred by the emotion with which Nan had unloaded everything to her. She became the only one of the Hardings from whom Nan felt she could expect a thoroughly sympathetic response, which Nan was sure Daisy could communicate to Carrie. ("Leave it to me," Daisy had written Nan [341]).

She vowed to provide the money needed for Elizabeth Ann's Kindergarten payment, plus another sum for her clothes. "You can count on me for K and C funds," Daisy wrote (348). The Kindergarten cost was $164, and Elizabeth Ann's winter clothes would require perhaps another $100. On seeing pictures of the child, Daisy thought she saw "the likeness which her brother's child bore to him." She believed the child would have been Warren's "greatest joy" (323f.).

The sticking point was Daisy's "concern…for the Harding name, [the need] to preserve it conventionally intact." Her compromise idea was that, as things stood, some years of delay might help relieve both parties of having to chance confrontation. Daisy's approach was: "It would be unfair to Elizabeth Ann…to tell her who she was until she became twenty-five years of age—and perhaps had had a love-affair of her own." This being wholly foreign to Nan's prospect for her daughter, she offered no comment. She didn't want her child to go through life "without knowing who she is" (346).

Nan's mind was insistently on the present practical matter of funding the cost for raising this child. As their discourse wandered into finances, Daisy made an interesting disclosure. The investment firm with whom Warren had owed the $90,000 was willing to settle for $40,000 (324f.). The Warren Harding estate was coming into an unexpected $50,000 windfall. Intriguingly, that, for Nan, should have been a way to open the matter of financial availability.

Much as both Harding sisters loved her, Nan had yet to get them interested in pushing for a settlement from their family, whose name Nan had protected, a feat which could become a bargaining chip. Finances being the hard part, dealing with that was particularly difficult for Carrie, married, as she was, to hard-lined Heber. In Nan's discourse with Jim Sloan, he brought up how much was paid to Carrie Phillips to secure her silence prior to Harding's Presidential campaign.[130] After all, Nan had held her silence. Carrie Phillips had not (351).

In any event, money was the one issue that neither of the sisters felt they could press with brother Deac. His adamant stance was intimidating, and other members of the Harding clan fell in line and were equally strong for protecting the family name. In light of the stone wall that Deac erected, as far as Nan would go was to ask the sisters for assistance with ongoing expenses for Warren's child.

Before Heber Votaw overruled any help for Nan's child and tried to suppress Carrie's instantaneous sympathy for Nan herself, Daisy had sent Carrie the whole of Nan's story and contemplated a fascinating possibility. Since Carrie's interest in children was even greater than her own, Daisy thought: "If Carrie Votaw knew this [Nan's story] she would want to go right out there and get that baby right away. She'd just love her" (Ibid. 323f.). Nan saw this as a perfect fit, since the Votaws had no children of their own (324). It was certainly a good deal better than Warren's haphazard conjecture about placement of the baby with, possibly, the childless, but affluent Scobeys.

For a while, there seemed to be hope that, with the Harding sisters on Nan's side, reasonable people would be able to arrive at a reasonable settlement of their differences.

PART X:

NAN VS THE HARDINGS

CHAPTER 72

"Warren's Sisters, Well-Meaning and Helpless"

In a letter to Daisy of 23 September, 1925, Nan recalled that Daisy had told her "how deeply sympathetic and interested Mrs. Votaw was bound to be if [Daisy] told her the whole story about Elizabeth Ann as [Nan] had related it to [her]" (343). Carrie's response was predicted to be positive. But she must have shared Daisy's letter with Heber. Following Nan's own letter to Carrie of the same date, she received a brief long hand note, in which Carrie answered that, since she was not feeling well, she was going to the Sanitarium. She was to be gone for a week, "taking treatments and fighting to keep on [her] feet" (247).

Earlier, Nan had naively visualized "Mrs. Votaw with her brother's child on her lap." "I had so prayed," Nan went on, "that I might see our child with her father, on his knee, but instead I was to see her with his sisters whom I also loved" (333). Actually, as Carrie was caught between her caring attitude toward Nan and the family view held by Heber, she sensed that her only remedy was withdrawal. If as ill as she said, Carrie's idea of taking a solitary trip to an undesignated Sanitarium (the Deacon's in Columbus?) sounded less like a probability than a dodge.

The fact was that, for all their sympathy toward Nan, the Harding sisters were helpless to assist with her plea for financial support. The more that help was contemplated for Nan and child, the more painful the situation became for the sisters and Nan together.

Daisy had found herself subject to the same dilemma Carrie was facing. It was not till 16 October, 1925, three whole weeks after Nan was told Carrie had been informed, that Nan received a letter from Daisy declaring, "I sent your letter on to sister but it didn't have the desired effect…but I'm glad I sent it just the same." Daisy went on to indicate how troublesome if would be for Nan to try to get through to the Harding men. "Somehow, I can't write it in a letter, the whole situation, resulting from the disclosure to her and her husband, especially in regard to him (Mr. Votaw) who just idolized E.A.'s father and therefore can't and doesn't want to believe it [i.e., that Warren had fathered this child] …." (358). Daisy had to break it off because there seemed to be no starting point from which she could see Nan proceeding.

Nan recalled that Jim Sloan had used that identical phrase: "they don't want to believe it!" (Ibid. Nan's itals.). Perchance, it took longer for Carrie to spell things out for Daisy than it had taken her to give Nan a hasty response to get herself out from under. In any event, Heber Votaw was the tough nut to crack. Warren, as mentioned above, had given Heber a well paying job as Superintendent of Federal Prisons, a position in which his poor supervision led to corruption at the Atlanta Penitentiary. In defending the Harding name, he defended his own.

After Nan told Daisy that she had received no answer to her letter written to the Votaws on 2 November, 1925, the date of Harding's birthday, Daisy replied, "I realize, my dear, how hard your lot, and the tremendous burdens you must be carrying. Pay no attention to the attitude of sister and husband. The situation is a difficult one and will come out all right, I'm sure." Daisy, in addition to offering payment for Elizabeth Ann's clothes (367) had also offered "expressions of solicitude for [Nan's] own health, in cautioning [her] not to overwork in [her] playwriting course at Barnard [College]." That "touched [Nan] deeply." The letter was signed "Lovingly yours." (Ibid.).

Daisy had been the first person to whom Nan divulged her story, "from beginning to end" on her return to Marion from Chicago, where she had gone to see her daughter following her return from Europe. Daisy was the sole Harding to accept completely all that Nan had told her, and she would have been one of the many others in Marion who totally believed Nan's story.

Her sister Carrie had been an enthusiastic ally, until she was influenced by her husband on behalf of the family. As Nan unfolded her account to Daisy, she had observed that her face "was a study," expressing "kaleidoscopically the varied emotions she must truly have experienced—amazement, pity, hurt, sorrow,—all there, *but never for one moment incredulity*" (323, Nan's itals).

Though Carrie had traveled abroad in her missionary work, she retained much of rural Ohio's small town culture, epitomized by up-and-coming Marion with a population that by the time of her youth, 1910, for example, had grown to just a little over 18,000. Carrie had been a friend of both Nan and Nan's sister, Elizabeth, and the girls were not just friends, but old friends, the Hardings having been familiar with the Brittons from youth. The Britton family had, in fact, been long standing neighbors, who lived just down East Center Street from the Hardings.

Carrie had trustingly believed in the truth of Warren's relationship with Nan. But, when Nan made her plea for support, even Daisy had to concede that the settlement Nan was requesting would, on slim evidence, create a financial problem for the family. Just as the sisters could not desert Nan, neither could they desert the family. That should have ended things, but Nan, obsessed with justice for herself and Warren's daughter, felt she was obligated to persist. So the sisters would be devoted to Nan, but not to her cause. It was painful for all three.

There was small comfort in Nan's remembering Carrie had told her she *knew* how close she and Warren had been, remarking, "You never really loved anybody but Warren, Nan" (98, 223). Carrie also very much wanted Nan to have Harding's wallet, which bore his name in gold lettering, and, in doing so she said, with affectionate recognition, "Here, Nan. You always loved Warren so much and I want you to have this. Brother Warren carried it with him right up to the time he died, and that makes it very precious" (339).

Nan recalled how in that "worn wallet" Warren "used to keep a certain snapshot of [her] to which he had taken a particular fancy." This wallet which had been held close to him also recalled thoughts of intimacy for Nan: "the leather fairly smelled of him" (341). The Hardings, having disposed of the snapshots, surely knew who the subject was. That part was not in doubt, but brother Deac was conceding very little, on the child nothing.

Daisy, on the contrary, was Nan's ally. She had been her high school English teacher, and was so convinced of the truth of Nan's relationship with her brother that she had sent Nan money, as needed, during Warren's lifetime and thereafter. What both sisters would, for obvious reasons, not want to articulate (out of respect for their deceased brother's memory, and regard for Florence) was that they knew their brother's love for Nan was fully as great as hers was for him.

The Harding sisters had an empathic attitude toward Nan, but, as with Warren's expression of helplessness, the sisters 'could do no more.' And so things stood with Nan's initial plea for help from the Hardings. What was difficult for the sisters was about to get more so for Nan.

CHAPTER 73

"Enter Deac: Open Conflict"

THINGS DID NOT GO WELL between Nan and the Votaws. In that letter of 16 October, 1925, Daisy wrote of Carrie's being perturbed that, if Nan "cared so much for their brother," why did she tell "so many people the story about Elizabeth Ann's identity?" (PD, 358). Nan, herself perturbed at Carrie's question, felt that for six and a half years she had been protecting "almost to inviolability a secret as colossal as ours" and deserved credit for that (Ibid., 359). This was the critical issue she wanted put to the Hardings. It served no purpose that Carrie, by that very question, indicated she was fully as convinced as Daisy was that Warren had fathered Elizabeth Ann.

But, meanwhile, regarding perturbance, Nan made the mistake of phoning the Votaws, to follow up on her volunteering to entertain questioning. She would come down to Washington from New York to do so, and rent a hotel room, assuring the Votaws of privacy and whatever time they wanted to have with her.

Unfortunately, it was Heber who answered the phone. To Nan's offer, its urgency calmly put, Heber acerbically answered that they had company (his brother, after a two year absence) and could not see her, which he repeated more sharply yet when Nan said she would take very little of his time. On her quietly adding it was all right if he didn't care to see her, Heber "bawled back" it wasn't that the Votaws didn't want to see her; it was that, just then they couldn't. With that, Heber abruptly rang off before Nan could get in another word (360). Aware that, with Nan having the power of disclosure, she was a potential time-bomb, Heber had to tread carefully, if not quietly.

Annoyance notwithstanding, Nan had to be put off, but without provocation, which was the tone adopted by Deac (Dr. George Tryon Harding II) when he took her up on the offer to be questioned. The face to face meeting was set up by Daisy, who had visited Nan in late March, 1926. It was to take place at Daisy and her husband's home in Marion on April first, which happened to have been the date when Nan had been planning to leave her job at the "Club" (i.e., Columbia University) to take up a new one as secretary to Richard Wightman of the Bible Corporation of America. That had to be postponed, however, and Daisy sent Nan a money order to cover transportation from New York to Marion.

Nan accordingly arrived on April first, and, Deac, who had a sanitarium in Columbus, had motored up to Marion, in a freak Ohio blizzard, which did not improve his mood. Daisy was optimistic that, if Nan could prove brother Warren's paternity, which Daisy herself believed to be true, she knew "the Harding family would do the right thing by Elizabeth Ann" (PD, 394).

On Nan's arrival, "the loving welcome" she received from Daisy gave her the ironic impression that the upcoming interview could not "be other than friendly" (396 f.). As the drama was about to unfold, Daisy forewarned her: "brother Deac intends to grill you unmercifully. Don't get angry. Just try to remain calm." The interview took place in Daisy's upstairs room, which Daisy gingerly departed, hoping for the best as the antagonists were to have their one-on-one exchange.

For Nan, it quickly became a prosecutorial ordeal. By begging leave to go back to the beginning of her "childhood background and adoration of [his] brother," Nan tried to deflect Deac's initial parry in which he wanted her to get right to the point, bluntly asking, "where" the alleged "first intimacy" had taken place. When Nan got into the initial "intimacies" followed by subsequent "all-night trysts" Deac kept interrupting with questions as to "when" and "where."

This went on for two long hours, during which Nan had shown him harmless early letters establishing that personal contacts had been made, and, with regard to the daughter, Nan showed George copies of the guardianship and adoption papers. However, since Nan and Warren had mutually agreed to destroy their love letters, that put her at a disadvantage in George Harding's persistent demand for hard evidence of intimacies.

Among other things, Nan volunteered to take George to the hotels where she and Warren had stayed in order "to trace for him the exact dates" of their all night trysts. She also described the "layout" of Harding's "senate offices" saying she "had been in both of them" and provided "the numbers on the doors" (399).

After showing "some irritancy at [her] frankness," and continuing to "squeeze" her for additional "wheres and whens," duly recorded in a notebook, Deac finally got to the question of her "idea of a settlement," at which "his face [was] full of consternation." On Nan's stating a claim of "$50,000" plus an additional "$2,500" to cover her indebtedness, "he stammered" that that would constitute, "all of the Harding Estate." Deac was angered at her wanting the "arrangement" of a "trust fund" for the child to be started "as soon as possible." He insisted that he had to verify the truth of what she had told him and was not to be hurried (396-401).

Though the atmosphere had run from tense to hostile, there was necessary civility in the aftermath, as Nan and Deac stayed on to dine with their hosts, Daisy and her husband, Ralph Lewis. Nan thanked Deac for coming up in a storm to talk to her, which he accepted with "impatience" (401). Nan felt she had provided all the "intimate detail[s] she could "crowd" into her conference with Deac, accompanied by the names of hotels and the dates of assignations, as requested.

Anxious for some response, Nan would endure a long wait, ending in unanswered dismissal (Honesty,10f.). As she saw it, the family's primary concern being to "shield their brother's name from…'scandal,'" Nan had to be "virtually repudiated" (Ibid., 36). For the Hardings, their silence signaled that that was an end of it.

In conferring with Jim Sloan, whom she drew on for information, Nan learned that a $50,000 trust fund for Warren's daughter was equitable, as his estate had been "variously reported at from $400,000 to $800,000" (PD, 395). She had wondered, when the subject had been broached with Sloan, whether the financial problem went back to his opinion that "it would be difficult to persuade [the Harding family] to part with any of their money." As Sloan had put it, excepting the President, his family members "were distinctly severe"—patently tight with their money (319).

Had Nan been able to present Deac with the letters she had received from Daisy, they might have helped her credibility, though they, just as likely, would have had little relevance for him. Inconsequential anyway, disclosure of Daisy's letters would have been a betrayal of Nan's vow to destroy them. Had Nan herself saved Warren's last letter—replete with endearments which only a lover writes—it would have cinched her case for the truth of their having had an intimate relationship. Lacking that level of proof, Nan had no case with the Harding family.

She put together a follow-up letter to Deac on April 4th, which, lacking his address, she sent to Daisy for forwarding. She added details she had been unable to assemble for Deac during his pressured interview, such as the birthday watch Warren had sent her on 11 August, 1917. She offered to give him the names and addresses of persons who could verify things she had told him, in addition to repeating her offer to take him to various hotels where she and Warren had stayed. She insisted that "this thing can be proven and I mean to keep at it until it is" (406). Like all else, her last ditch effort to gain the Harding family's (i.e. Deac's) approval of her appeal for support of Warren's child was destined to be futile.

Great as Daisy's sympathy was for Nan, she had to write her of the crux of the problem for the Hardings. With "the details of the $90,000 brokerage matter," weighing on them, "now then on top of that, your claim is put in." Therefore, "Do you wonder that the whole family are up in arms against a thing that is too hard to prove?" (385).

Comfortless as it was, Daisy had to give Nan the bottom-line. Immediately, however, Nan was outright short of cash. She had told Daisy on her April first visit that she couldn't pay her $130 rent bill, due on the 10th of the month (407). Daisy continued sending Nan money, and she signed her letters "Lewis," (no longer "lovingly") to disguise evidence of her having been in contact with Nan and giving her financial help. That great a pariah had Deac made of Nan.

Daisy's attitude having changed, she suggested that Nan should look for cheaper lodgings. Also, indicative of a need for frugality (likely Deac's idea) Daisy added that expenses could be paired if Nan sent Elizabeth Ann to live on Grandmother Willits' farm, a heartless separation for Nan (408). Despite the money Daisy sent her, Nan became well aware that her sentiments were not the same. Nan was finding the door more tightly closed on her entertaining any expectation of a settlement.

She was so caught up in her financial crisis that it was difficult for her to appreciate the tight rope Daisy was walking, on the one hand, dedicated to the family's position, while, on the other, solicitous of Nan's, and doing what she could for her financially. As all of this played out, there was sadness enough for both.

CHAPTER 74

"The Drama Plays Out"

THE CONFLICT WOULD GIVE RISE to a drama in which the antagonists had to be careful of how they treated one another: hostile, but doing their best to suppress overt hostility. There was unspoken anger during periods of confrontation, sparring of the kind that had taken place between Nan and Heber. There was much anger, outspoken off-stage on Nan's part, particularly over her interview with prudish Deac. Disgust over his inability to evade consideration of his brother's lust, he had no kind words for the "gold digger" who had been its object.

Typically, in such situations, communication, such as it was, was best conveyed by messengers, with Daisy happening to be the logical interlocutress for the Hardings, and Jim Sloan pitching in off-stage on Nan's behalf. In between, there were periods of relief, distraction, even much needed ironic detours of good feeling.

To project a summary of the drama that dragged on for almost four years after Warren's death, climaxing in Nan's blatant publication of their affair, the drama, in rough outline, went like the following, based mainly on data set forth in The President's Daughter, plus her postscript in Honesty or Politics.

Prelude: Going back, then, to the beginning of Nan's travail—on her return from Europe, she typically had little notion of all that would lie ahead for her. It became a journey of disappointment to end in a vale of tears over the prospective fate of her daughter, based on the need to fund her upbringing.

Act One, Scene i. Except for the period of good feeling she enjoyed with the Harding sisters, and with their aged father, Nan encountered nothing but frustration. She was chagrined, in the first place, because there was not so much as a note left for her from her lover. She tried to think that maybe the child's father had left a bequest that would yet come to light.

Scene ii. For a while, she had thoughts of getting a clerical position with the Harding Memorial Fund, thereby doing something to advance his Memorial, while getting paid for it. She contacted Judge Gary, who had a prominent role in the Fund, but got no reply. She also tried Mrs. Harding, and was told she could not be of service (PD, 289f.).

Scene iii. When nothing materialized, neither a bequest nor a job, Nan sought an alternative that would both make provision for her child and avoid conflict with the Hardings. She decided to marry the Norwegian seaman, Captain, Magnus Cricken [Nielsen] on his offer to provide the $25 to $30,000 that she requested in advance, as a trust for Elizabeth Ann.

Scene iv. When Cricken, a ship's master, and, on the side, ship-broker, failed to come through, Nan started legal proceedings, to get their marriage annulled. It was not that he hadn't given her money from time to time prior to their marriage; it was just that its availability was not consistent and fell short thereafter. In any event, they had been married in January, 1924, but, it being a mariage de convenance, Nan, lacking what was promised, got herself an annulment, declared legal in March, 1926.

Scene v. In between, she was so hard pressed, being in debt to various persons (mainly on promissory notes to Jin Sloan) she had to pawn the Captain's wedding ring, along with the watch he gave her, for which she got a meager $75 (305f.). Not much help when she was over $500. in debt and had just 7 cents (sometimes listed as 6) left in her purse. (345, 305).

Act II, Scene i. [A build up to crisis one.] Nan had the impression that the Hardings were concerned with two matters: sordidness and secrecy. On the matter of compensation for secrecy—namely, the sum she quoted to raise Elizabeth Ann, even Daisy finally had to let her down. She had had to acquiescence in the family's resistance to compensation.

Scene ii. Having failed to receive a reply to a letter written to Daisy, Nan, after "a lapse" of over a month, on 3 August, 1925, wrote a brief inquiry wanting to know if Daisy had notified Carrie of Nan's situation. In her reply, Daisy offended Nan by getting into such things as their "different ideas about men and [their] relations to them," when, as Nan privately interjected: [Shouted Off-Stage.] what she had really "sought was [Daisy's] counsel, her help!" [Here, as throughout, Nan's itals.]

Scene iii. Daisy, as messenger, had offered the well-meaning hope that Nan would be happy and "attain the desires nearest [her] heart," which, at the time, was the best that she could do for her. Exasperated with Daisy's avoiding the obvious need of an "active interest [in her cause] instead of …inactive acceptance of a tragic situation," Nan's impatience mounted. Daisy, on the other hand, was making a polite statement that, on the "action" Nan wanted Daisy to take with her family, their resistance was insurmountable.

Scene iv. By then somewhat frenetic, Nan took "Lots of love, dear Nan" as having "failed to carry the usual note of sincerity" (321f.). The passages from Daisy's letter that Nan quoted did not really suggest a lack of sincerity, but could be taken as a kindly brush off: "I want so much to see you happy and attain the desires nearest to your heart. …My heart goes out to you in any of your suffering, relative to B—-" ["Bijiba," the child's self-selected nickname] (342). Anything less than action (on Daisy's part) to shake the Hardings—actually Deac—into meeting Nan's demand, she considered as the equivalent of betrayal.

Scene v. [Rage voiced in soliloquy.] Feeling that Daisy had given up, Nan sensed that things had reached the stage where she believed she had to bring the Hardings explicitly to the issue they were avoiding. Concerning Daisy in particular, Nan wondered, "Could it be that she had failed to understand that my revelations to her had been for the express purpose of bringing the Harding family to a realization that there existed an obligation on their part to Elizabeth Ann, and not merely to solicit sympathy and discuss the intimate details of my relationship with her brother?" (342).

Act III, Scene i. For a while there was a hiatus in Nan's pursuit of her cause. She had much else to think about, like, at one point, falling behind in rental payments, of $130 monthly. Her low paying secretarial job at the "Town Hall Club" [fictitious name for a Columbia University office] in New York, at $35. per week ($140,monthly), left her barely able to scratch out a living. Fortunately, she was receiving occasional guilt checks from Daisy. The "Club" did give her contacts with persons engaged in the literary world, which inspired her to think about writing a play around her experiences with Warren Harding.

What she really wanted was to find a way to get a small apartment in which she could bring her mother out to care for Elizabeth Ann (316f., 334f.). Come September, nothing had developed, so, unable to approach other Hardings, Nan tried to reassert her case with Daisy.

Scene ii. When Daisy had written her of their different relationships with men, it seemed to Nan that she might have been citing the problem of indecency as something that got in the way of the resolution Nan was entitled to. In her letter to Daisy of 23 September, 1925, Nan indicated that, if the seamy side of her relationship with Warren inhibited Daisy from getting through to the Harding family, she had an answer.

She wanted it known that in her "unconventional relationship" she would "never be able to attach one iota of sordidness to the beautiful, natural, and finely impelled love...which resulted in God's giving [them] Elizabeth Ann" (Ibid., 343). [Her anger mounts.]

Scene iii. [Off-stage Rage, Followed by Go-Easy Approach.] Since Daisy's sending the Votaws Nan's disclosure resulted in an off-stage hostile rejection made in defense of the family, Nan wanted to rise up with a defiant desire to tell the Hardings to just harken: Give me the money to raise Warren's child, or you risk exposure.

On the other hand, holding out the palm of a peaceful agreement, she promised, "If they would make possible to [her] the possession of [her] child," she would do all in her power to protect the secrecy they wanted. She had, after all, made that explicit pronouncement in her long letter to the Votaws of 18 October, 1925. She had not only included her desire to be questioned, but had also asked whether they cared "to help [her] to help Elizabeth Ann," as "a moral obligation to [their] brother's child" (361f.).

Scene iv. Nan felt Heber was an important player in negotiations, as she recalled there were times when she had called Warren at the Senate Office Building, and it was Heber who picked up the phone (360f.). Heber had to be brought in, particularly since he "felt so bitterly resentful about the whole matter." This had been confirmed by her phone call about the questioning. First, however, the family had to be convinced that her child was Warren's. So, included in her letter were snapshots of the child, which showed that "even as a mere baby she was he [sic,Warren] all over" (363).

Scene v. Finally, there was the critical interview with Deac, set up by Daisy to take place in her room at her home, on April first, 1926. Nan was continuously interrupted during Deac's snappish grilling, in which he skeptically wanted to know of the first and later intimacies she had had with Warren. And, from that point on, Deac posed abrupt questions of "where" and "when" trysts had taken place. In short, he felt his demand for proof had not been met, though Nan had offered to take him to hotels, and also Senate offices, where the trysts had occurred. Her proposals fell on deaf ears. Deac, having motored up in a freak springtime snow storm, had been sufficiently irritated to begin with.

Scene vi. [Chorus and Goading Messenger.] Nan had loved the two Harding sisters, and the love was mutual, but, as shown, they had buckled under to the men dictating the family's interests. They had Nan's resolve that she would be honor-bound to protect the Harding name in exchange for a settlement. Besides, there was the fact that Warren had been $90,000 in the red to a brokerage firm that would settle for $40,000, which left the $50,000 Nan was asking for.

Jim Sloan had been reminding Nan she could have gotten a handsome sum for her silence prior to Warren's embarking on his Presidential campaign—something in the range of, say, $200,000, to be paid for by his rich backers. Sloan cited all that had been paid out to Carrie Phillips (351).

Act IV, Scene i. [More Off-stage Rage.] That sort of deal (Carrie Phillips style) was not something Nan would think of, its being "foreign to [her] thoughts" (Ibid.). She did have an idea of how a settlement could be done by means of a trust fund established for Elizabeth Ann, with she and her child living on the interest (352). But her patience was wearing thin.

Noting that the "line of thinking" on the part of the Votaws as well as Daisy, "led straight to the fear of exposure," Nan's righteous indignation began to build. She made a series of arguments, a version of which was what she wanted presented to the Hardings.

As previously asserted, she had assiduously kept from the world the secret she and their brother Warren had shared, which she was "ready to further guard," though she had one far more important interest at heart: "I rated my child's future and my own sense of justice for her far above the continued consideration of protection of the Harding name" (365). [Expressed in rage.]

A lot of this, as reported in PD, was frustration that Nan was getting off her chest. She resented the Hardings' arrogance. There was not so much as an outright 'No' from Deac. Assumedly, a legal precaution At any rate, they (he) just let it hang-fire; her request unapproved. Nan had had enough.

Scene ii. [Off-Stage Rage Anticipating Climax.] After having presented Deac with as much convincing evidence as she could directly give him, Nan observed that all she had earned for her pains was "virtual" repudiation (Honesty, 36) [An off-stage stab in the air.] However, as Nan continued to spell out her side of the matter, it sounded like she was prepared to give them an ultimatum, in so many words, a last ditch blackmail: Enough! Give her the funds she had requested on behalf of the daughter she had had with Warren, or she would tell all. Or, pay her off and they'd have absolute silence.

[Nan's Soliloquy.] "It lay with them and their sense of right toward Eliabeth Ann whether or not the story they wished to conceal were further revealed. I had assured them of my co-operation, and, except they fail me, I would continue to suffer the fictional explanations which surrounded the identity of Elizabeth Ann's father. … If …the story leaked out, I would know that I had done everything in *my* power to keep it intact, and that only the refusal of Warren Harding's own brothers [sic] and sisters to sponsor the cause of his own daughter had precipitated such revelation. *I would sacrifice myself, in dedicating every remaining shred of nervous energy to protective efforts, in their behalf, if they would make possible to me the possession of my child"* (op. cit., 365, Nan's itals.).

Scene iii. [Her outrage is boiling over. Soliloquy picked up.] "I would not forever tolerate unjust criticism of past conduct…any more than I would countenance the figurative drawing away of skirts from the child who had every right in the world to tug at them in her rightful demand, through the voice of her mother, for recognition and equity" (365f.).

Nan receives a postal money order of $110 from Daisy with a request that Nan destroy her letters to Nan.

Act V, Scene i. [Climactic Blow Delivered. Nan shakes her fist in direction of her antagonists.] Nan was fed up with the silent treatment from Deac. Had Warren's brother no sense of courtesy? Having heard the essence of Nan's argument and rejected it as lacking the evidence needed for him to comply with Nan's terms, the family (i.e., Deac) forced her to do the alternative, which was to put the whole story out for the public to judge her credibility.

Scene ii. Hence publication of *The President's Daughter,* more accurately the story of the daughter's mother in her love affair with Warren G. Harding, the girl's father. The publication date was 25 June, 1927, and, very shortly thereafter, Nan revealed to her daughter that she was her true mother, not her aunt, and that Warren G. Harding had been her true father. (*Honesty,* 99, 102).

Her book has good sales, accelerated after H.L. Mencken's review.

Curtain.

CHAPTER 75

"How Nan And Her Book Were Received"

After Warren G. Harding's death, nothing was more difficult for Nan, than the consequences of her publishing the love life she had enjoyed with him, an answer, as it were, to Deac's rejection.

Nan suffered a number of immediate hurts on her coming back to Marion, none quite as bad as the slings and arrows that she encountered when she became controversial. It seemed that people believed what she wrote, but disliked the fact that she wrote it. In Ohio, as in other states, it was not a good idea to make a favorite son look bad. Nan, however, felt she had to press a libel suit against Charles A. Klunk, for his publication of The Answer to her President's Daughter, in which book the deceased author (Joseph deBarthe) had called Nan a blackmailer and a woman of loose morals (Shadow, 642f. Murray, Era, 490).

Predictably, Nan lost her suit. She had had a difficult case to make, when local opinion could condone Harding and condemn her, particularly when the case was being tried in the Toledo Federal Court, before a jury of three. For her to have been Warren's mistress was more of a disgrace than his adultery. Nan had apparently outraged enough Ohioans to lose her suit, on the basis of that alone. Since the case was tried as late as October, 1931, her book had aroused lasting memories.

However, there had been exceptions to the general bias from

Marion, one previously from among the Hardings themselves. Throughout Nan's problems with them, Daisy had remained Nan's constant advocate. In March, 1926, she had set up Nan and her daughter in a three room furnished apartment in New York, whereby, for only the second time since the death of the child's father, Nan had been able to live independently with her daughter in a place they could call home. The child, aged six, would go to school with Nan's mother who came East to live with them (Honesty, 3).

Seen from a larger perspective, her book brought to light the treatment she had received from the Hardings. Deac's renunciation of Nan's claim for support was tied to a hypocritical attitude of the post-war era regarding sex morality. It was reflected in the same mentality that gave Nan the brush-off when she tried to interest major publishing houses in her manuscript.

The fall-out from the trial was actually mixed. However much she might have thought the heartfelt sincerity of a couple in love would override the claim of a tawdry exposé, her book nonetheless added to the scandal already heaped on President Harding's head.

Sexual revelations attached to the private life of a President, recently deceased and dishonored, had to be avoided by a major publishing house. Finally, however, with financial assistance from a sympathetic commercial printer, Steven U. Hopkins of the Polygraph Company, Nan undertook the risk of self-publication, and the rest was history.

Nan had lost her case, but she had won the approval of numerous readers. For her purposes, publication itself meant vindication. It was for her a love story truly told. As for depravity, there was not the slightest indication of salacity in the telling. Nonetheless, it was obviously a questionable decision for Nan to bring a libel suit that got tried in Ohio, in 1931, four years after publication. The only good her case did bring was that it prompted her in the following year, 1932, to publish a list of mostly favorable responses from the reading public, plus the favorable view of some reviewers.

Sexual revelations attached to the private life of a President, recently deceased and dishonored, had to be avoided by a major publishing house. Finally, however, with financial assistance from a sympathetic commercial printer, Steven U. Hopkins of the Polygraph Company, Nan undertook the risk of self-publication, and the rest was history.

Prior to being taken up by Polygraph, Nan's book actually had been rejected by several publishers. T.R. Smith of Boni and Liveright told her that the harsh reception given publishers of Samuel Hopkins Adams' Revelry had poisoned the well for her. As Smith frankly put it, "If...Revelry, which is fiction, gave [publishers] trouble, they probably figured that your book of facts would put them out of business!" (Honesty, 63).

That her book was presented as factual made it riskier than fiction, thought to be harmless. Readers could shrug off make-believe, but not a memoir derived from actual experience, particularly one about a major public figure, indeed a deceased President. There was the fear of legal action. However, the Harding family's reticence, their, above all, shying away from publicity worked to Nan's advantage. Once word was out about the content of her book (thanks to Mencken) it became a best seller.

Nan herself was given an interested reception from the reading public, and she published a thirty-three page "Addendum," to Honesty or Politics containing passages selected from letters that were almost all complementary. Those which she cited were universally accepting of her credibility, and, by and large, backed her cause: "That every child born in the United States of America be regarded as legitimate whether born within or without wedlock" (Honesty, v).

She wasn't given much coverage from reviewers, but she quoted one favorable review from a reputable critic, Robert Morss Lovett, writing in the New Republic: "The truthfulness with which these circumstances are recorded leaps out from every page. ... The book tells a story perfectly symptomatic of American life of the present day; tells it with a frankness and simplicity which shames the efforts of Mr. Sumner's league to suppress it, and of literary magazines and departments to boycott it..." (Honesty, 228).

Nan would have contested the idea that she dealt the coup de grace to her lover's reputation. She, in fact, would implicitly make that point in quoting excerpts from over one hundred of the letters "taken from thousands of like opinions" that readers had sent her (Honesty, 339-372). Contrary to what might have been expected, many wrote feelingly of her ordeal, and of Warren's as well. On reading Nan's book, they mainly came away with an enhanced opinion of him, seeing Warren Harding as a human being they could relate to; their President, true, but not a distant persona.

Representative was a woman who felt Nan had created "a great deal of love, sympathy and understanding for President Harding." Another wrote that she had "always had an intense admiration for Warren G. Harding, and [that] reading such an intimate story of his life only deepened that admiration." Yet another "ardent admirer," of his became "much more so" (Ibid., 343, 341, 353).

Importantly, Nan's book was accepted as factual, based on a true-life poignant romance. Typically, a woman who had read the book a second time wrote that she "could not get it off [her] mind for a long time," adding, "I believe every word you have written and agree with you in every way in your entire situation" (355).

Satisfying the "ring of truth" criterion used by approving biographers, most of the letter-writers Nan quotes saw the veracity of her memoir as self-evident. It was a common sentiment for a woman to write, "I have just finished reading your book…and wish to tell you I am convinced of its truth." There were other similar examples, as with a woman who, having "just read" the book, had to tell her "No one could ever doubt a word of its authenticity nor your sincerity" (349).

Most women respondents heartily endorsed Nan's announced cause on the legitimacy of children born out of wedlock, and she herself was regarded sympathetically. She was "congratulate[d]" alternately for her "courage," "honesty," and "inspirational" effect (353, 359, 347). She earned multiple variations on empathy, as with, "my heart bleeds for you…. I could not check my tears throughout the reading, especially when you appealed to the Hardings and were so misunderstood" (344).

One letter went right to the point of how Nan wanted her love to be understood: "It is my personal belief that your associations with our honored President were far more holy and pure than are the relations in millions of homes that are supposed to be shrines of chastity" (349).

She won approval for writing the book itself, a sentiment which probably was not universal with the general public, and was not true of some Ohio reviewers. She did, however, strike a chord with like-minded Ohioans. She gave clips from twelve letters from Ohio residents, all of whom strongly sided with her, one from a destitute single mother from hometown Marion itself. There was another from a lady who lived "less than fifty miles from Marion," and looked askance at the Hardings, referring to "this great wrong done by people who should have helped" (359).

While Ohio women might have been sympathetic toward Nan, she could not have expected many favorable reviews from newspapers in her home state. A woman reviewer for the Dayton Daily News declared that The President's Daughter was "a book without a reason for its being...a blot—a most disfiguring blot on one woman's escutcheons!" (op. cit., 229).

Looked at more generally, Nan received vindication from various parts of the country. The collective inference one takes from those letters is that, although her memoir wasn't going to get her anywhere with the Hardings, Nan could have the satisfaction of knowing she had made a strong case with an understanding readership.

Of major importance, was the favorable treatment Warren Harding himself received, particularly from women readers, who were the majority of the respondents that Nan quoted. Of the 109 letters she excerpted comments from, only seven are identifiable as having come from men, though nine additional letters—some from doctors—seem also to have been written by men, who thereby comprised about 1.5% of the aggregate that she quoted—not very impressive perhaps, but enough, considering the low expectation from a source not prone to write her.

One can anticipate that women would be charitable in their attitude toward Nan, and unsympathetic toward Harding, but that seems not to have been the case.

Nan directly anticipated the possibility that it would be charged that her book defamed Harding, and she confronted an Arkansas Congressman (John N. Tillman) who came out with that view. He wrote that she "was greatly besmirching the name and memory of [her] child's father." In answer to this, Nan gave excerpts from six letter-writers who, on the contrary, held that her book greatly brightened their view of Harding (Ibid., 260).

One excerpt, from a man from North Dakota, addressed the problem even more explicitly than those she used to refute Tillman's criticism. The point this man made was: "...if one ever entertained an unkind thought of our dear departed president you have done everything possible to you to dispel it. Certainly your readers...must acknowledge his inherent honesty, his great natural kindliness and his deep love for you" (Ibid., 359). Another male reader held that Nan gave him "a much higher regard for President Harding than [the reader had] had before [he] read [her] book" (350).

Typical of other responses were those which indicated that the "intimate story of [Harding's] life has only deepened [the writer's] admiration," of him (341). Although Nan had written the story of a President's illicit love, there seems to have been a significant number among her correspondents who saw none of that, and instead credited her with inspiring "a great deal of love, sympathy and understanding for President Harding" (343).

Ordinary folks, those who had regarded Harding as one of them, voted for him on that basis, and cheered him on his cross country trip to Alaska, would seem to have been among those who responded most sympathetically to Nan's account. On the other hand, Nan's sampling of readers' favorable responses overlooked the fact that a goodly number of those who had once favored Harding would also have been disillusioned by Nan's disclosures. To that extent, it is likely that the responses Nan provided were a sampling from people who perhaps did not represent the opinion of a silent majority of her readers.

Nan does quote several adverse comments which sound like they may reflect the attitude of a larger readership. The New York Telegraph, for example, made an editorial statement that her book was "a disgusting revelation in the eyes of decent people." The Telegraph's reviewer took it even further, declaring: "That a mother can expose her child to the world as an illegitimate for any reason leaves an impression of unnaturalness. …there is only one mother in a million that would sacrifice her child for the betterment of the world no matter how badly it needs it."

Nan also reprinted insults that referred to her book as "a 'Harlot's Progress,'" or called her a "jade." In a review that was otherwise favorable, one finds a crucial question: "How could she have written the book, revealing the affair, if she loved Harding as she declares she did?" (Honesty, 228-230).

She changed some minds, but, country-wide, she probably left herself open to that type of criticism. Among readers with a Comstockian persuasion, most would have focused on the issue of morality. On that basis, a large enough segment of the population would likely have tended to agree with the Arkansas Congressman's opinion of what Nan did to Warren Harding. Nonetheless, Nan had made her point in quoting readers of an equally moral persuasion, who wrote Nan from the heart, offering vindication based on the disclosure of Harding's humanity.

For some readers, her book obviously did nothing to change the impression of him as our singularly worst President. As registered by one historian, Nan's revelations magnified Harding's sexual adventures, real, rumored, and imagined: "From the common talk of club and bar it might have been inferred that Harding's lecheries ran up into the scores" (Adams, Incredible Era, 430). Nan could well have understood that, among those who did not write her, there existed a portion of the reading public who would be unforgiving.

The President's Daughter is high drama. What Nan heard from a substantial number of people who wrote her about it leaves the reader with a sense that these lovers deserved better. On the day of their last meeting, Warren told Nan that, much as revelations of corruption weighed on him, their "matter" superseded "the combined worries of the whole administration" and was "on [his] mind continually" (PD, 237). After the love-from-the-heart experience that he and Nan had shared, many readers were left with the hope against hope that a solution could have been found, when, poignantly, one knew it couldn't.

This type of response was recognized by a respected reviewer of that day, Harry Hansen, writing in his column, "The First Reader" in the New York World for 3 October, 1927, which Nan quotes. Hansen begins by calling The President's Daughter "one of the greatest surprise packages on the book market today." Continuing, he represents PD as credibly truthful:

"Coming to it with the expectation that it was a second-rate recital of scandal…I find it a highly romantic and thrilling story of a love affair. …It is an astounding romance, a tale that even if all names were erased would sweep the country as the story of a woman's tremendous preoccupation with love and motherhood, one of those documents that could hardly have been concocted out of a blue sky, that must have been lived" (Honesty, 171).

CHAPTER 76

"Considered Worthy At The End, and Calmed"

Warren Harding was not at his best in January, 1923. Nan, in her recollection of it, was psychologically just as bad off. Dogged by depression, Warren was frustrated to the point that he neglected to take common-sense care of his precarious health. Equally frustrated was a hope that the love he shared with Nan Brittan might come to a fitting conclusion. Heart-rending for both, that indicated why one reader would call Nan's memoir "the greatest love story of the century" (Honesty, 342).

That much was private, but there was a carry-over of heart into other relationships. It was part of Harding's nature that he felt for people in distress, unfairly treated, or under a cloud politically. The latter applied to the "friend," most notorious for having betrayed his trust, Albert B. Fall, his ex-Secretary of the Interior, a self-aggrandizing politician under suspicions which Harding chose to ignore.

When his westward journey took him through Kansas City, he made a point of having a personal meeting with Fall's wife Emma and asked her to dine with him and Florence, who, on Albert's retirement, had assured Emma of "unbroken friendship" (Florence, 503).[131]

Though Senator Robert LaFollette's initial call for an investigation of the Teapot Dome oil leases had not gone anywhere by the middle of 1923, it was sitting there offering Democrats the temptation for a trouble-shooting expedition that would incriminate Fall. Several months after resigning from his Interior post, he had gone off to Russia with Harry Sinclair, in pursuit of leasing oil fields on Sakhalin Island, a venture on which Harding had wished Fall well.

Although he could expect a meeting with Mrs. Fall might be disturbing, he felt obliged to see her. Nothing might be going on with Teapot Dome, but there still was enough ambiguity surrounding Fall that it would have been hurtful to Emma. Also, Harding must have felt some guilt over his having countered Fall's desire to exploit Alaska's natural resources. Secretary of Agriculture, Henry C. Wallace, a staunch opponent of Fall's plan, would shortly be joining Harding's entourage in Denver.

Senator Arthur Capper (of Kansas) told William Allen White that, prior to the speech Warren was to give, he stayed closeted in a room with Emma for almost an hour, and emerged, "obviously frustrated, worried, and excited" (Autobiog, 24). Whatever had transpired, the conversation couldn't have avoided the matter of Teapot, which, since it reminded Harding of things he'd prefer to forget, made this charitable visit an uncomfortable one. Regardless of the cost, fidelity to friendship, had moral equivalence for Warren and was instinctively observed.

For all of his solicitude over the distress of others, Warren and Nan had no way to escape from their own. Like all of the world's great love stories, in fact and fiction (e.g., pre-and post-Abelard and Heloise[132]) Warren and Nan's romance not only ended sadly, but, as with the history of tragic lovers, theirs had been foredoomed to prototyically end that way.

Despite the negative impression Nan's memoir may have created, taken as a genre love story, there was much on the positive side. Given her disclosures, what Warren and Nan had retrospectively to depend on for a recovery of the magical attraction of their romance was that Love-Lost has historically claimed greater empathy from readers than love that ends in fairy-tale fulfillment, in which case the striving, longing, and excitement are forgotten. Whatever scorn their romance may have suffered from moralizing commentary, many of the letters

Nan received showed there was a readership for whom her love story had lasting appeal.

One reader told her, "You have written a love story that in my opinion will be retold in prose and poetry in ages to come." Another wrote, "The greatest thing which you have accomplished is something you may never have thought of. It is you who have built the monument to Warren G. Harding that will breathe and have life" (Honesty, 364). Like the poet who needs but one receptive reader to complete the meaning of his poem, Nan would have had reason to believe that, for sensitive readers, Warren G. Harding, had, by her hand, been passionately memorialized.

The remarkable aspect of Harding's career is that none of his personal travail, acute as it was, would impact on his ability to function as Chief Executive. If his role was not always carried off lucidly and well, still, the sum total of his actual record, as has been shown, surpassed that of Presidents accorded a higher place in history. Save for the mess he had made of his personal life, as President, he performed the job far better than the little he has been credited for. He got more done, in fact, than Buchanan types who were rated above him.

As for what effect the women had had on his role as President, whatever could be said of Harding's affair with Carrie Phillips, though its shamelessness might be condoned for extenuating circumstances, the fact of its having been known had no bearing on his public life. Fear it though they did, the same could have been said of the Nan Britton affair, even if revelation of it during his Presidency would have been career-ending. There was no recorded instance of Warren's neglecting business to be with Nan. He indeed shuffled her off—usually to her sister's in Chicago where she could be with their child—when Presidential business required all of his attention.

A failed lover and undistinguished Senator, Harding became an accidental President. On one level, it might be said that whatever good he did as President was because he was President. The Office itself got him to work hard at deserving it. His leadership was such during his first year on the job—dominating Congress when necessary—that he made a hit with the Press, and had the electorate in tow. As a reputable historian like Ellis Hawley pointed out, if judged by results, Harding greatly exceeded expectations of him.

Interestingly, Mencken felt that the true story of Warren Harding had not yet been written—as of 1927. So he came up with one really pertinent suggestion, of a type which has been acted on by several of the sources I have cited in this study. "What is remarkable," Mencken wrote, "is that, so far, no adequate history of the Harding Administration has been done. … The thing that is needed is an impersonal and well-documented account of the whole sorry business, written by someone with no thought save to record the truth" (Op. cit.).

Considering that Mencken had such vitriolic contempt for Harding, he would assumedly have been looking for a rigorous, if harsh, treatment of Harding's career. There were times when Harding himself became rather glum about what he was seeing, belatedly. Beginning in May, 1923, he felt that, with Charlie Forbes and Jess Smith having run wild, he could sense he was losing hold of his Presidency. He suddenly found himself responsible for the irresponsible activities of his staffers and feared that more of the same would yet to come to light.

Things were growing bad enough that, much of the trouble having already happened, he sensed it was already beyond his control, and that was why, in his helplessness, he couldn't bring himself to a catharsis by telling all to Nicholas Murray Butler. There was no remedy. Where was he to begin? Where end? Nan had to remain secret. It was no accident that Harding's embarrassing disappointments created a paralytic after-effect.

The unspeakable were foreseeably mortal to his Presidential reputation. A single blessing in all of this was that he did not live to see his accomplishments swept aside once Congress became intent on exposing scandals.

As for Nan's memoir, the sales promoted by Mencken's lengthy review may have been helpful to her, but they also got the attention of the sensation seekers, bound to make a superficial judgment of Harding's character. As Nan felt publication was a necessity, she had to have felt that the highly sympathetic portrait she gave of Warren would counteract the negative aspect of acutely personal revelations. And with representative readers she succeeded.

Of the various ironies that marked his career, the very last one told him there remained some appreciation for him yet, as Florence read to him on his death bed from a Saturday Evening Post article entitled, "A Calm View of a Calm Man." In his parting, this gave Warren Harding the idealized vision of himself as a President, who, in January, 1923, was represented as an able leader who in steadfastly doing his duty would stay above the fray. He could very well ignore his critics, personally assured that he had made a laudable use of his abilities, which in the long run could be looked back upon as successfully employed in the achievements of his Administration.[133]

If people knew the sorry state that Warren Harding was actually in during January, 1923, it would have been apparent that this President's leadership was anything but "calm." He was ailing with the flu, but refused to rest it out, suffering from high blood-pressure, was overweight, given to insomnia, and worried about yet another resurgence of his wife's kidney problem. Nor were things going smoothly in his Administration, as Harding had a month earlier gotten an eye-opening account of Charlie Forbes' free-wheeling thievery in running the Veterans' Bureau. The unwitting President got more than a hint of outrages going on behind his back.

However, with none of this being publicly known, if nothing in his Presidency had changed toward the end of January, 1923, or even at the time of his death in August, and with little criticism aroused by the suicides of Jess Smith and Charles Cramer, chances are that the Harding Administration would have gone out on a positive note. Since the people were sympathetically inclined in their grief over the untimely death of a publicly appealing President, for a while, things didn't look too bad politically.

Commenting on Harding's standing with the American people immediately following his death, an adulating Willis Fletcher

Johnson wrote of the public's adulation for a President beloved with "unexampled unanimity" (op. cit., Life, 13).

Having died before he could be assailed by scandals that didn't touch him personally, he could have gone out an honored President, personally liked by both the Press and the Public. For, in sum, though obviously flawed, Harding actually became a far better President than he was perceived to have been.

Looking back from 1938, long after Harding's bottom rank had become fairly well entrenched, William Allen White recalled his personal observation of a Harding quite different from the image that clung to him.[134] Significantly, White was returning to notes taken in 1923, by all odds the most stressful period of Harding's tenure.

Yet, there was this hardened, unsentimental reporter vividly highlighting President Harding at his engaging best, when neither he, nor anyone else, could have possibly foreseen how this seeming pillar of self-assurance would shortly be looking mortality in the eye and barely escaping disgrace in his time.

Thus, as I re-quote White's remembrance of this President in 1923, it serves as a capsule portrait of him commanding center stage. Harding would have appreciated its being used to enliven his obituary:

"No one could have been more genuinely earnest in the manifestations of his public desire to be a good President than Warren Harding. He was frank in confessing his limitations, disarming in his candor to his friends, and even to casual acquaintances and always to newspaper men who crowded into his press conferences every Friday. He stood before them bland, charming, even jovial at times, but with an actor's quick sense of dignity; a fine, well set up figure of a man, clearly of the emotional type with the eager wistful lineaments of a friendly pup written on every flexible feature, with the warmth of a woman's cordial glow in his eyes" (Puritan in Babylon, 230).

CHAPTER 77

"In Memoriam"

ON HIS UNTIMELY DEATH, HARDING was mourned nationally. Emphasized in the grief of ordinary people, who could identify with him, he was universally loved, as signified by Willis Fletcher Johnson. No one gave a better first hand description of this outflow of feeling than Herbert Hoover, who witnessed it on the "long slow four-day journey to Washington" of the funeral train.

"Uncovered crowds came silently at every crossroads and filled every station day and night. There was real and touching grief everywhere. The newspapers announced from Ohio that Mr. Harding's favorite hymn was 'My Redeemer Liveth.' Soon at every station and every crossroads the people sang it as we passed. At the many places where we stopped a moment to give the people a chance for expression, bands and orchestras played it. My chief memory of that journey is of listening to this hymn over and over again all day and long into the night.

"At that moment, the affection of the people for Mr. Harding was complete. Had it not been for the continuous exposure of terrible corruption by his playmates, he would have passed into memory with the same aura of affection and respect that attaches to Garfield and McKinley." (Memoirs, II, 52).

ABOUT THE AUTHOR

I AM AN EMERITUS PROFESSOR of English at Kent State University, and have previously taught at the University of Missouri, the College of William and Mary, Ohio State, and the University of Akron.

I did my BA (with honors) at the University of Missouri, my MA at Yale and my PhD at Columbia University. I had Fulbright Professorships at Copenhagen University (Denmark) and Tubingen University (Germany). I was Guest Lecturer at several European Universities, some including Lecture Tours @: Coimbra (Portugal), Rome, East and West Germany, and the Netherlands.

I have published over 40 articles in major scholarly journals (e.g., PMLA, American Lit., Modern Philology, New England Quarterly, American Quarterly, Early Am. Lit.) on, among others, Whitman, H. James, Twain, Stephen Crane, Harold Frederick, E.W. Howe, W.D. Howells, Hemingway, Steinbeck, Eliot, and C.B. Brown. I did a book, "Mark Twain As Critic," with Johns Hopkins, and was General Editor of the MLA-sealed Edition of the "Novels of Charles Brockden Brown," America's first professional novelist, for which I did "Historical Notes" and a "Historical Essay" for Edgar Huntly, Vol. IV.

In World War II, I served as a Combat Infantryman with the 4th Infantry Division, an outfit that made D-Day, liberated Paris, and was first through the Siegfried Line. I Joined them in the latter and went through their two most bitter battles; namely Hurtgen Forest and the Battle of the Bulge (in which we saved Luxembourg) was wounded during our pushing back the Bulge. I have published a Memoir of my experience in Combat entitled, "Falling Out and Belonging: A Foot-Soldier's Life," 2006. My book on Warren Harding is a major effort in my retirement.

END NOTES

1. Burl Noggle, Teapot Dome: Oil and Politics in the 1920's (Baton Rouge: Louisiana State University Press, 1962). There have been significant studies of the Harding Administration since Noggle's assessment, which I cite, but all uniformly take note of Harding's status as our worst President.
2. The Available Man: The Life Behind the Masks of Warren Gamaliel Harding (New York: Macmillan, 1965) 297.
3. The Shadow of Blooming Grove: Warren G. Harding in His Times (New York: McGraw-Hill,1968) "Foreword," xv. Hereafter, Shadow.
4. Incredible Era: The Life and Times of Warren Gamaliel Harding (Boston: Houghton Mifflin, 1939) 190, 245, 189.
5. Only Yesterday: An Informal History of the Nineteen-Twenties (New York: Harper & Brothers, 1919) 126.
6. Dead Last (Athens, OH: Ohio University Press, 2009) 156, 223.
7. The ranking was done by C-Span in a survey conducted from December, 2008 to January, 2009, and was based on ten leadership attributes. The complete list appeared in numerous newspapers, as, for example, the Richmond [Virginia] Times Dispatch, February 16, 1994, A-2,4.

   Gerry Ford's opinion of Carter was given in private interviews with his hometown newspaper, to be released after his death. Ford's statement was: "I think Jimmy Carter would be very close to Warren G. Harding" ("Ford's Opinion of Other Presidents Is Revealed," New York Times, 13 January, 2007, A, 12).
8. Murray, The Harding Era: Warren G. Harding and His

Administration (Minneapolis: Univ. of Minnesota Press, 1969) 530, 536f.; hereafter, Era. Russell, Shadow, xiv.

9. Francis Russell, "The Four Mysteries of Warren Harding," American Heritage, XIV (April, 1963) 83, 81.

10. Nan Britton, The President's Daughter (New York: Elizabeth Ann Guild, 1927) 388. Hereafter, PD.

11. The Strange Deaths of President Harding (Columbia, Mo: University of Missouri Press, 1996) 58, 65. Presumably, Ferrell would have it that the content of the PD narrative had been provided by Nan, and that Wightman wrote the book. This assumption has no factual support.

12. Carl Sferrazza Anthony, Florence Harding: The First Lady, the Jazz Age, and the Death of America's Most Scandalous President (New York, William Morrow, 1998) 153. Hereafter, Florence. I shall be adding new information about Harding's relationship with Carrie Phillips from James D. Robenalt's The Harding Affair: Love and Espionage During The Great War (New York: Palgrave Macmillan) 2009. Hereafter, Affair.

13. Wilson made a number of barbed comments in the same vein, saying it will be "very difficult...to stand...Mr. Harding's English." A remark by Wilson's Secretary of Agriculture, David Houston, typically reiterated the put-down of mindlessness: "What a trial it will be to have to witness Mr. Harding's efforts to think and his efforts to say what he thinks." August Herkscher, Woodrow Wilson (New York: Scribner's Sons, 1991) 668. David F. Houston, Eight Years with Wilson's Cabinet, 1913-1920 (Garden City, N.Y: Doubleday, Page, 1926) II, 148, 93.

14. Selected Letters of William Allen White, 1899-1943, ed. Walter Johnson (New York: Henry Holt, 1947) 11. The Autobiography of William Allen White (New York: Macmillan, 1949) 586-588.

15. Masks in a Pageant, (New York: Macmillan, 1928) 389. Murray, Era, 62.

16. John Dean cites accounts in the New York World and The New Republic which portrayed Harding as the least qualified

candidate since Buchanan. Warren G. Harding (New York: Henry Holt, 2004) 67.

17. Murray, Era, 52; Harding papers, White to WGH 5 October, 1920. For all subsequent reference to the Scobey-Harding correspondence, I am indebted to the Ohio Historical Society for permission given to read and to quote from their letters to one another, plus several letters to Scobey from other persons. Citations to this correspondence are given in the form established by the Ohio Historical Society. Occasionally, for some indirect quotes and items summarized from their correspondence, or for another use of a prior reference given in the standard form, Scobey is identified as FES, Harding as WGH.
18. References to the Times are given by date and page in the body of the text, rather than in multiple endnotes.
19. Sullivan, The Great Adventure at Washington: The Story of the Conference (Garden City, NY: Doubleday, Page, 1922) 225.
20. Regarding the poker analogy, John Dean has it that Harding might have offered the same idea in slightly different terms, saying, "I feel like a man who goes in with a pair of eights and comes out with aces full" (Warren G. Harding, 66).
21. MIC 3 Warren G. Harding Papers [microform], Letter to Frank Edgar Scobey, 20 January, 1920: Ohio Historical Society.
22. Our Times, The United States, 1920-1925, VI, "The Twenties" (New York: Scribner's Sons, 1946) 209f.
23. Unsentimental Harry Daugherty on meeting Debs for the first time, on 24 March, 1921, had said afterwards, "I never met a man I liked better"—though, as Daugherty later remembered the incident, he toned down his reaction. (The Inside Story of the Harding Tragedy (New York: Churchill, 1932) 115-121).
24. Ray Ginger, The Bending Cross , (New Brunswick, NJ.: Rutgers Univ. Press, 1949) 407, 415. Eugene V. Debs, Writings and Speeches of Eugene V. Debs (New York: Hermitage Press, 1948) 468-469.
25. This idea came up in a pre-inaugural talk Harding had had with Butler. Across the Busy Years (New York: Charles Scribner's

Sons, 1939) I, 401. He had input from Secretary Hoover on working conditions for steel workers. The Memoirs of Herbert Hoover (New York: Macmillan, 1952) II, 103.

26. A Puritan in Babylon (New York: Macmillan, 1938) 230. Though this was a book White was doing on Coolidge, he couldn't resist giving two chapters to Harding, a more interesting figure. The fact that Harding had been a newspaper man himself doubtless had something to do with his upbeat mood in the presence of reporters.

27. Carl Anthony provides an example of how a well informed biographer might accept as factually true Daugherty's falsified account of what he said that Harding supposedly had told him about the information he had gotten on Smith (Florence, 404).

28. One can get an idea of what such a sum would amount to in today's dollars by checking out the cost of ordinary items of clothing in Harding's time. It was possible, for example, to buy a pair of Women's Oxford shoes in July, 1921 for $5.85. Harding told Nan Britton, his check came to $15.00 for dinner and a cocktail for each, to which he added a $1.50 tip. He considered the total rather pricey, in fact, "ridiculous[ly]" so (PD, 64f.).

29. White, Autobiography, 619.

30. "Professor Pens Thoughts on the Harding Unknown," Marion Star, 4 March, 2006, p. 3A.

31. Murray, Era, 399-400. Randolph C. Downes devotes an entire Chapter (XXII) to the subject of Harding and "Negro Rights." The Rise of Warren Gamaliel Harding, 1865-1920 (Columbus, Ohio: Ohio State Univ. Press, 1970) 535-561.

32. Hawley, The Great War and the Search for a Modern Order, A History of the American People and Their Institutions, 1917-1933 (New York: St. Martin's Press, 1979) 58.

33. For many of the details of Teapot Dome set forth here, I follow parts of the analysis given by Burl Noggle, who traces its overall developments from a Conservationist point of view, in his Teapot Dome: Oil and Politics in the 1920's. Additional pertinent information, which I use in connection with Albert Fall, is derived from David H. Stratton's Tempest over Teapot

Dome: The Story of Albert B. Fall (Norman, Okla.: University of Oklahoma Press, 1998).

34. White, Forty Years on Main Street (New York: Farrar & Rinehart, 1937) 244f.
35. Revelry (New York: Boni & Liveright, 1926) 313.
36. Joe Mitchell Chapple, Life and Times of Warren G. Harding, Our After-War President (Boston: Chapple Publishing Co., 1924) 293-300.
37. MIC 3 Warren G. Harding Papers [microform], Letters from Frank Edgar Scobey, 29 December, 1920; 31 December,1920. Letters to Frank Edgar Scobey, 4 January, 1921; 31 January, 1920: Ohio Historical Society.
38. M. Nelson McGeary, Gifford Pinchot (Princeton, N.J.: Princeton Univ. Press, 1960) 270-71. An "insider" like Scobey had also been counting on Harding's being persuaded to take the right direction. His case, though, was to support Daugherty's effort to make a Presidential Candidate of him. MIC 3 Warren G. Harding Papers [microform], Letter from Frank Edgar Scobey to Warren G. Harding, 8 December, 1919: Ohio Historical Society.
39. MIC 3 Warren G. Harding Papers [microform] Letter from Frank Edgar Scobey to Harry Daugherty, 23 February, 1920: Ohio Historical Society.
40. MIC 3 Warren G. Harding Papers [microform], Letter from Malcolm Jennings to Frank Edgar Scobey, 22 March, 1920: Ohio Historical Society. Harding's early aversion to getting into patronage had come out at various times, as in his letter to Scobey of 25 November, 1919.
41. MIC 3 Warren G. Harding Papers [microform], Letter to Frank Edgar Scobey, 20 January, 1920: Ohio Historical Society.
42. MIC 3 Warren G. Harding Papers [microform], Letter to Frank Edgar Scobey, 25 November, 1919: Ohio Historical Society.
43. MIC 3 Warren G. Harding Papers [microform], Letter to Frank Edgar Scobey, 30 December, 1919: Ohio Historical Society.
44. MIC 3 Warren G. Harding Papers [microform], Letter to Frank Edgar Scobey, 30 December, 1919: Ohio Historical Society.

45. MIC 3 Warren G. Harding Papers [microform], Letter to Frank Edgar Scobey, 7 February, 1919: Ohio Historical Society.
46. MIC 3 Warren G. Harding Papers [microform], Letter to Frank Edgar Scobey, 14 January, 1919: Ohio Historical Society.
47. MIC 3 Warren G. Harding Papers [microform], Letter from Frank Edgar Scobey to Mac Jennings, 8 December, 1914; Letters from Warren G. Harding to Frank Edgar Scobey, 7 February, 1919; 14 January 1919: Ohio Historical Society 1901.
48. MIC 3 Warren G. Harding Papers [microform], Letter to Frank Edgar Scobey, 16 December, 1919: Ohio Historical Society.
49. MIC 3 Warren G. Harding Papers [microform], Letter to Frank Edgar Scobey, 24 March, 1920: Ohio Historical Society.
50. MIC 3 Warren G. Harding Papers [microform], Letter from Frank Edgar Scobey, 20 April, 1921. Letter from Harry Daugherty to Frank Edgar Scobey, 27 December, 1919 Ohio Historical Society.
51. MIC 3 Warren G. Harding Papers [microform], Letter from Frank Edgar Scobey, 29 December, 1920: Ohio Historical Society.
52. MIC 3 Warren G. Harding Papers [microform], Letter to Frank Edgar Scobey, 14 December, 1920: Ohio Historical Society.
53. MIC 3 Warren G. Harding Papers [microform], Letter to Frank Edgar Scobey, 4 January, 1921: Ohio Historical Society. My itals.
54. MIC 3 Warren G. Harding Papers [microform], Letter to Frank Edgar Scobey, 12 January, 1920: Ohio Historical Society.
55. MIC 3 Warren G. Harding Papers [microform]. Letter from Frank Edgar Scobey, 21 May, 1921. Scobey was quoting Harding's letter of 12 May.
56. MIC Warren G. Harding Papers [microform], Letter from Frank Edgar Scobey, 7 May, 1921; Letter to Frank Edgar Scobey 12 May, 1921: Ohio Historical Society.

    It was in Scobey's letter to Harding of 20 April, 1921 that he reported on the meeting at which Creager had been elected Chairman of the State Republican Committee and Eugene Nolte Vice-Chairman.

57. MIC Warren G. Harding Papers [microform], Letter from Frank Edgar Scobey, 29 December, 1920: Ohio Historical Society.
58. MIC 3 Warren G. Harding Papers [microform], Letter from Frank Edgar Scobey, 18 March, 1921: Ohio Historical Society.
59. MIC Warren G. Harding Papers [microform], Letter from Frank Edgar Scobey, 20 April, 1921: Ohio Historical Society.
60. MIC 3 Warren G. Harding Papers [microform], Letter from Frank Edgar Scobey, 20 April, 1921; Letter to Frank Edgar Scobey, 12 May 1921: Ohio Historical Society.
61. MIC 3 Warren G. Harding Papers [microform], Letter to Frank Edgar Scobey, 25 August, 1921: Ohio Historical Society.
62. MIC 3 Warren G. Harding Papers [microform], Letter to Frank Edgar Scobey, 21 March, 1922: Ohio Historical Society.
63. MIC 3 Warren G. Harding Papers [microform], Letter from Frank Edgar Scobey, 21 March, 1921: Ohio Historical Society.
64. MIC 3 Warren G. Harding Papers [microform], Letter from Frank Edgar Scobey, 7 May, 1921: Ohio Historical Society.
65. MIC 3 Warren G. Harding Papers [microform], Letter to Frank Edgar Scobey, 4 January, 1921: Ohio Historical Society.
66. Meanwhile, Scobey, also finding MacGregor "friendly," saw that the reason he wanted to be with a winner was that it would enable him to maintain his position as National Committeeman. MIC 3 Warren G. Harding Papers [microform], Letters to Frank Edgar Scobey, 16 December, 1919, 12 January, 1920. Letter from Frank Edgar Scobey to H.M. Daugherty, 23 December, 1919. Letter from H. F. MacGregor to Frank Edgar Scobey, 11 February, 1920: Ohio Historical Society.
67. MIC 3 Warren G. Harding Papers [microform], Letter from H. M. Daugherty to Frank Edgar Scobey, 4 December, 1919: Ohio Historical Society.
68. MIC 3 Warren G. Harding Papers [microform], Letter from Malcolm Jennings to Frank Edgar Scobey, 22 March, 1920: Ohio Historical Society
69. MIC 3 Warren G. Harding Papers [microform], Anonymous

letter to Frank Edgar Scobey, 15 December, 1919: Ohio Historical Society.

70. MIC 3 Warren G. Harding Papers [microform], Letter from Malcolm Jennings to Frank Edgar Scobey, 22 March, 1920: Ohio Historical Society.
71. MIC 3 Warren G. Harding Papers [microform], Letter to Frank Edgar Scobey, 16 December, 1919: Ohio Historical Society.
72. MIC 3 Warren G. Harding Papers [microform], Letter to Frank Edgar Scobey, 22 November, 1919: Ohio Historical Society.
73. MIC 3 Warren G. Harding Papers [microform], Letter from Frank Edgar Scobey, 29 December, 1920: Ohio Historical Society.
74. MIC 3 Warren G. Harding Papers [microform], Letter to Frank Edgar Scobey, 4 January, 1921: Ohio Historical Society.
75. MIC 3 Warren G. Harding Papers [microform], Letter from H. L. Beach to Frank Edgar Scobey, 31 December, 1920: Ohio Historical Society.
76. MIC 3 Warren G. Harding Papers [microform], Letter to Frank Edgar Scobey, 10 January, 1921: Ohio Historical Society.
77. David H. Stratton, Tempest over Teapot Dome: The Story of Albert B. Fall (Norman, Okla.: University of Oklahoma Press, 1998) 111, 212. This biography of Stratton's throws a different light on Fall's character from that advanced by Scobey, and also by Daugherty.
78. Daugherty strongly denied that Fall had ever asked to use his name, insisting that Fall had sent the telegram on his own initiative, "without saying anything to [him] about it." Fall did not just use his name, but to Daugherty's amazement—and chagrin—Fall "signed" Daugherty's name to the telegram, and charged it to Daugherty's "personal account" (Inside Story, 80f.).
79. MIC 3 Warren G. Harding Papers [microform], Letters from Frank Edgar Scobey, 29 December, 1920; 20 April, 1921: Ohio Historical Society.
80. MIC 3 Warren G. Harding Papers [microform], Letter to Frank Edgar Scobey, 31 January, 1920: Ohio Historical Society.

81. This was how Fall was looked upon by his Director of the Bureau of the Mines. The Memoirs of Albert B. Fall, ed. David H. Stratton (El Paso, TX: Texas Western Press, 1966) 6f.,

82. "Saturnalia," Baltimore Evening Sun, 18 July, 1927, p. 15.

83. Russell, 383. Willis Fletcher Johnson, George Harvey, A Passionate Patriot (Boston: Houghton Mifflin, 1929) 278. There were several versions of Harvey's putting the critical question to Harding. The one reported by Johnson is simpler than the one Russell quotes. Randolph Downs, who made a careful inquiry into the "smoke-filled room" episode, suspects this dialogue may never have taken place (The Rise of Warren Gamaliel Harding, 415-425).

84. Here, as elsewhere, I have been selectively indebted to Francis Russell for information about Harding's relationship with Carrie Phillips, since, prior to 2009, when James Robenalt came out with the book in which he recorded excerpts from the Warren-to-Carrie letters, Russell had been the only person given the opportunity to peruse those letters before the package was pulled from public view.

85. Jack Warwick, "Growing Up With Warren Harding," 31. This pamphlet compiled from eighteen installments of Warwick's story originally published serially in the New York Evening Post in 1920 was reprinted in Warwick's self published, All in a Lifetime, 1938.

86. This look is discernable in a photograph of Harding as an undergraduate at Ohio Central College, on the back cover of Warwick's Growing Up with Warren Harding Power of the White House (Philadelphia: Winston, 1923) facing page 21. Since Johnson dates Harding's age in the photograph as 21, that would put it at 1886.

87. MIC 3 Warren G. Harding Papers [microform], Letter to Frank Edgar Scobey, 26 March,1915: Ohio Historical Society.

88. MIC 3 Warren G. Harding Papers [microform], Letter from Malcolm Jennings to Frank Edgar Scobey, 22 March, 1920: Ohio Historical Society.

89. MIC 3 Warren G. Harding Papers [microform], Letter from Florence Harding to Mr. and Mrs. Frank Edgar Scobey, 20 January, 1919: Ohio Historical Society.
90. An unsubstantiated incident is cited by a reporter who claimed that the child of Harding's widow neighbor took the reporter upstairs to show him Harding's toothbrush, saying, "He always stays here when Mrs. Harding goes away" (Shadow, 401).
91. First Ladies (New York: Random House, 1995) 233.
92. Carl Sferrazza Anthony, First Ladies, the Saga of the Presidents' Wives and Their Power, 1789-1961 (New York: William Morrow, 1990) 393. .
93. On Harding's frequent trips following his election to the Lieutenant-Governorship in 1903, Assistant Treasury Secretary, Charles Hilles observed that Florence was Warren's rather frequent traveling companion.
94. MIC 3 Warren G. Harding Papers [microform], Letter to Frank Edgar Scobey, 9 March, 1918: Ohio Historical Society.
95. This meeting, which was the initiation of their affair, took place in May, 1917. Thereafter, Nan records the exact day on which their intimacy was consummated, 30 July, 1917 (PD, 49).
96. Scobey's denial that he ever knew a thing about Nan came after he had seen himself mentioned in her book. He claimed his name had been taken in vain, as he had "never heard of this woman." MIC 3 Warren G. Harding Papers [microform], Letter from Frank Edgar Scobey to W. K. Leonard, 14 November, 1927: Ohio Historical Society.
97. MIC 3 Warren G. Harding Papers [microform], Letter to Frank Edgar Scobey, 30 December, 1918: Ohio Historical Society.
98. Nan does not give a precise date for her remembrance of this pronouncement, but, since she, in retrospect, records its occurrence as having taken place during Harding's Senatorial tenure, that would probably put it in late 1917, as she writes, he had gone to see her in New York, during one of Florence's earlier near-death sieges (PD, 232).

99. MIC 3 Warren G. Harding Papers [microform], Letter to Frank Edgar Scobey, 18 November, 1918: Ohio Historical Society.
100. MIC 3 Warren G. Harding Papers [microform], Letters to Frank Edgar Scobey, 12 July, 1915; 13 December, 1915: Ohio Historical Society.
101. Harding reports that, despite the banning of the Hulu, he and Florence were given a privileged performance, attended by the Governor of Hawaii and the Mayor of Honolulu. The dance wouldn't have been sufficiently attractive to Scobey, he notes, as the women had to wear those grass skirts. However, to satisfy the interest of Scobey's wife, Harding had to draw her attention to a certain detail: "Mrs. Scobey will be interested to know that the fatter a Hulu dancer is the more perfectly she describes the naval circle." MIC 3 Warren G. Harding Papers [microform], Letter to Frank Edgar Scobey, 26 March, 1915: Ohio Historical Society.
102. MIC 3 Warren G. Harding Papers [microform], Letter to Evaland Scobey, 20 February, 1922: Ohio Historical Society.
103. MIC 3 Warren G. Harding Papers [microform], Letter to Frank Edgar Scobey, 25 October, 1919: Ohio Historical Society.
104. MIC 3 Warren G. Harding Papers [microform] Letter from William C. Fordyce to Frank Edgar Scobey, 18 December, 1918: Ohio Historical Society.
105. MIC 3 Warren G. Harding Papers [microform], Letter to Frank Edgar Scobey, 12 July, 1915: Ohio Historical Society.
106. Russell referred to Burton, Harding's Senatorial predecessor, as "a bachelor and scholar, a reactionary of rectitude" (<u>Shadow</u>, 125). Scobey, writing Mac Jennings about his survey of Senators with Presidential timber, thought well of Burton's ability, but called him "Old Grandmother Burton." MIC 3 Warren G. Harding Papers [microform], Letter from Frank Edgar Scobey to Malcolm Jennings, 8 December, 1914: Ohio Historical Society.
107. MIC 3 Warren G. Harding Papers [microform], Letter to Frank Edgar Scobey, 2 December, 1914: Ohio Historical Society.
108. MIC 3 Warren G. Harding Papers [microform], Letter to Frank Edgar Scobey, 7 May 1917: Ohio Historical Society.

109. MIC 3 Warren G. Harding Papers [microform], Letter to Frank Edgar Scobey, 3 January, 1918: Ohio Historical Society.
110. MIC 3 Warren G. Harding Papers [microform], Letter from Frank Edgar Scobey, undated [1914?]: Ohio Historical Society.
111. MIC 3 Warren G. Harding Papers [microform], Letter to Frank Edgar Scobey, 12 July, 1915: Ohio Historical Society.

     Harding had met Roy Campbell during his visits to the Scobeys in San Antonio. Campbell was a close friend of Scobey's and a strong Harding supporter, whom Scobey, in one of his patronage coups, got appointed Collector of Customs for his San Antonio District.
112. MIC 3 Warren G. Harding Papers [microform], Letter to Frank Edgar Scobey, 5 April, 1917: Ohio Historical Society. At age 75, 1911 was the last year that "Uncle" Joe Cannon, of Illinois, was Speaker of the House of Representatives. Harding, born on 2 November, 1865, was 52 in 1917, and Scobey, born on 27 February, 1866, was 51, both middle-aged, bordering on old for their time.
113. MIC 3 Warren G. Harding Papers [microform], Letter to Frank Edgar Scobey, 7 February, 1919: Ohio Historical Society.
114. MIC 3 Warren G. Harding Papers [microform] Letter from Malcolm Jennings to Frank Edgar Scobey, 18 December, 1917: Ohio Historical Society.
115. MIC 3 Warren G. Harding Papers [microform], Letter from Malcolm Jennings to Frank Edgar Scobey, 24 October, 1914: Ohio Historical Society.
116. MIC 3 Warren G. Harding Papers [microform], Letters to Frank Edgar Scobey, 13 December, 1915; 12 July, 1915: Ohio Historical Society.
117. MIC 3 Warren G. Harding Papers [microform], Letters to Frank Edgar Scobey, 14 December, 1916; 31 May 1918: Ohio Historical Society.
118. MIC 3 Warren G. Harding Papers [microform], Letter to Frank Edgar Scobey, 18 June, 1914: Ohio Historical Society.
119. MIC 3 Warren G. Harding Papers [microform], Letter to Frank Edgar Scobey, 4 December, 1916: Ohio Historical Society.
120. As I have indicated, for much of the Carrie affair that I cover here, I make judicious use of information from Francis Russell,

sticking to verifiable matters. Much of the Carrie affair is covered by other biographers that I cite, eminently Carl Anthony. I have made use of James Robenalt's quotation from Warren's letters to Carrie, which provide fresh details previously unavailable.

121. Carl Anthony holds that Harding had a personal interest in the possibility that Carrie Phillips might be questioned about her pro-German remarks, since he was anxious regarding "what Carrie might reveal under pressure" (Florence, 152).
122. Sam Janus, Barbara Bess, and Carol Saltus, A Sexual Profile of Men In Power (Prentice-Hall: Englewood Cliffs, N.J., 1977) xix, xx. Harding was in good company, adultery having been a common enough phenomenon among American Presidents. No need to consider the roster of Presidential adulterers, but Harding's predecessor, a very devout Presbyterian and lofty intellectual—none other than austere Woodrow Wilson—was known to have had a relationship with Mary Peck.
123. R. W. Apple, Jr., "Nan Britton Lives in Seclusion in Chicago Suburb," New York Times, July 15, 1964, p. 18. In the comment on Nan, Apple reports, "Francis Russell, a historian who read the letters [to Carrie Phillips], said last week that they tended to give credence to Miss Britton's claim that she had been Mr. Harding's mistress from 1916 to 1922 and had given birth to his child." Apple misdates the beginning and end of their affair by a year each way.
124. MIC 3 Warren G. Harding Papers [microform], Letter to Frank Edgar Scobey, 19 October, 1917: Ohio Historical Society.
125. They quote Harold Lasswell to the same effect, as he points out that, "Much social and political life [of these men] is a symptom of the delayed adolescence of its propagators…." Psychopathology and Politics (New York: Viking Press, 1960) 188. (Janus, et al., 6-7).
126. White, as cited above (Puritan in Babylon, 230) had declared that Harding had had a two year "honeymoon," but that was with the Press. His on-the-job "honeymoon," when things were going exceptionally well for him both as President and with Congress, was of shorter duration however.

127. Dwight Lowell Dumond, America in Our Time, 1896, 1896-1946 (New York: Henry Holt, 1947) 377.
128. Her disillusionment occurred in a moment of stress, when she saw things coming apart. With time, hopelessness would, however, be softened, for, in her more sober retrospect, Nan wrote that she felt Harding would certainly have declared his paternity once his term as President was over (Honesty, 14).
129. There is no record of a $50,000. debt independent of the $90,000. figure, which was the amount of the stock losses for which compensation was owed to Harding's brokerage firm.

131. As Emma was the wife of a friend, Warren evidently felt, she merited more than a courtesy call. Outside of White and Daugherty, his meeting with Emma Fall was the only such personal contact of record that Harding made on this trip.
132. No need to strike a parallel to the legendary twelfth century lovers, but Heloise was around twenty years Peter Abelard's junior. She bore him a child out of wedlock and, at first, refused to marry him on grounds that it might disgrace him and injure his reputation as teacher and philosopher. It was the exchange of love letters, discovered in a fifteenth century manuscript, that created the lovers' iconic fame.
133. Samuel G. Blythe, "A Calm Review of a Calm Man," Saturday Evening Post, CXCVI (28 January, 1923) 3-4, 73-76.
134. Interestingly, White was reversing a vision he had had of Harding ten years earlier, when he had regarded him as humbled by the responsibilities suddenly being thrust upon him (Masks, 412). But that original view was of a neophyte Harding just entering the Oval Office. White's later reminiscence was of an experienced and fully confident President who had mastered the Office and felt himself in charge. Ironically, this was not long before his psychological decline and his fatal decline in health would set in.

[*N.B.: The End Notes jump from 129 to 131 due to the elimination of two Notes.*]

INDEX

A

B

C

D

E

F

G

H

I

J

K

L

M

N

O

P

R

S

T

W